THE GREEDY

OLD BASTARDS

A Systemic War on Women in the U.S.

SUSAN MORRIS-CARTER

Library of Congress Control Number: 2014913979

Morris-Carter, Susan
    The Greedy Old Bastards: A Systemic War on Women in the U.S.
Includes bibliographical references and index.
ISBN 978-0-9906567-0-8

Cover and Interior Design: Delaney-Designs

Published by SuProCo Publishing
1300 Army Navy Drive, Ste 1101
Arlington, VA 22202

ISBN 978-0-9906567-0-8
Printed in the United States of America

DEDICATION

I dedicate this book to
My tall, handsome and sweet husband, Vondell Carter.
and
To the intelligent, strong and beautiful women in my life
My grandmothers, Helen Smith-Wright and Mary Huryk-Krawchuk, and
My mother, Helen Wright-Krawchuk.

ACKNOWLEDGEMENTS

I take full responsibility for the contents of this book and thank all those who have contributed and assisted me in my need to share my thoughts on what it's like to be a woman in a "man's world." Not by any means a "shrinking violet," I owe a debt of thanks to my family and friends who have tempered me and stuck by me as I tried to get from the inception of the manuscript to the end of this journey. It's a long and painful road to be an author and I couldn't have gotten here without the loving support of my husband of 17 years, Vondell Carter. He has shared his intelligence, kindness and patience, which often made it difficult for me to write about the abuse and treachery of the truly bad men in the world and the Greedy Old Bastards.

Fortunately, my manuscript was brought out of the depths of male flagellation into a hopefully coherent and interesting book for women and "enlightened men," by my editor Andrew Szanton. I owe Andrew a lot for being honest enough to keep me on the right track without changing my message. My thanks to Kevin Berends, a fabulous writer and friend, who started me out when I was stuck.

I appreciate the strong and intelligent women and men in my family who made me a feminist. Without them and my friends, a highly diverse group of people, I wouldn't be who I am today – it's just not been easy being "me." My gratitude goes to my female friends forever for reviewing some of my chapters and telling me to hurry up: my sister Nancy, and my girlfriends, Susan Ralston, Alice Varga, and Mary Redfield. For support and sustenance when I needed it, I want to thank my friends Bob, Morris, Margena, Michele, Paul, Andy, Davy, Laszlo, Segun, Alease, and Royal. I have been especially blessed to have my sister's children and their spouses, Carl, Jacqueline, Tina, and Peter, give me much-needed telephone breaks during my writing sessions. A special thank you goes to my dear friend Marsha Coleman-Adebayo, who made me do it - finish writing and publish my book.

Finally, I don't know what I would have done without my two constant feline hairball companions, Little Bits and Sweetpea, a Raffamuffin and Main Coon. They were never far from my writing space, peacefully resting, purring and making their independent contributions.

Writing this book for you has been a great pleasure, so I hope that you enjoy it.

PREFACE

I am neither a misandrist nor misanthrope; there are millions of wonderful men and people in this world. We couldn't or wouldn't want to live without the men in our lives. Most of those in my life have been exceptional – kind, gentle, considerate, hardworking, and loving - great sons, husbands, fathers and friends. A few have been rough, aggressive, and violent. The following Chapters cover a myriad of topics, but are mainly about those other men – the ones who use and abuse women and children. Even though the Good Old Boys and The Greedy Old Bastards may not appear to be part of that ilk, they are because they are the ones who have the power and wealth to make the U.S. and the world a better place for women, children and the disadvantaged.

Instead, they continue to use strategies against us, particularly the middle-class, women and specific groups so that they remain often overworked, underpaid, overtaxed, and exploited. I have taken on many areas and many groups - Democrats and Republicans, Liberals and Conservatives, Pro- and Anti-Movements, and the Gun Lobbies. I tried to uncover the Big Boys in all their ignominious greed and glory as they lie, deceive and manipulate us. Some areas I felt compelled to cover, such as the continued racism experienced by blacks that imprisons, ghettoizes, and victimizes them, then blames them. As a nation we have lost our way.

It's not easy to understand and know what is right, just, and fair in our highly complex and diverse country. We have the wealth, resources, and opportunity to take a new direction that utilizes and maximizes the strength of all our people instead of a select few. For every person we abuse, we pay the consequences. American people are not a homogeneous group, and have their various faiths, customs, and beliefs. This is what keeps us from coming together as a major force against the more powerful who set aside their differences to stay in control. Until we use our strength as a majority, we will continue to be skillfully manipulated by an elite group of Good Old Boys and Greedy Old Bastards.

I ask to be pardoned for any offense given or leeway taken in order to get my views across on behalf of women and our most important asset – our children.

TABLE OF CONTENTS

CHAPTER 1

1 Portrait of a Jackass

"Do not put such unlimited power into the hands of the husbands. Remember all men would be tyrants if they could."

Abigail Adams

I had nothing planned after work, so I stopped at my best friend Natalie's house to say hello. I knocked on her front door, it flew open and there I was eyeball to eyeball with her irate, red-faced, inebriated husband, Charlie. He was a muscular 6'2" brute, and he caught me off guard.

"What do you want?" he bellowed, gritting his teeth.

"I was just stopping by to see Natalie."

"Bullshit!" He hit me with the screen door, yelling in my face.

"I'm fed up with you and all your feminist crap!"

I was accustomed to being hated by Charlie and a bunch of other lowlifes who had somehow managed to woo and marry some of my best friends. I was used to getting blamed when some of my friends began sticking up for themselves in troubled relationships. And, I was used to Charlie's drinking and becoming violent. I had a lot of alcoholics slurring through my friends and family: "sleeper" drunks who drank themselves into oblivion before falling asleep; and "violent" crazy drinkers like Charlie.

I turned to leave, but Charlie wanted to punish me because I was independent, educated, happily divorced from my ex-husband, and on good terms with the world. He shoved me hard from behind to show me who was boss. He couldn't call me a "stupid bitch" as he called my girlfriend and other women, so that further enraged him. I was thinking about how Charlie had once thrown a small middle-aged Jewish guy halfway across a barroom for the crime of saying a few words to my girlfriend. I knew I was about to get thrown somewhere, and I was hoping it wouldn't be face-first into the big oak tree in their front yard. I had plenty to fear from this abusive, racist, anti-Semitic misogynist. To him, I was the epitome of what was wrong with male-female relationships in the U.S. and the world. I was like the female anti-Christ.

And then here came my girlfriend Natalie tearing out her front door, jumping on Charlie's back, and trying to choke-hold him. Natalie's powerful for a woman her size and Lord knows she's had enough experience fighting this man. But Charlie just tossed her off like a piece of lint, and turned to his victim for the day – me. He was hissing and huffing, his beer-soaked eyes bulging. As I tried to escape, he kept coming. Natalie ran back into the house and came out the door with a baseball bat.

Charlie snatched it from her and threw it in a neighbor's yard. Out again she came with a second baseball bat and slammed it into Charlie's right arm. That didn't stop the creep; it just raised his adrenaline a little more. I was thinking: 'Damn, Natalie's tough.' I was also thinking: 'How many baseball bats does she have in that house? If I was married to Charlie, I'd hide every knife, gun and baseball bat in the State of New Jersey.' Here she came again with baseball bat number three, and I thought just for a minute: 'She's getting as crazy as he is!'

When you're not guilty of anything, police sirens sound really sweet. One of the local cops, probably with a crush on Natalie, was sitting in a parked car down the street, waiting for the next Charlie-and-Natalie brawl to break out. Seeing and hearing the ruckus, the cop hit the siren and skidded up to the curb. I felt a sense of relief and took the first opportunity to escape, fleeing down the street in my car, with my hair flying, happy to put distance between myself and the madness.

I reached my safe haven, a two-bedroom townhouse on the other side of town. My heart was still thumping; I was relieved and happy to have escaped without injury. But the small joy I felt didn't last. I started to worry about the danger my girlfriend was still in from the beast she married. After calling to find out she was okay, I began to relax. But deep into the evening, I thought about all the Natalie's around the world, tied to vicious bullies and buffoons like Charlie, by blood or by marriage - men who use their strength and weight to intimidate and often destroy the women and children who depend on them. I finally fell asleep from sheer exhaustion, but awoke the next morning pissed off at the world.

I was determined to write the book you are now reading. But I need you to know that I am writing about the Good Old Boys or, as I call them, the Greedy Old Bastards. Charlie is one of them, but he's at the lowest level. As my girlfriend has always said, "His God is money." He has no attachment to anything but getting and keeping money. He will lie, steal and cheat to get it and keep it. Charlie is a phony, a manipulator, and a user. But he is at the bottom of the barrel of greedy men who are raping and destroying this country (and other countries) for their own ends – and punishing women and children in the process. They work at staying at the top rather than making the U.S. a better place for all of us. Greedy Old Bastards come in every shape and size. They are in every segment of our society. And they keep us in our "place," persuading or beating us into submission and subordination. It's all from the same misogynistic mindset.

So, here it is – the book I hope will help women change things for the better for ourselves, our children and the less advantaged in the U.S. I want American women -- and not just celebrity women -- to become powerful and politically astute, so we can help homeless and abused women and girls in our country and throughout the world. I believe if we join together we can make things happen. So, I am going to share some of my experiences and thoughts. I know there are many good men out there, who are enlightened and will join us. Many others may not like what I have to say. So be it. It's my right and I'm taking it.

Things should be so much better than they are today. We just have to use the brains God gave us. We have the intelligence and the chance to change things and break down the organizations and systems that maintain the status quo. We need to understand and tear apart their strategies. We'll get back to Natalie and Charlie later.

Let's start with the conditioning that goes into making Greedy Old Bastards (GOBs) and their male progeny – the GOBlins. Then we'll move into the various clubs built, controlled and maintained by them. So that you don't become totally depressed, I've inserted some humor and finally I'll suggest some ways we can try to make a difference.

2   It's A Boy – My Son, My Son

"The emotional, sexual, and psychological stereotyping of females begins when the doctor says: 'It's a girl.'"

Shirley Chisholm

We were enjoying a girls' Saturday afternoon, ignoring all the football games, when Sarah's labor pains began and her water broke. She was two weeks early, so we weren't expecting to be the ones to rush her to the hospital, preferring to enjoy the champagne and *hors d'oeuvres* she'd prepared for us, struggling back and forth between her den and kitchen.

"*Somebody dial 911. Get the ambulance or we're going to have a baby right here!*" Mary yelled as she held Sarah's hand.

"*Where the hell is Matt?*" screamed Jacquie, frantically.

"*Who cares, we can't wait – someone call his cell phone!*" several of us chimed in at once, including Sarah, who was now screaming in pain and stress.

"*Let's just get the car and take her to the hospital. It's just down the street,*" said Alice.

We piled Sarah with the soon-to-be baby, a prepared bag, and a blanket into the back of my car, the rest following in another car. Alice, sensible at first, decided it would be great fun to deliver the baby in the car. We disagreed vehemently, sighing in relief when we made it to the hospital and the doctors and nurses took over.

When Matt finally arrived, he pranced, preened and crowed like a rooster. We women were commiserating about how easy it is to insert sperm and then show up to celebrate. But we were as happy as he was, especially when the male doctor announced "It's a boy!" He could just as well have said, "It's a member of the Good Old Boys Club." Thankfully, we were not in another country delivering a valueless girl, who might have been killed for coming out the wrong gender.

We were now ready to play our parts in the life of this new tiny human being and his rite of passage, as described by LaTorre in *Sexual Identity: Implications for Mental Health*:

> *The sex of your child and his health are about the only things your doctor tells you about him. In fact, besides... (length and weight) and a name...From this moment on, you treat the child as though he were a member of his sex, which he is, and as though he possesses qualities of his sex, which he does not.*

I was raised with a brother and a cousin who lived on the first floor of a three-story house and neither of them were the brightest bulbs in the chandelier. Besides being as stubborn as a mule, my brother was neither spiritual nor sweet, and once he married his second wife his character flaws got even worse. In spite of this, our mother fawned over him as though he were a combination of Christ, Gandhi, and Albert Einstein. "My son, my son..." was the refrain I heard all my life.

Almost all of my girlfriends said they heard it too – or admitted they were the same way towards their sons. Boys are anointed as kings, and given sainthood, which is further confirmed by their mothers and fathers. Many daughters experience this bias all of their lives, so they come to believe they must accept that the son is the heir to the throne. This "anointment-by-parents" is crucial to understand because it sheds light on the fact that male preference is not simply a system that men enforce on women – although it is that too – it is something we also learn from our mothers. While it doesn't have to be that way, it starts so early that it's hard to reverse once it begins. Even the most privileged women suffer in their marriages from this "malady."

When Diana Spencer married Good Old Boy Prince Charles of England, she was young, innocent-looking, and beautiful. Prince Charles, a homely specimen with huge ears who talks as if he has a broom up his butt, needed an heir and a spare so he used a young, naïve Diana to bring some beauty and flexibility into an otherwise staid, worn-out British monarchy. But, he evidently continued to drool over his long-term love, Camilla, who is more in line with his age, looks and stuffiness.

In the beginning of the "Once Upon a Time" fairy tale, Lady Di thought she was marrying her Prince Charming; she and her children would live a life of royal luxury. Her first son would be the King of England and her fairy tale marriage would last forever. Instead, she suffered from bulimia and maladies that befall a woman when they marry the wrong man and have to stand by him as he indulges in the sins of a spoiled, privileged mama's boy – my son, my son of the Queen of England.

When the Royal Wedding was over, reality set in for Lady Di. Prince Charles wasn't Prince Charming after all, and he was in love with Camilla Bowles. After Charles and Diana divorced, Lady Di finally found love with Dodi Fayed, but they both died in that horrible car crash in Paris that is still being investigated as an "accident." And what did the press say about Charles and Diana then?

Most blamed her for the break-up of the royal marriage. They said the "world's princess" was flighty (unstable), not too intelligent (stupid), anorexic (sick), a spendthrift (extravagant), and a spoiled brat (bitch). She was portrayed as a badly messed up, adulterous wife because of spare Harry's red hair. And how did the press describe Prince Charles? He was a highly-educated, sophisticated, and trained-for-the-throne man-of-the-world. The behavior of Charles is no different from that of many other males, accepted because it is the male's prerogative and God-given right to bed whomever he wishes, without ramifications.

3 Competitive Little Creatures

"After the game, the King and pawn go into the same box."
Italian Proverb

Everything that happens after the birth of a child is standard operating procedure. We could probably write a manual for it. The process begins with orientation, indoctrination, conditioning, and disparate treatment of boys and girls. Although it is less prevalent now, we usually dress our boys in a deeper color and tell them to go off and have great adventures. We dress our girls in pastel or soft colors and tell them to be careful of what they do. Boys are handled less than girls and given more independence as they play. We read books to boys about young men who fight wars and slay dragons; we read books to girls about Cinderella meeting her Prince. We praise boys for being strong, discourage them from admitting weakness, while we allow girls to cry and appear weak and needy. We send boys outdoors, and then feed them, hug them and dote on them when they return home. Girls learn to nest, so they are often indoors, learning how to cook and clean the house, and praised for being giggly and coy "good little girls."

We put boys in competitive sports, while the girls are their cheerleaders. We train the boys to think of themselves as leaders to believe that problems can be solved by brute force. We tell girls that getting married and having babies is paramount to their happiness and success as a woman. The nurturing and nesting process begins early with their dolls and doll houses, just as birds prepare their nests for new baby chicks. Women are the gatherers or shoppers, who cook the food and clean the cave as housekeepers. We are the caregivers. While much of this may be less prevalent today than in the past – it still goes on.

Research into our "hunter-gatherer" ancestors shows that it was actually the opposite – "gatherers-hunters." The gatherers (women) provided about 85% of the food and the hunters (men) hunted only for the other 15%. Granted, hunting was more dangerous, but gathering was more useful and sustaining. The hunters were also probably relaxing for most of the day in their primitive "man caves" until it was time to hunt and bring in the bacon, while the women were doing the rest of the work. Things don't seem to be much different today than in those long-ago cave days.

Boys learn to appreciate the benefits they have and those they get from women. They get them without having to endure the pain of "women's work," or jobs that are often repetitive and thankless. Women's work has always been denigrated, while their pursuits are praised and rewarded. As they get older, most men have built-in sex, nicely decorated homes, well-kept heirs, sustenance, and bragging rights. They don't realize or care how time-consuming and hard it is to maintain a house – buying groceries, fixing meals, mopping, scrubbing, dusting, vacuuming, doing the laundry and changing the bed sheets and towels.

Another disparate, and sometimes desperate, area between men and women is sex and their view that anatomy is related to destiny. Boys come to appreciate their obvious sex organ, while girls hide or ignore their sexual parts until they can be used by someone else, generally a male. We let the boys know that their penises are very, very important - some are even circumcised in a special ceremony with religious overtones. And, boys are made to understand that they are going to use and enjoy their penises throughout their lives. Every little penis is treated with reverence, inside and outside the home. And women are part of fulfilling their sexual fantasies and needs.

A century ago, famed neurologist and psychoanalyst Sigmund Freud talked about women's envy of penises and the restrictions on female lives dictated by their anatomy. Some of Freud's theories are still with us today and still used by men to maintain the unequal status quo.

4 The Father of Love

"The fact is, women are in chains, and their servitude is all the
more debasing because they do not realize it."

Susan B. Anthony

Women's lives are dominated and circumscribed by their sexual reproductive organs and functions. That's what the "Father of Psychoanalysis" and "Father of Love" Sigmund Freud said. We suffer from penis envy, blaming our mothers for the missing appendage. Therefore, he opposed our emancipation. Freud's views have screwed us up for over a century and his progeny of theoretical clones are still spouting out some of that same nonsense today.

Freud believed the innate physical differences between men and women determined their destiny and that we women are, of necessity, subordinate to men. He also appeared to know about and believe in the benefits of the "my-son, my-son syndrome." He said that those who were preferred (or anointed) by their mothers (as he was) have lives filled with a "peculiar self-reliance and an unshakable optimism" leading to their success. A self-fulfilling prophesy and a long-lasting advantage.

Feminists have said that Freud's theories have diminished women and preserved the status quo between the sexes. Others have said there should be a distinction between anatomy and gender or physical and biological traits, along with socially ascribed norms. I believe it's all of the above. There is no reason women's anatomical differences are not considered far superior to men's. Instead, childbirth is denigrated to a lesser status even though it ensures the continuation of our race.

Despite the contributions he made to psychology, I'm not impressed by Freud's work. His biased and misogynistic theories tick me off. He called women suffering from horrible societal restrictions "hysterical." He bemoaned the fact that after 30 years of research into feminine souls, women were still unfathomable to him. He sure had a lot to say for a guy who admitted he couldn't figure women out. So, he cried: "What does a woman want?" His answer was a penis, but, he also said, "turn to the poets," or wait for science.

This gave men the golden opportunity to subordinate women further because of their anatomy and allowed men to throw up their hands and dismiss the needs of women. Women were impossible to understand or satisfy. If Freud the expert couldn't do it – how the hell could other men do it? The mysterious female is beyond complicated; she's unfathomable. And, we can't get something from men if they don't know what we want – it's a beautiful Freudian Female Catch 22! Even well-known comedian Steve Harvey, all these years later, is singing the same tune.

5 Down & Dirty

"If I'm not interested in a woman, I'm straight-forward. Right after sex, usually I say, 'I can't do this anymore. Thanks for coming over!'"

Vince Vaughn

Women envy men's penises and are hysterical. That's what Sigmund Freud said, and comedian Steve Harvey has added more problems to our state of mind. He tells us we need to give men what they want if we ever hope to get one and keep him. Dimpled-faced, likeable, well-dressed Steve says he wants to help women who feel "disappointed, disenfranchised and disillusioned because of their failed relationships." Further, he agrees with Freud that "Men cannot read minds, and we are completely incapable of anticipating what you want." How can we not believe this man and the advice he gives in his book, co-authored with Denene Millner, *Act Like a Lady, Think Like a Man*? Right off the bat, when I heard the title, I wondered why a woman had to act like a "lady," but should think like a man. That's just the typical double standard coming from a rich 21st century Black male.

I really enjoy Steve Harvey in his many roles on television these days. But he's not a scholar or so hot himself. His former wife, Mary

Vaughn, was arrested and thrown in jail for contempt of court when she spoke out about their divorce. She and Steve were married for 16 years and had a drawn-out bitter custody battle in 2005. The divorce was sealed with a gag order, probably so it wouldn't hurt his illustrious career. Vaughn said she had no money for an attorney as she fought Harvey's legal team in court. So while she struggles, fast forward to Steve and his gorgeous third wife, Marjorie.

Steve and Marjorie appeared on the cover of *Essence* magazine under the caption of the "25 Most Influential African-Americans." In the article, he said Marjorie changed his life, helping him to become a more "honest, loyal and respectful man." He admitted he was never loyal and credits her, dripping in diamonds on her arm, finger and ears, with turning him around. Evidently, she wouldn't take any of his nonsense and forced him to curb his poor treatment of women. So now he feels confident in telling women what they have to do to get and keep a man. He was also saying the other two wives were not able to do this because he needed a woman who thought more of herself. But then that was before he became rich and famous.

Steve Harvey says that women are often clueless about men and can't understand their deception and the games they play. (Evil little creeps!) His solution is not to treat them in-kind, but instead give men what they want and deal with them "on their terms, on their turf, in their way." All this time, I thought that was what women were already doing! Now, a full-fledged comedian psychologist, Steve says love means three things for men: "Profess, Provide and Protect." And, in return men need three things from women: "Support, Loyalty and the Cookie." It's a kind of a "tit for tat" approach.

Further, a woman should treat a man like a King and give him sex, which he needs more than "air" itself. Then, if a woman doesn't give sex to her man for a month – he's going elsewhere. She gets special dispensation if she's pregnant with his child. Thank you, Steve. He says he's not the only man that thinks this way. Men in Clubs, such as motorcycle, country, Elks, Masons, and fraternities, understand what men need from women. He even outlines in detail a woman's exhausting day as she rushes to take care of a sick child, gets the kids ready for school, drives in traffic, works all day, and does the cooking and laundry when she gets home.

This is happening while Steve says the husband may not do much (Steve's a comedian after all). He still wants sex, while she just wants to watch her favorite TV show. Your man doesn't want to talk, so I guess you should be quiet and just "put out." His other chapters are filled with more insults to women, such as the Chapter on "Sports Fish vs. Keepers," in which he likens women to fish that are thrown back into the water like chum, or kept. He says women are at fault when a man cheats and I think he is trying to commiserate with us when he tells us that women "…have to lie back and allow a foreign object to enter your body."

How disgusting can you be? It made me think of the gross use of objects pushed into women's vaginas during some rapes. A foreign object is defined as an object that "intrudes where it should not be," like having something in your eye. A penis into a vagina is where it is supposed to be for procreation and recreation. Women do not "have to lie back and allow" a penis to enter her vagina, anymore than a man has to "stick his penis in any hole." Then he has the nerve to say that men "respect standards" so women should get some. Who in the world is Steve talking to here? Women are usually not the ones who lack standards. This is beyond pitiful! So – enough of Steve.

6 Finding a Good Man

"I've dated the sweet mama's boy, the musician rocker, the struggling artist – basically a lot of people without jobs."

Alyssa Milano

It's not easy to find a good man. And men have ideas and attitudes about the women they select. Pornography is supposed to warp men's minds when it comes to the type of sex they want. So do other things regarding women built into our society. Hugh Hefner of *Playboy* fame became a sexual icon because he knew what men wanted and needed; he gave it to them and it wasn't for good reading material. If anyone believes that, they will believe that women select men for their brains, not their looks, sexual appeal, or money. We've all been told the old adage, "It's just as easy to marry a rich man as a poor one!" But, did we listen – no. We had to learn the hard way.

We were also told to believe that if a man is good to his mother, he'll be a good husband. Another view is that men who are "Mama's Boys" have something wrong with them because they are under their mother's thumb. We just can't win. Personally, I have found that men who love their mothers seem to care about women more. They still have to be good-looking and sexually appealing, sensitive, kind, and have a job. Many women select older men to replace dear old dad, and some men do the same when it comes to replacing their mothers. They want a chief cook and bottle washer. Of course, most middle-aged and older men like to choose the younger models. Either way, the men to avoid are like the one below.

A miserable young misogynist said he went out to dinner with his mother, referring to her as "this ignorant female." He was angry because, in their discussion, his mother said you need money to date women, in other words - get a job. She basically said "Romance without Finance is a Nuisance." He was incensed and said he was fed up with the bullshit of women like his mother who mix love, finance and material possessions. Duh – since when is money not King? His tirade means he had no job, no money and a bad attitude – so no girlfriend. He blamed materialism on feminine bitches like Hulk Hogan's wife who manipulated poor Hulk emotionally, then took his money. Further, he said women will "manipulate you until your balls are dry…."

With men, it always comes back to their penises and balls. I haven't met any dried-balled men, but I've met many women who have been squeezed dry and used up by men, then traded in for juicier, wetter, and much younger ones. This young ass had no respect for women or his mother. At one point in his vituperative blog-a-thon, he said he could "slap" his mother, but he wouldn't. I guess his mother should be grateful. This is what she raised - a sexist pig and misogynist loser. She probably even paid for his meal. He needs to be bitch-slapped by a real bitch! I'll do it.

I talked to a young woman with three daughters who said she has only been divorced for a year and her ex-husband was lower than being married to a homeless guy. She said she wouldn't be dating for awhile and hasn't seen anyone worthy of shaving her legs for. Many women are out there looking on websites – the new bar scene. It's not easy to find that man in a million. And many women are just settling in order to get and keep a man, which comes back to haunt them later. Instead, we have to learn to live alone and be at peace with ourselves first. If a male comes along who is made of good material, then we can share our life with him. If not, we should live happily, alone.

7   There's a Shortage Out Here!

"I used to be Snow White, but I drifted."

Mae West

The U.S. is not like a candy store where we can pick from one manly, delectable treat or another. There are just not enough men to go around for all the women looking. And never mind asking the Fairy Godmother for a good one; she's probably out looking for a Godfather herself. The sex ratio for the entire world is 101 males to 100 females, but infant mortality rates are still higher for male babies than girls in most parts of the world. The number of males available also falls because of the environment, wars, imprisonment, early death and homosexuality. Environmental factors are supposed to impact on sex differences and morality rates. A research biologist friend of mine believes environmental pollution has affected testosterone and estrogen levels in the fetus, which can be corrected and reversed right after birth, thereby reducing homosexuality; hence, more available males.

There is either an enormous increase in the number of gay men or there were more hiding in the closets than we thought. Some say 21% of U.S. men are gay and 22% of U.S. women are lesbians. So that should pretty much even out the gender imbalances. Surveys and other estimates are that 4 to 9 million (close to 4% of the population) are gay, lesbian, bisexual and transgender (1.8% bisexual and 0.3% transgender). Anytime there's a 5 million statistical gap, then it's a big guess. Some of those who believe in reincarnation think that transgender people just came back into the wrong bodies.

The Director of the U.S. Office of Personnel Management (OPM) under President Obama was openly gay. He decided that a survey should be conducted asking Federal employees to voluntarily designate if they are lesbian, gay, bisexual or transgender (LGBT), now LGBTQ or Questioning for the Q. This voluntary designation is already done for affirmative employment purposes to collect data covered by statute, such as age, sex, race and national origin (RNO).

It would not only be illegal to ask an employee's sexual preference, but would open up an entirely new discriminatory avenue. RNO data is supposed to be private and confidential, but we know it's easy to obtain and is often given out freely in some agencies, which was the case at the U.S. Environmental Protection Agency. So, a homophobic supervisor could learn that one of his/her employees is LGB or T, and then take an adverse action against them because of it. An employee's sexual orientation, hetero- or homosexual, is just not a valid criteria for employment, yet EPA has recruited from colleges and universities with high numbers of LGBT students for years.

When I was single for many years, I found there was an extremely limited supply of good heterosexual men who wanted a feminist like me. I didn't cook, but liked to clean and iron; I didn't want children, but I liked them as long as they belonged to someone else; I was ambitious, hating lazy shirkers; I worked hard, despising goof-offs; and it took me forever to get my education, so I hate dumb asses who think they are smarter than others (as do many attorneys). As a white-collar professional from a mixed-collar (white and blue) family, I became a white collar, but sided with hard-working blue collar. I also sided with the unemployed and underemployed. I despise hypocrites and misogynists and I'm a die-hard feminist.

"Feminism" and "feminist" became dirty words used against females who fought for or wanted equality. A feminist is someone who advocates social, political, legal and economic rights for women. Does any woman have a problem with that or do they consider those rights strictly reserved for men? Denigrating feminism and feminists was a strategy used to pit women against each other – the anti-feminist against the feminist, just as working women are pitted against homemakers. I've always been proud to be a feminist, fighting for the rights of my gender. And, I have never been against women who want to live differently or work at home, which is often unappreciated and harder to do.

There just weren't that many men out there looking for a beauty like me. So for many years I found out what it was like to be in the mainstream of single life in the U.S. filled with misogynists and bullies. One time, a male I met at a local restaurant-bar near my home said aggressively to me, "Sit Down!" after getting ticked off by something someone said to him, probably that he was an unmitigated asshole. I must have looked shocked by this oblivious moron. I said I needed to use the restroom and high-tailed it out the front door to my car and home. I always seemed to be running for home and my two cats. Another time, while visiting my girlfriend in Arizona, a group of young men in the local restaurant-bar were being obnoxious and vulgar. I asked one of them if this was typical of all of the men in the area or was it just him; he said there were five women to every man in Phoenix, so get used to it. He was just another lying jackass.

Good men are snatched up by women right away – leaving the not so good out there to pick from. I think it would help if we had a website for our discards listing their faults, personally annoying idiosyncrasies, and deviant behaviors. Without that – it's a shell game. The U.S. has more females than males and the female-male ratio differs by state and location. For example, based on the 2004 U.S. census, Alaska has 103.2 males for every 100 females in comparison to the U.S. average of 95.8 males for every 100 women. So, if you need a man, start packing your Parkas.

This is not the same case in other countries where there is a shortage of girls because of femicide, women/girl trafficking, and other horrific abuses. The U.S. engages in wars, declared or undeclared, authorized or unauthorized, cold or hot, so we are killing off or disabling many of our young men, and reducing the young male population. If we are not doing that, we are imprisoning them, particularly Blacks and Hispanics. So, women spend a lot of their time dreaming about men, looking for them, or going it alone. Vibrator sales are probably on the rise.

Eventually, I just stopped looking for a decent, good-looking, clean, and nice guy. If a man threw himself at me, I would consider him, but otherwise, I got used to living alone and enjoying myself. I found that when I stopped looking, I became more independent and content.

And, my neat-freak Virgo personality made me even more particular when it came to my selection or rejection of the men I met.

8   A Lid for Every Pot

"Our dog died from licking our wedding picture."
Phyllis Diller

Many men are just plain slobs. Since statistics are so poor, I would guess it's 100 slobs to every neat freak, higher if there is no woman around in their life, and then it probably soars to 5,000 to 1. I'm especially neat and can't seem to do anything until I clean up. This may have been a holdover from my youth when we were required to finish all our chores before we were able to go out to play. I still feel that way, which may not be a good thing. A person's energy only stretches so far, and cleaning and repetitive household chores may prevent us from doing more interesting or important work.

Most men don't have that problem – they just head out and do their thing. They assume things will be in order when they get home, unless they live alone. Then, generally, his place is either a pig sty or he has someone take care of it - a girlfriend, his mother, or a housekeeper. This should get a rise out of neat men out there going it alone. It's probably why married men live 10 years longer than their single friends. I've often felt that I didn't need a man as much as I needed a good wife.

I've always been amazed at how dirty men can be and have chalked it up to sports and sex – rolling around in the dirt and as they say, "doing the nasty." When I was younger, I was shocked and disgusted when I saw an extended family member pull out his "member" at a ballgame, go behind a tree, and pee on the tree roots and bark, as if he were a dog. He didn't bark like a dog, he just peed like one. He had to pee, so he did. Some men have to spit, fart and burp, so they do, making it a tremendous joke on all of us in the vicinity. There was a civilian executive in the military who regularly "passed gas" whenever or wherever he wanted, even sitting with female employees on the train when they travelled. Those who knew this executive pig learned to sit in a different car.

Spit and we walk in it; fart and we smell it; pee and it kills the trees. I can still envision the peeing old man. This all sounds so harsh and gross to say, but imagine, we're living and trying to endure it. I've encountered men who readily pick their noses, jiggle their penises, openly belch, admittedly don't wash their hands after using the toilet, take their socks off to smelly, disgustingly unkempt feet, and don't wash their clothes. Some throw their dirty underwear on the floor, smell of body odor and bad breath, use foul language, tell filthy jokes, engage in premature ejaculation, and are just slobs and pigs out looking for female companionship. They need a woman who will tolerate them, clean up after them and clean them up. There's supposed to be a lid for every pot and from Steve Harvey's perspective – these are your Kings.

A young girl at the dentist's office told me her husband just throws his clothes on the floor when he gets home from work and puts his briefcase on the dining room table. It drives her crazy. My suggestion was for her to buy large baskets and either throw his things in them or make him do it. The other option was to leave them there, but she's probably a Virgo and can't do it. I have baskets all over the house for my paper- and magazine-collecting husband and it works – it's either that or the booby hatch. Thank goodness for the "World Market" with all those baskets, making me think this may be happening all over the world.

A male professional friend of mine used to blow his nose at lunch and put his snotty handkerchief on the table. We were all grossed out and the employees I supervised said they could no longer take it. I asked him to blow his nose away from the table and not put his soiled handkerchief on the table. He proceeded to lecture me on why we used handkerchiefs in the first place. In the old days, he said, men would wipe their noses with their shirt sleeves at the table, so King Richard II of England invented the handkerchief. Did I know he was just carrying on as he was supposed to as a King? I wouldn't be getting anywhere with him, so I talked to his wife. She said it was a lost cause -- he never listens to her, either. Then I noticed when his handkerchief was not handy, he would use the napkin -- which now makes me want to bring my own napkins to restaurants. I already bring my own salt and pepper shakers. If this keeps up, I'll need a satchel filled with kitchen wares.

9 Freeloaders & Married Men

"I looked up my family tree and found out I was the sap."
Rodney Dangerfield

I'd rather feed my cat and clean his litter box than feed and clean up after some of the men I've dated. Some of them were pitiful human beings! A great many were looking to freeload off me. Others just wanted a quick roll in the hay, but I didn't live in a barn. Lots of the men lied about almost everything, from not having a wife and family to their real professions. A few wanted to move in with me when they found out I owned my own townhouse and car. Some just dreamed they had sex with me and spread that rumor; a few wanted to hit me up for money – basically, they wanted to hit me up any way they could.

But, mother didn't raise a fool. If these jerks needed something from me, they were in really bad shape, and I didn't need any more baggage to carry. A friend of mine calls some of the women he dated "a load." That's so crude, but I realized I didn't want any loads either. I consider myself lucky not to have ended up with any of the true beasts and brutes out there who use and abuse women unmercifully. I'd have probably ended up in jail. But, what's a girl to do?

Many of us, females and males, can relate to being something close to stalkers or "tree-sitters." These are the poor souls who are going with married men or women and spend all their holidays and free time sitting alone at home, spying on them from their car, or hiding behind trees or bushes with binoculars or night-vision goggles. Men just lie and hope they won't get caught. They say they aren't married when they are. Some say that their marriage is over because their wife "doesn't understand" or have sex with them anymore. Most say they will be leaving their wives any minute. Don't hold your breath......

This will often go on for years until the mistress gets fed up or meets someone else who treats her with respect. There are men in the same boat, but there is no antonym for Mistress – so how about a new word – Misstash because stash means hidden and both relate to hair as in "tresses" and "mustaches." Mistress and Misstash – sounds good to me. The movie *Bridesmaids* has a great skit about a selfish married man, his attitude and the impact on his single mistress. The 1987 movie *Fatal Attraction* about a married man's one-night stand put the fear into many men, just as the Lorena Bobbitt's "cut off your penis" case did. Going with a married man is a losing proposition, to be avoided at all costs. There may be a shortage out here, but that doesn't mean you have to settle for seconds – and don't believe a word he says.

An article in American Association of Retired Persons (AARP) on "Why Men Cheat" said that everyone knows why men cheat: quite a few men are pigs; and they "disingenuously identify themselves as hunters.... biologically incapable of monogamy." The reasons the article gives as to why many men don't cheat include: being incredibly lazy, startlingly ugly, cheap, or afraid of getting caught. Affairs are time-consuming and they saw the movie *Fatal Attraction*. I knew it!

Statistics on how many cheat on their spouses are no better than any other data collected. Who's admitting it, anyway? In one estimate, 3% - 4% of married people have a sexual partner other than their spouse in any given year. Up to 22% will have an affair while in a monogamous relationship. Affairs increase when the hormones are raging, during our younger years; as we get older, the number declines. So it seems like a good idea to get your sexual drives and needs out of the way before you marry and marry later rather than earlier – but while your clock is still ticking for having babies. Who knows how many people are having affairs? It's mainly important when it's your spouse or significant other. Get smart and alert – no sense in making yourself open to cheaters or what they can bring into the relationship, like Sexually Transmitted Diseases (STDs).

I've always been alert to losers and users. The latter is evident without much time elapsing. He is needy and wants what you have without coming up to the table with anything. He probably identified you as a caring giver - a user's dream. Before you blink your eyes, he will have moved in with you, gotten into your bank account, borrowed money and used you unmercifully. The losers are no better because they drag you down with them. Both of these types will empty out more than your refrigerator.

10 What's Wrong with Mr. Right?

"When I eventually met Mr. Right
I had no idea that his first name was Always."

Rita Rudner

It's a fact of life that a man must love a woman more than she loves him! Any woman who doesn't believe this will be in for a rough time. Only when we value ourselves, as much or more than men value themselves, can we be sure to avoid really bad-acting, nasty men just looking for their next female sucker.

Men always have an opinion on why women can't find good men. It's invariably our fault. And, there are always handy lists that we can follow to be successful husband hunters. One list was so inane, I had to share it with you and added my suggestions in a "he said, she said" way.

He says: Do what he asks you to do, without question – If a man asks you for a favor and you question him and say 'Why?'....he will instantly feel like you just don't want to do it.

She says: Don't do what he asks you to do without a good reason – and don't do what you don't want to do. Life is short and often dirty. You are not a doormat. If he asks you for a favor, always ask why; you are not his fairy Godmother, or his MasterCard.

He says: Maintain yourself – Men are visual, which means if you let yourself go, he will lose interest. He doesn't want to commit to a woman who is only going to get worse.

She says: Women have eyes, too, which means if his pot belly is hanging over his penis, she will lose interest; if he is a premature ejaculator, she will lose interest; if he doesn't have a job or ambition, she will lose interest. He is not your father and he will not be getting any better as time goes on either.

He says: Be financially dependent (sic) – It can help a man to know that you aren't going to take every last penny he has.

She says: Don't be independently useable, so he can take every last penny you have, then go on "Judge Judy" and say it was a gift. Keep your money under lock and key. If he has no money, yours is still not his.

This diatribe went on and on with: trust him, be there for him, compliment him, accept responsibility for a fight, and learn to take a joke and criticism. Then the inevitable -- maintain his interest by being sexually pleasing to him, being honest and making him laugh! What are we – 21st century sexual clowns?

Surveys are taken constantly about male-female relationships because they are so poor -- both the surveys and the relationships. One said that the most significant difference was in ranking what each gender found important: women ranked their desire for home and children 4th; men ranked it as 9th; men ranked ambition for women as least important; women rated character and personality much higher than physical attractiveness. Of course, when it comes to considering a man sexy, power and money grabs women's attention.

Another survey of 20,000 men and women said the traits desired differed from the first meeting and the long-term. At first glance, women want kindness, a sense of humor, ambition, sexual chemistry, good teeth and lips. Over time, they still want kindness and a sense of humor, but they shift those physical traits for proximity and stage in life – or bad teeth and companionship. Initially, women want to be sexually attracted to a man; but later she's more interested in whether or not he has the skill and interest to satisfy her sexually. We also crave companionship with men since we know we'll be mainly with women later in life and may spend at least 10 years alone.

Whatever all the surveys say, the success and happiness in a woman's life depends on her self-esteem and independence. These things allow her to better evaluate partners and to avoid bad, morally sick, abusive, over-sexed, lying, cheating, self-centered, egotistical, and misogynistic men. There will always be some of these ready to destroy or kill you, and your children, if you let them.

11 $10 on Number 5, Please

"All right everyone, line up alphabetically according to your height."
Casey Stengel

You have a better chance of picking a winner in the Kentucky Derby or the Preakness than you do in picking your first husband. Over the years, I learned that a "happy wife and happy life" depends a lot on the first man a woman marries. In countries with arranged marriages, many women have no choice in the matter and many such marriages work out because the families involved help to make them succeed. We like to think of ourselves in the U.S. as far more advanced, yet our divorce rate is close to 60%. Most American marriages fail, and many others that last are enduringly unhappy.

We are optimistic as a people, and American women believe in fairy tales showing a world filled with good men who are like most of them – generous in spirit, kind, gentle and caring. Generally, a woman wants to build her nest, raise her progeny with a nice man, and live happily ever after in their home with its white picket-fence. But it's just not that way.

My parents had a 52-year marriage. Every time Mom and Pop hit a rough patch, they took a cruise together – and there were so many cruises we lost count. Marriage is never easy. I think my parents' long marriage was what made me a "10-year itch" person. I was scared of a long marriage that would sink into boring sameness or swampy muck. And I have motion sickness, so cruises were out. I had a wonderful first marriage until the 10-year itch hit me after marrying too young to see and touch the world. Once I got out there on my own, I was ill-prepared, indecisive and insecure.

I recall a beautiful morning when the sun was shining in the windows of my high-rise apartment. I wanted to paint the living room – but what color? I called my ex, a skilled artisan and decorator with an eye for color and design. We were divorced and good friends, possibly because we had no children and he was a nice Irish guy who loved life and his mother, Dolly.

"Hey, I can't decide what to paint the large wall in the living room. Can you help me out?" I asked nicely.

"We're not together anymore, remember?" he said, laughing. *"That's your space. Just pick a color and live with it. If you don't like it, you can always paint it again."*

"Yes, but you're the expert -- so please give me a hand," I begged.

"Nah," he said. *"You're on your own and it would be good for you to do it yourself."*

So much for our being friends after divorce! In a fog of indecision, disgusted with myself for having my freedom without knowing what to do with it, I drove to the local paint store, and asked the young salesman to recommend a color. I was independent and free – but couldn't cope with making decisions without a man's help. It's funny when I think back on it now – but it wasn't funny then.

I finally bought a huge wallpaper mural of a forest with fir trees and evergreens that covered the entire living room wall, floor to ceiling. I made a colossal mess with the paste and paper, water, and glue. I fell off the ladder twice, and the mural was a wrinkled mess. With these giant evergreens and firs, my apartment looked like a cock-eyed Yosemite National Park. It's fair to say I couldn't see the forest for the trees.

I knew I'd been a fool not to make a careful paint selection. The guy managing the apartment complex was a macho man who already hated me. Now what would he do when he saw this mess? A wise friend of mine once said, "If you find yourself in a hole, the first rule is: 'Stop digging.' So I did. I lived with that wallpaper until I moved, or snuck out, because I was unemployed and broke. I hoped whoever moved in after me liked to go camping in the woods. During my down years, I realized I was extremely naïve and had been sheltered from the harsh realities of life in a man's world.

My ex fared much better than I did – he looked great and had women hanging all over him. Not that he was very particular about the women he selected to have sex with after divorcing. He seemed to be making up for lost time. He would come by to visit me in my tree-lined abode so he could rub in how well he was doing compared to me. It was a silent and smirking, "I told you so." I tossed him away and ended up on my ass in the woods every day, wondering where I was going. My financial and emotional independence took a nose dive too. As my brother would say, there was no one to count on but the three of us: "me, myself and I." But, some of my girlfriends were even in worse condition when they were dumped, and many of them also had children to raise.

CHAPTER II

1 Yes, Dear

Housework can't kill you, but why take a chance?"
Phyllis Diller

A woman's life is drudgery smothered in perfume. One female blogger said that women are strong and unique, to be compared to no other. She said women handle everything with ease, divine wisdom and strength – from menstruation pains, childbirth, sleepless nights, post-natal blues, shopping, cleaning, providing, and dealing with relatives, yours and his. She believes women are very diplomatic by nature with pure hearts and a sense of purpose. Woman is a consummate person, sacrificing all for her family, and will even relinquish her outside job, as well as professional and personal goals, for her family. She will still have to satisfy her man sexually and emotionally. I just don't think the same way, so the women who want to be self-sacrificing martyrs will have to do it without me.

Life is all about competition and strategy – who's going to get what and from whom? Winner takes all. Loser gets zilch or close to it. Since a man's mindset is competitive, they accept that fact – the goal is to win! They even do it to get a quality woman as their wife and compete against other men for her. Men like to feel (and often need to feel) that they have won a competition for their woman. Just as Steve Harvey is proud to have won Marjorie. During the competition, the wooing period, men are prepared to change their personalities and put their best foot forward. But once the competition is over and they have won the match, men expect to be able to revert to their natural selves.

The before-marriage scenario is not the same post-marriage, when he feels, "I got her, no one else can have her, she is mine, she meets my basic needs for sex, a nest, food, and heirs, and if you are a Princess, a "spare." The latter phase is the "I'm so confused about what she wants" so I can't possibly give her what she needs or desires. Generally, the expression "familiarity breeds contempt" often refers to long-term relationships, such as marriage. Yet, there are many couples who become closer after they stay together for a long time. Distain in relationships may be caused by the partners becoming too comfortable so that they no longer maintain the same degree of respect, romance, and support for each other.

Where did all those flowers go? Men seem to become complete idiots and lose their minds post-marriage, if they had any before they said "I Do." So, what do we women want? How about equality here? How about some heavy-duty support? How about time for ourselves since we're now working full-time outside the home yet the burdens of the household are still ours? How about doing your share? We want a little cooperation – is that too much to ask? We are trying to negotiate with often non-negotiating men and husbands. And we are barraged with messages, such as: 'Do what your man asks… keep your looks… trust your man… please him sexually… and be there for him.' What about us?

There are not many women who haven't heard, "Can I help you, dear?" This means the job is yours and you can get some assistance if he feels like it. If he doesn't – tough! Many women complain about men saying they will "babysit" their own children if she needs to go out or take a break. He's like a fill-in, assistant or temp worker, usually needing guidance up the kazoo, until you throw up your hands and do it yourself. This is a very effective strategy: Mess up the laundry by turning the clothes pink; lose one of the children while watching sports; slop water all over the floor when doing the dishes; tear up the kitchen while cooking. Then, step aside while someone who knows how to do it does it. Guess who? That does not mean that if a man likes to do something, such as cooking, he shirks that – if he likes it, he does it. If he doesn't like it – it's yours. If he does it, it's the greatest achievement since sliced bread. If you do it – good luck – don't expect any accolades or credit.

2 To Beget or Not to Beget

"I knew I was an unwanted baby when I saw my bath toys were a toaster and a radio."

Joan Rivers

Everyone knows the decision to have children affects women much more than it does men. Women's entire bodies and lives change when they have children - sometimes for the better, sometimes not so much. We have a predisposition to procreate so we don't die out as a species, just as we have a strong innate drive to avoid or prevent death. So wouldn't you think that women who are responsible for our futures, bearing, and raising our children would be held in the highest esteem and considered indispensible?

Women are constitutionally stronger in ways that allow us to endure the pains and health risks of pregnancy and childbirth. Yet, the myth lives on that men can endure more pain than women because they are stronger and fitter. Anyone who's had to care for a sick man or husband can tell you that many men are worse than babies when they are sick. They whine about the smallest amount of pain.

British philosopher Herbert Spencer said that fitness does not refer to whether an individual is bigger, faster or stronger, but instead a physically fit person must just be "fit enough." And, women are certainly fit enough and constitutionally stronger in ways that allow us to endure the pains and health risks of pregnancy and childbirth. As comedian Carol Burnett said when asked to describe childbirth labor pain: *"Take your bottom lip, pull it over the top of your head, and that's what labor pain feels like."* I don't know many men who would endure that even for the good of man- and woman-kind, do you?

Women in childbirth are also pointlessly working against gravity. Did the 18th century English physicist Sir Isaac Newton say that gravitational force only pertains to men? Women giving birth are lying on their backs with their legs in stirrups waiting for the baby's head to emerge. If the baby refuses to come out easily, the doctor may use forceps to pull the poor baby out of her womb as she screams, grunts, pushes, sweats and groans. She is trying to push a 7-pound baby out the small birth canal, against gravity, while her doctor is rolling around on a stool. Let's not make it easy for her.

Bearing a child is impossible for a man, so most men candidly admit they prefer not to do it or witness it. This is why there are so many jokes about men having babies, such as:

- Maternity leave would last two years with full pay
- Natural childbirth would become obsolete
- They'd stay in bed during the entire pregnancy, and
- The human race would die out.

Unfortunately, pregnancy among unwed celebrities, who have money and help, has been touted in the media. This may be why the U.S. now has the highest teen pregnancy and birth rate in the Western industrialized world. The rate was higher in the 1950s, 1960s, and 1980s, but women were marrying younger then. Most of today's teen mothers are unwed (79%) with about 820,000 teens becoming pregnant each year. There are more young women waiting before they have children to finish their educations. But it is that other large group of girls getting pregnant in their teens that we are not properly dealing with. And with the shortage of men in this country – good men – girls and women are not waiting to have children until they find the perfect man. Instead, because their clock is ticking, they are having children alone -- or adopting before their birth clock winds down.

As a female who consciously chose not to have children, much of what the average woman goes through as wife and mother missed me. I give other women a lot of credit for walking around for nine months with an enormous belly, backaches and hormonal imbalances. We childless women are busy keeping our attention on ourselves, what we like, what we want to do, with only our partner's wishes and needs to consider, when and if we feel like it. When we choose ourselves and our careers over having children, we invest ourselves less emotionally and financially than our sisters who decide to have children. We use our money and time for ourselves: lunches and dinners out without cooking or washing dishes, housekeepers, facials, massages and spa days. Our bodies don't change much so we don't have stretch marks, varicose veins and other pregnancy effects. Our lives are also very different with our partners and spouses. But, we also lack major rewards and benefits from having those glorious little human beings that represent our future.

3 Super-Women – That's Us

"I hate housework! You make the beds, you do the dishes and six months later you have to start all over again."

Joan Rivers

Women have achieved their rights -- the "right" to work, work, and work to exhaustion. We are "Superwomen," trying to be perfect in everything, at our jobs, in our homes, for our bosses, for our children, for our spouses, and for our country. We've retained our old jobs -- and got lots of new ones. Whoever said 'Women's work is never done' knew what she was talking about. Men are tactically and strategically smarter than women when it comes to getting out of doing work. Many men say they cannot take care of house maintenance, as my father's generation did, because they are just not handy (just randy). They have their main jobs and can only "assist" or "help" little "wifey-poo," when she asks. She now has to wear the pants and the apron, at the same time.

Women moved back into the workforce, as they had after the World War II years of "Rosie the Riveter," but we did not effectively compete, negotiate or insist on *quid pro quo* for taking on another full-time job. We should have agreed to bring home a second paycheck only in exchange for relinquishing our duties in housekeeping, child-rearing and -caring, food shopping and cooking, clothes washing and driving the kids. While many women like to do things at home, the trade could have been based on preferences, but fairly distributed. Instead, men became our little helpers, just like the kids.

I had hope when I heard the response of a young girl in South Carolina. My friend Muriel asked her son's latest girlfriend what she did at home. Sweet as could be, she said, "*I don't clean or cook, or anything like that, but I do a little dishes.*" From then on, we called her "Little Dishes." She was in college and being a housewife for Muriel's son was not on her agenda -- nor on his either. He changed women as often as dish towels. But, most men are doing what she is doing, a little dishes, unless they are the exception to the rule – and there are plenty of those guys out there, too, so don't get your drawers in a bunch. But, for most women, what happened?

What else could they do but proclaim and brag about their "super-woman" status – as if it were a badge of honor or a reward given to good girls who learned to do everything perfectly, without whining or nagging. And, before we fail to address this nagging thing most women are accused of – I know many men naggers and whiners, along with control freaks and domineering idiots. If men did what they were asked to do the first time, instead of feigning stupidity or procrastinating, nagging wouldn't be necessary. I don't know about other Virgos, but I get tired of hearing myself.

We were told we could attempt to achieve as much, or even more than our male counterparts, more than we've ever dreamed was humanly possible, without having a total nervous breakdown. Freudian hysteria is nothing compared to this. As an attorney once said to me when he learned that I worked instead of shirking my responsibilities: "We like people like you who do the work because that's less for us to do. We let them, we thank them, and then they appreciate us for letting them."

He appreciates and thanks us for bringing in that second paycheck, but that doesn't mean he wants to clean the toilet.

And don't expect the men to be around when it's time to take care of our elderly parents. More than 42 million of us today are in the "Sandwich Generation" caring for children and aging parents; almost 90% of the time it's a woman who cares for the elderly parent. Another 20 million families are caring for a disabled family member at home with a greater burden again falling on women. Since we are living longer, the window of care-giving continues to grow, along with the financial and emotional costs. Yet super-women in their middle years tend to have salaries and benefit packages smaller and more vulnerable than those of men. Most males, particularly siblings, don't even offer help or refuse it when asked. They're busy.

So we women try to do it all. We want to be considered indestructible – able to fly through houses at breakneck speed and still have energy to care for everyone, fix dinner, and have unbridled sex. This is so we can feel that we, our roles, and functions are important, needed and appreciated. We are super strong and virtuous goddesses, always trying to smell good for our man. We are what every man wants - a good, clean, pure woman who can put in a hard day's work -- and then screw like a rabbit. As comedian Billy Crystal said, "*Women need a reason for sex. Men just need a place.*" Joan Rivers answered for women by saying, "*It's been so long since I had sex I've forgotten who ties up whom.*"

4 Marital Recidivism

*"I love being married. It's so great to find someone special you
want to annoy for the rest of your life."*
                                        Rita Rudner

Women bore sexually more easily than men. With all the burdens
falling on the middle-class, it is any wonder that the emotional and
physical energy required to maintain a lusty, high-flying, relationship
wanes -- for some, quicker than others. Sexual compatibility is essential
if you want a marriage to last. If he wants sex and you don't, there's
trouble. If you want sex and he doesn't, more trouble. If he wants
kinky sex, and you don't, real trouble. The number of scandals of men
engaging in sex outside marriage should enlighten us as to what's really
going on. Many wives have just detached themselves and gone on to
other things, or the children start to come first, so he can take "it"
elsewhere.

A girlfriend of mine had a husband who made his "day job" the
watching of pornography. It was on the main TV in the living room
when I arrived, and I had to tell him to turn it off. My friend told me
he wanted sex several times a day, every day. I told her I'd rather throw
up than have sex every day, never mind several times a day. That's just
crazy. I also told her to tell him to get a job, but she didn't.

Another friend has a husband who stays in his upstairs room on
the computer every night, ignoring her. He says he's writing a best-
seller. Come on. Since they aren't having sex, he's middle-aged, and
she's overweight, he's probably on the Internet doing his thing. I told
her to check his computer. She ignored me too. So, shut up and live
with it as many women do.

Lots of women close their eyes and ears, go about their business
and retain their security, a house, kids, and money. Females who were
surveyed said they would consider marrying someone they were not
"in love" with if the mate had everything else they wanted. With
90% of us marrying, 50-60% of us divorcing, and a high number

unhappily married, you would think we'd learn from our mistakes. But no, we go right out and do it again, like Elizabeth Taylor and her serial monogamy. At least she got rubies and diamonds.

About 70% of us remarry, which is marital recidivism, or "the tendency to relapse into a previous undesirable type of behavior or crime." Sadly, chances are high of marrying another dud, but divorce is easier the second time around. First marriages will more likely result in a second marriage, but the second marriage will not increase the odds of them staying married. This is attributed to Americans being optimistic when it comes to selecting a partner – 'til death do us part, which has come to mean death of the marriage, not our own death.

The median age now for a first marriage is about 26 for women and 28 for men. A century ago, the median age at first marriage was 22 for women and 25 for men. More young women and men are pursuing their educations and careers before plunging into marriage and having babies. This is even reflected in the new health care program that insures young adults until age 26 who are still living at home. The number of kids living at home, off of Daddy and Mommy, has increased since the economy took a nose dive. Also, kids are lazier. Why not have Mom and Dad pay and do everything, while we enjoy ourselves? Past generations were kicked to the curb when they reached 17, 18 or 19, or they would have to pay steep rent for room and board.

People used to stay in marriages for the family and children, surviving all the ups and downs, often enduring misery for decades. In our current throw-away, here-and-now society, couples are more likely to divorce than to remain together. Some will stay together until the children leave the nest – then they fly out looking for something exciting and new. Men still want "laid back," sensual, supportive, and un-materialistic women. In other words, don't nag me, ladies; be sexy, and don't spend my money. Many of my girlfriends have cheap husbands and they live with it, scrimp or spend their own money. I don't get it.

As the years pass, the longer couples are married, the less important their sexual drives become and the more important their security, companionship, and commitment to each other become. Through their years of give and take, hardships, tragedies, happiness, love, joy, trials and tribulations, they learn to satisfy each other's basic needs. It sometimes becomes, "It's cheaper to keep her/him, than it is to get rid of her/him." Many of my divorced and single girlfriends say they don't want to be responsible for an older, possibly unhealthy, needy man later in life – it's just too much trouble. Other women say they would enjoy companionship but they don't want the problems that go with it, meaning sexual relations, or putting up with a cheap, controlling, lazy couch potato – a big-bellied load.

5   It's Nobody's Fault

"We sleep in separate rooms, we have dinner apart, we take separate vacations – we're doing everything we can to keep our marriage together."
Rodney Dangerfield

Divorce is a lousy game for everyone but divorce lawyers. Infidelity, children out of wedlock, cancer of the throat, herpes, STDs, AIDS, desertion, beatings – it's nobody's fault but your own!

After all the dust settles, not surprisingly, men do much better in divorce than women. Many women are just not paying enough attention to what's going on while married, allowing men to hide assets and engage in other shady "get out of marriage" business. Added to this are the "No Fault" divorce laws that generally benefit men. Neither spouse has to prove "fault." It's enough to state that they are incompatible or have "irreconcilable differences." No fighting, no derogatory testimony, no finding of guilt or innocence, no misconduct by either party aired in public -- it's just over. Every state but Illinois and South Dakota has the No Fault laws in place. A copy of the state's divorce laws should be given to every couple when they buy their marriage license.

A couple's marital property or property acquired by the two during the course of their marriage is generally divided equally based on the state law. There is always the hope that parties are treated fairly. But no matter what the laws are, women do worse even when the settlement looks fair and equitable. Women were typically awarded custody of the children, but not anymore. Even though women still do most of the child-caring and -rearing, there are custody battles. Unfortunately, women's lack of earning power often makes it more difficult for them and the children – when they are fighting the divorce and afterwards.

After divorce, many men start a whole new life with a younger wife and a second family, while the ex-wife struggles with the old life. This inequality is exacerbated by the fact that we have family-unfriendly work policies and environments, which have been created and managed by men for men. Wages and promotions are for the full-time males who will not be getting pregnant, needing any special treatment, or taking time off to give birth and care for children.

Divorce settlements take none of this into consideration, so splitting 50-50 is a joke on women. The man still earns his pay without cramping his lifestyle or having to make a major contribution to the family's expenses. The quality of her life and the children's diminishes while he sends a monthly check to cover child support and/or alimony. That's if he sends it at all. His time is his time, his money is his money, and his life is his life after divorce. Meanwhile, *her* life is often a struggle because she takes on more without adequate help.

The No Fault laws have made women's lives even harder because the grounds no longer count. Causes for dissolution of marriage are no longer considered, such as: Adultery, Desertion, Abuse, Incarceration, Insanity, Impotence, Substance Abuse, and Transmitting Sexual Diseases or Infections. And men account for most cases involving these reasons that would turn it in favor of women. Even walking out the door and leaving everyone behind has no legal consequence.

The courts consider child and spousal support, property and financial division, not the overall trauma that a deserting spouse puts on the other party and their children. In No Fault divorces, no matter what the other party does, he/she is not at fault – live with it and get over it! Moving to South Dakota and Illinois sounds like a plan since they don't have No Fault divorce laws yet.

We must have been asleep when the divorce laws changed in this country. In a contentious divorce, women can no longer be assured they'll have the right to retain a child after carrying the fetus in their wombs for nine months. A little sperm goes a long way. We often lose because we lack the financial or political means to put up a good fight and to hire a good attorney, which is hard to find anyway. Many women select bad attorneys because they pick someone who makes them feel comfortable, probably a Good Old Boy. The bias and greed of this bunch - lawyers - is astounding.

Shakespeare said, "When law can do no right, let it be lawful that law bars no wrong….," and Charles Dickens said in *Oliver Twist*, "The law is an ass." And, you can forget "common-law marriages" that are no longer recognized in 27 states and 13 states never allowed it. There are only 9 states that allow common-law marriages to be contracted and the rules are so stringent and differing, you need an attorney again. If you remain together that long, something's wrong anyway. You lose.

6 Singing the Blues

"God bless the child that's got his own, that's got his own."

Billie Holiday and Arthur Herzog

Women who have achieved their own financial and emotional independence rarely want a man who has less than what they've achieved. Billie Holiday said in her autobiography that the famous song "God Bless the Child" was written after she had an argument about money with her mother who made the comment, "God bless the child that's got his own." When you're young, your choices are better than when you get older. But, we're born alone and we'll die alone – and we'll spend many of our middle years with strangers.

Women earning money can now be sued by their spouses for alimony and child support, even though for centuries women had almost no chance to get any support from their spouses. The courts and institutions have shifted to ensure that women are given the inalienable right to pay males. Even "Lady Justice" is balancing her scales in their favor after she turned her blind eyes against her sisters for centuries. The legal system and courts are filled with GOBs taking care of their own. Many celebrities are now fighting their spouses who are suing them for alimony and custody of the children and engaging in the typical name-calling.

Beatle Paul McCartney's divorce was the usual mud-slinging. His wife called him abusive and a violent drug user; he called her a gold digger and high-class prostitute. Christie Brinkley was called driven, angry and bitter by her husband, Peter Cook, after he was caught having an affair with his 18-year-old assistant. Poor David Gest said Liza Minnelli beat him during her alcoholic rages so he suffered neurological damage and severe headaches, and she gave him herpes; she said he stole $2 million and tried to poison her. They settled on a truce and No-Fault divorce.

One of the worst cases recently was that of celebrity Michael Douglas and his gorgeous wife, Catherine Zeta Jones. He said he had throat cancer from oral sex, not saying when or where he got it – leaving his wife out there. After all the publicity, he changed his story to say his doctor told him to lie about it when he actually had tongue cancer. Michael must have learned his tricks from the 1989 movie *War of the Roses* he starred in with Kathleen Turner. These divorces are no prettier, only more public with more money involved. But what is the alternative? No Fault divorce?

I am grateful that I was able to find my husband out of all the frogs I dated. He was a die-hard bachelor, but after a few serious tangos we learned to dance together without stepping on each other's toes – too much. It's an ongoing dance and my feet hurt sometimes, but if you play you've got to pay. Age is a great teacher and leveler; we also mellow out and mature – so we just spread out and find our own space. But everything is easier for the "Girl who has her own."

7 Lying – A National Pastime

"Men are liars. We'll lie about lying if we have to. I'm an algebra liar. I figure two good lies make a positive."

Tim Allen

Men lie and women believe them – that's the way the game is played! Of course, women tell lies, too. I worked for a female boss who was evil, sick, and a pathological liar. As a black female, she had it in for me because I married one of "her" handsome, successful men. She married a dud. I have also come in contact with many other women who live a life of lies, but it appears that men and women lie for different reasons. Many men lie without conceding that their lying is a betrayal.

Men see themselves as "handling" a situation, handling a woman's emotions by concealing things from her which "she's better not know-ing." Men can rationalize because there are all types of lies: The big lie, a little white lie, a barefaced lie, a strategic lie, sins of omission and commission, hyperbole, deceptive statements, half-truths, evasions, misrepresentations, and perjury. There's no end to the type of lies they can tell and be believed. While they are reaching for the moon and stars, going as high as they can in their lives and careers, maximizing their talents, income and status, men figure they may have to lie. That's just the way it is.

One of men's major lies revolves around infidelity, which tends to destroy their marriage. Staying in love with someone you can't trust is almost impossible. He's thinking he can "handle it," even if it's another woman's breast. The main example that comes to mind is our former President Clinton and all his GOBligook that included a man is not having sex unless he's inserting his penis into a woman's vagina. Oral sex under his desk in the Oval Office does not constitute having sex "with that woman," -- or was that the other woman? Monica is finally coming out of her shell to tell her side of the sordid tail – I mean tale. Getting ready for Hillary's run for President!

There are so many scandalous examples that it's hard to keep up with all of them. It's actually titillating for those of us stimulated by gossip, but devastating and damaging to all the women (and men) involved in these scandals. And, instead of using our independence and intelligence to stand our ground, women have become part of the problem.

We all laugh about the way men tell you they "love" you just before, during, or after they get into your pants. That's "just a white lie" for him, but probably a big lie to her because they are coming from different places. He's just trying to "get his rocks off," and she is emotionally moving toward love and forever. It must be related in some way to estrogen and the working of our brains.

Is it any wonder that relationships rooted in inequality only get worse? The fairy-tale dust and serotonin-driven lust wears off, the children are pushed through the birth canal, and everyday life seeps slowly and imperceptibly between the couple and the sheets.

Whatever happens, lying is so deceptive and hurtful because it means the other person thinks you're an idiot – stupid enough to lie to and be believed. Lies are ethically and morally wrong. They take away the other person's right to make a choice if the truth were told. But many people believe that lying well is a necessary art -- a way to contain the damage. If you think a person's lying – as was that horrendous boss of mine – they probably are, so check it out. We caught her lying so many times, she just started to admit them – but it never stopped her because prevarication was in her blood.

KAREN CARPENTER

A marriage gone horribly wrong because of lying and deceit was that of the famous musical legend, Karen Carpenter. She and her brother Richard formed the hit musical duo, The Carpenters. Her voice was unique and beautiful and their song, "We've Only Just Begun," is still an all-time favorite. Karen was an example of a talented and successful woman in the cutthroat music industry.

As was Lady Di, Karen married the wrong man and suffered from an eating disorder that eventually killed her. Her husband, a divorced real estate developer nine years her senior, blatantly lied to her. Even though he knew she desperately wanted to have children, he concealed the fact that he had a vasectomy and there would be no children during their union. He destroyed her dreams by manipulating and lying to her. And, this happens to many other women who date and marry men who lie and deceive them.

MARYANN

You just can't believe anything on the internet. My dear friend MaryAnn believed an idiot she met on one of the dating-mating Internet sites. Fast forward – they were getting married, buying a huge townhouse using the equity from the sales of her small townhouse and his house. They were going to live happily ever after. Her strategy should have been to marry first, then buy the new townhouse. You already know the end of the story….. Instead, she sold her place, put the equity on the new nest, and he slivered out like the snake he was at the last minute.

Off to counseling for her, and back on the internet dating service for him. It was a costly mistake that devastated her, but she had her own and the wherewithal to recuperate. She said she just stared at the ceiling for six months wondering where she went wrong. 'After all,' she said, 'I didn't know I was so desperate to get married at my age. It's hopeless when I couldn't even get a disabled mixed-race guy with one eye as my spouse.' We laugh about it now, but it was not funny at the time. It was a costly and hard lesson to learn – so be sure to watch out for a one-eyed mixed-race disabled guy on the internet looking for his next female sucker.

8 Standing by Your Man

"Never go to bed mad. Stay up and fight."
Phyllis Diller

Men believe it's okay for women to look like fools. After all, they think we're generally stupid. It's a shame women stand by their man after he's lied, cheated and gotten caught. The number of men having affairs or resorting to prostitutes is nothing new; what is new is that they expect their wives to stand by their sides for "moral and political support."

Anthony "The Weiner" Weiner had his problem exposed and his wife, Huma Abedin, stood by his side -- defending him after he texted photos of his penis to women. A Hillary Clinton protégé, Huma tried to use the excuse "It's a family problem" not a public one, but the public wasn't buying it. Weiner wanted to remain in the race for Governor of New York in spite of his public exposure. "The Peter Tweeter is a Repeater," joked Jay Leno on the *Tonight Show* as Weiner first denied, then admitted to continuing his perversion even after being "outed." On various newscasts, Weiner was shown admitting his sexual problem, then standing back defiantly, his arms across his chest, letting his wife take over to defend him.

The message being conveyed was that if his loving wife could tolerate him and his lying, so should we, the American public. So what if he was elected and continued to Tweet his Peter. This model of public service is not what we have in mind. And the impact on our children is mind-boggling. Our society is becoming more corrupt and morally bankrupt as we take these scandals for granted and view Miley Cyrus's ass in our face almost daily. She is quite the role model for young girls. If Anthony Weiner was on the street exposing his penis, he'd be arrested for indecent exposure, and Miley wouldn't be getting richer for hanging from a pole or exposing her private parts.

Former New York Governor Eliot Spitzer's now ex-wife Silda Wall Spitzer, a Harvard Law School graduate and a Wall Street attorney earning more than he was, stood with her cheating husband as he told the public he had spent thousands of dollars on a call girl at a Washington, D.C. hotel. A political analyst said she was part of a political team and just "taking one for the team." I guess she was doing what Ronald Reagan said in the movie *Knute Rockne, All American,* "…Some time, Rock, when the team is up against it, when things are wrong and the breaks are beating the boys, ask them to go in there with all they've got and win just one for the Gipper…."

Actually, she was doing what was suggested in the 1980 movie *Airplane*: "Win one for the Zipper." Spitzer humiliates her, but she defends him "so that she can hold the family together during the crisis, support the man she loves, and provide some sort of political viability for her man." This kind of GOBligook and humiliation should have ended decades ago. Wake up, women!

Spitzer's not alone, either. Louisiana Senator David Vitter's name appeared on the Madam List; Idaho Senator Larry Craig was arrested "tapping his toe" in an airport bathroom for a homosexual tryst; and New Jersey Governor James McGreevey announced he had a gay lover who was also a state employee. Former North Carolina Senator John Edwards really screwed up. He impregnated a campaign videographer while his wife, Elizabeth, was suffering from cancer. Edwards was indicted, but found not guilty on one count, the judge declared a mistrial on the other charges, and the Justice Department dropped the case. He's a Good Old Boy home free and Elizabeth is gone, along with his paramour and their child. He's moving on.

Hillary Clinton has been credited with providing a media template for how to behave when all hell breaks loose and you are standing by your lying man in politics. *Politico* reported: "It was a familiar scene… Once again, a politician was apologizing (sort of) and once again his wife was standing right there by him with impeccable makeup and unmovable hair." The Republicans will pull this out when and if Hillary decides to run for the presidency in 2016, along with Benghazi and many other tidbits. She's busy doing her up-front work right now.

Even African American Good Old Boy Herman Cain couldn't contain himself. A business executive and Tea Party activist from Georgia, Herman ran for the 2012 presidential nomination touting his 9-9-9 tax plan. He claims his plan came from a bank employee, but others say he took it from a *SimCity* video game that came out in 2003. The game taxed players 9% for industrial, 9% for residential and 9% for commercial taxes. It was easy to remember so it resonated with the Tea Partiers, and he became the conservative black Republican front-runner to beat Barack Hussein Obama in the polls. Cain later withdrew because of allegations of a decades-long affair with a woman.

The Good Old Boys of all races have strategies for everything and use games or even vaudeville acts for inspiration. Cain used a video game; others use the vaudeville skit from The Three Stooges, appropriately called "The Niagara Falls" routine. It goes like this:

"Slowly I turned Step by Step": Step 1 – Denial; Step 2 - Defiant; Step 3 - Wife Stands By Man; Step 4 - Unnamed Enemies; Step 5 - Sorrow and Hurt; Step 6 - Let Me Get Back to Work; Step 7 - Ask forgiveness from God, Family and Friends; Step 8 - The End or Re-emerge from the Ashes.

This is nothing new, but it should have at least diminished by now. I've researched some of the more salacious scandals of Presidents, Congressmen, Senators, Governors and Mayors and grouped them into categories. As far back as President Grover Cleveland, there have been "illegitimate" children. (I've put "illegitimate" in quotes because children are never illegitimate; it's their daddies who are.) After Cleveland came Presidents Jefferson and Harding; U.S. Senators Thurmond and Edwards, and Governor Schwarzenegger. These are only the ones we know about.

Going with under-aged girls includes two who went to prison, Congressmen Mel Reynolds and Buz Lukens, and then Gerry Studds and Governor Neil Goldschmidt. Interns have to watch themselves because these included President Clinton, Congressmen Gary Condit and Dan Crane. And, to set the record straight: Interns are young and taken in by the power around them. It's up to the dirty old men to make sure these incidents don't happen. Yet, our society blames the intern.

At a recent party, when Monica was mentioned, a female attorney called her a whore, said she was not innocent and knew what she was doing – giving the President a blow job under the desk and she heard Lewinski was paid $12 million. This attorney didn't say much about Clinton, just castigated a member of her own gender. He's still giving out advice to the country and supporting Hillary in her run for the presidency in 2016. They would go down in history as the first husband-wife Presidents if she's successful.

When we elect a President, they have four or eight years to put their policies in place and serve the American public. They are residing in our house, the White House, with their families. We understand Lord Acton's aphorism that "Power corrupts, and absolute power corrupts absolutely." But is it too much to ask the male Presidents to keep their penises in their pants for a few years and their eyeballs in their "heads" where they wear their glasses?

It's always about the penises – so let's talk about them.

CHAPTER III

1   Man's Best Friend

"God gave men both a penis and a brain, but unfortunately not enough blood supply to run both at the same time."

Robin Williams

"Men are dogs. I know what men are and how they think -- I'm telling you, they are dogs! This was blurted out by my girlfriend's husband, a conservative, highly-religious man, while we were dining out and discussing the men their daughter was dating. My girlfriend and I nodded in agreement, our heads bobbing up and down. But what were we really agreeing to – the fact that everyone knows that men are dogs?

Almost all the dogs I've ever known have been loyal, protective, happy, wagging their tails and jumping for glee when they greet you. They love you unconditionally, unless taught otherwise. While there are exceptions in all animals, dogs remind me of my sister's dog, a sweet Shih Tzu named Harley who loves her no matter what is going on in her life or what condition she's in. Admittedly, Harley picks up his leg and pees everywhere on anything; and if he were not neutered, he would go after female dogs indiscriminately and constantly want to shag. He often stinks unless he goes to the groomer; and he rotates on his back end on the floor when his glands are swollen and need emptying, making me think of boys with "blue balls."

Men love their balls - golf, baseball, football, basketball, tennis, soccer.... So is it any wonder that they are enthralled with their own balls? I, and many of my girlfriends, have heard about blue balls since high school. It was probably a 1960's thing. I've never seen any blue balls myself, probably because I was not looking. When guys in school wanted to have sex, they would use the "blue balls excuse." As one male friend laughingly said, "We always used that as a way to get girls to have sex because we would moan about the pain we were in, and it usually did the trick." Another friend said that as a black male, they used the "black and blue balls excuse."

Blue balls is a slang term referring to testicular aching that may occur when blood fills the male's genital vessels when he is aroused, but not dissipated. It probably came from the "bluish tint that appears when the blood engorges the vessels in the testicles." Blue balls were an effective empathetic tool used on naïve and inexperienced girls. One of my girlfriends fell for it. When I asked her why she had sex with her boyfriend, against her principles, she said he was in pain and she didn't want him to suffer anymore.

I don't know if men still use this as a sexual ploy or they have so many new tricks it's no longer necessary. I assume men, likened to dogs, with their natural proclivity to fuck often and indiscriminately, make sure that their balls don't turn a shade of blue, which interestingly enough is the color designated for boys. How vulgar - but that's the way it is and how the game is played!

2 Big Balls Braggadocio

"I'm thinking balls are to men what purses are to women. It's just a little bag, but we feel naked in public without it."

Sex & the City Quote

Men are preoccupied with their penises. They are unduly concerned with their physical stature and prowess in comparison to other males, their competitors. It's crucial to know that men see themselves as fundamentally independent creatures -- who must prove themselves in a competitive world that swirls around them, and which poses danger to them, and their family. The very phrase "to measure up" conveys the male preoccupation with size. Men are the protectors, who want to produce children and to protect them from harm. This is all built into their psyches, but is often used as the excuse for the inequality between the sexes. He has to protect her, not only from others, but from herself, since she can't do it.

In contrast to men, women are fundamentally non-violent and attached beings, attached to their parents, their friends, their children, their husbands, and their extended families – it's probably why they live longer than men. Although, the gap in life expectancy between men and women is dropping because men are giving up heavy manual labor and women are taking on the stress of work and "super-women-'dumb'." But, there's still a 4-year gap that will increase if women go home again and men go back to heavy lifting. Don't count on it.

Women also want their children safe from harm but they believe this can be managed in a cooperative, noncompetitive way. In times of great danger, women are grateful for a man's protection. But in most situations, women are more inclined to see shows of force for what they are: totally unproductive "macho bravado," "male gorilla-like chest-beating," "big balls braggadocio," -- and the main ingredient: "My penis is bigger than yours."

As a psychology major, I feel that if Sigmund Freud could bloviate about "penis envy" in women, I know more than enough to talk about male penises. We are a country that loves to count and measure things – we count our money, we count (or miscount) votes, and we count on our hands and toes. We even count sheep to sleep. Why sheep, I don't know; it makes me think of mattress sales ads. One of the things that boys' measure is the size of their penises. Male penis size is one of men's (hence women's) major concerns, yet information has been "short" in coming, double pun intended.

In 1948, famous sex therapist Dr. Alfred Kinsey decided to find out the average size of a penis. So he asked 3,500 men to return a postcard with the length of their erect penis. Obviously, this was not a very well-controlled or –handled scientific survey because a man's honesty about his penis size is like a woman's honesty about her weight. What are a few more inches or pounds among friends and surveyors? Anyway, Kinsey said the average size of a man's erect penis was 6.2 inches. This - over half the size of a 12" ruler - stood for 50 years, crushing many men's egos over the decades and making many women feel they were missing out on something. Take out a ruler and tell me that a 6.2-inch penis is not scary for petite or average-sized woman.

There's a lot of information and photos on the internet and other media about penises, but this is my take on the subject.

3   Every Inch Counts

"Men read maps better than women because only men can understand the concept of an inch equaling a hundred miles."

Roseanne Barr

Leave it to capitalism and the private sector again! In 2001, a condom manufacturer wanted to determine the true sizes of men's erect penises. So they asked college students in Cancun on spring break to take part in an erect-penis study. About 400 bored or well-hung males agreed to take part in the study. Tents were set up so the males could do what they had to do -- after which nurses had the chore of measuring their erect penises. Hard work, but someone had to do it. This may have been why 100 volunteers dropped out, leaving only 300 male-measured penises. I don't think any of the nurses dropped out. Drum-roll please!

The average length of the surveyed erect penises was 5.88 inches, less than Dr. Kinsey's 6.2 inches. Most penises (59%) were between 5.2 and 6 inches; the average thickness was 4.97 inches. Only 1 male in 4 had a penis longer than 6 inches and only about 10 men had penises 7 inches or longer – thank goodness. Of course, the statistics were probably skewed – not screwed. But, this still won't prevent men from feeling that a smaller penis, under 5.88 inches, is really bad news. I'm only trying to help here and build some self-esteem.

So, another area to consider is that there are two types of penises: Short, fat, elastic-type that stretch (these men need lots of money); and long, flaccid ones that barely change size when erect. When men are peeing at urinals, in athletic showers, or in the great outdoors, they may be jealous for nothing. Flaccid penises look larger, but actually range from 2 inches to over 5 inches; they just fill up and remain the same size. The former elastic types are usually smaller, but fill up and enlarge.

Everyone wants to measure in on erect penis sizes, so Masters and Johnson later reported that they range from 4.9 to 6.9 inches. Finally, surgery is only recommended for males whose penises are below 1.6 inches flaccid and 3 inches erect. Generally, lengthening surgery is offered mainly for congenital abnormalities, bad surgery after cancer or other diseases, and trauma from accidents or amputation. As a woman, I believe what's important is not the size, but whether or not a man satisfies a woman and does what he's supposed to do with his entire body. The "slam bam, thank you, ma'am," with a big or small penis, is just selfish and pitiful. And, too big is also frightful.

Years ago, one of my friends told me he had an enormous, long, thick, penis. He said women were so terrified when he unleashed it on them that they refused to have sex with him. He struggled to find a compatible female sexual partner. I was a good listener, but that was the size of it. I also had a girlfriend who had an affair with a paramour who was impotent – that's almost an oxymoron. But they managed somehow through 10 years of infidelity to have sex without an erection. They considered pumps and other equipment for him before they finally broke up. Sadly, he also had a heart problem, so I asked her what she would do if he died during sex in their 8th-floor apartment hideaway. I've never forgotten her response: "I will drag him down the hall to the elevator, put him in alone, and push down." So much for that decades-long love affair!

Of course, we all know there are those penises that are circumcised and those that are not. Circumcision, meaning to "cut around," is the surgical removal of the foreskin from the penis. It hurts even thinking about it. One third of males worldwide are circumcised for religious or personal reasons. Circumcision is most prevalent (almost universally), in the Muslim world, along with parts of Southeast Asia, Israel, South Korea and the U.S.

About 56% of male newborns in the U.S. were circumcised a decade ago, which has declined since the 1970s and 1980s. The causes cited for the decline are: the increase in Latin American immigrants, who are less likely to circumcise; Medicaid no longer reimburses for circumcision; and, the risks are more obvious than the benefits. While there are good reasons NOT to circumcise (somewhat less sexual pleasure and a tendency to get inflammation at the opening of the penis), there are also solid medical reasons TO circumcise. These include lower rates of cancer of the penis (and of cervical cancer for sex partners); somewhat lower rates of STDs; and, fewer urinary tract infections. And, we all know urinary tract and yeast infections are a problem for most women throughout our lives.

Years ago, there was a large group of us in the gynecologist's office being treated for recurring urinary tract and yeast infections. After talking to each other, we learned that we had all been prescribed with a broad-spectrum antibiotic that kills a wide range of disease-causing bacteria – good and bad. A side-effect of antibiotics is the change in the body's normal microbial content that attacks indiscriminately both the beneficial and harmless bacteria found in the intestines, lungs and bladder, often destroying the body's normal bacterial flora so that it can lead to secondary infections. While broad-spectrum antibiotics are appropriate and necessary, narrow-spectrum antibiotics are used to prevent major secondary problems. Asking your physician what you are being prescribed and the side effects is the way to go, along with the girls' best friends: cranberry juice and yogurt.

4 What's in a Name?

"Do you want to know why men name their penis? So the most important decisions in their life aren't made by a stranger."

Linda Howard, *After the Night*

Men love to name their penises: flog stick, best friend, one-eyed monster, Johnson, Niagara Balls, the Big Kielbasa, pecker, love machine, salami, schlong, dong, woody, prick, dick and junk. I'm sure men could add a few more gems. They name their balls too: cojones, nuts, the globetrotters, gruesome twosome, dumb and dumber. His possession is prized and powerful. He celebrates how often he has gotten to use it on women; the more conquests - the more notches on his belt. Bragging rights come with higher numbers. Even Mariah Carey's husband, silly, lovable Nick Canon, bragged about the women he'd screwed as if it were a badge of honor when he's married to one of the most talented women in the world. Women are screwed no matter what their fame or status.

While men's private parts are glorified, women's private parts get lots of nasty names: cunt, twat, snatch, pussy. And women are referred to as bitches, whores, tramps..... Women must be attractive to men, yet women often hear that they are too fat and their vaginas smell like fish. Funny, I haven't heard women say much about men's smelly crotches. "Feminine products" are advertised on TV for taking care of these female odors, while products for men are for increasing their libido, protecting them from impregnating women, and preventing sexually transmitted diseases. Women put up with men's smells because they seem… part of being a man.

In locker rooms, barbershops and beauty salons, women are portrayed as sexual playthings for horny men – he's a "Whoremonger." We see this in video games, Hollywood movies, and in ads for everything from insurance to automobiles. In movies and TV shows over the past two decades, men are shown peeing and talking to each other at urinals. Personally, I'm tired of it. A recent TV advertisement for a toilet maker had a mother in the bathtub taking a bubble bath. Her two very young sons walked into the bathroom, passed by her and went directly to the toilet to pee together. Daddy came to the door, smiled at his wife; she smiled back, because it was so cute to see their two sons peeing together. The boys turned and left with their father, while mother basked in all her glory in the bubbling tub, happy about her two sons team-peeing.

If you count the number of times you now see men at urinals, you'll be surprised. Even balls are no longer off limits. A pitifully disgusting Kmart holiday ad depicted men swinging their balls in boxer shorts and ringing bells, which was called the "Show Your Joe" Jiggle Bell ad. It was disrespectful to viewers generally, and specifically sacrilegious during the holidays. We all should take offense at men's penises being flaunted in our faces daily, literally and figuratively. Unfortunately, many men would probably not mind having our vaginas in their faces every day, and they love their penises and balls. It's a problem that seems to grow larger every day, way beyond six inches. We need to call a halt to this constant penis glorification and exposure that harkens back to Sigmund Freud's obsessions.

I believe we also have to stop the constant emphasis on the homosexual community and sexuality. A recent awards show went way beyond acceptance and was downright vulgar. Television shows, movies, and everything Hollywood does not have to be filled by and for the LGBT community. Hopefully, it is a pendulum swing that has gone too far and will come back to center sometime in the future after that community believes it has won the war against homophobia. And even these statements can get an American in trouble, personally and professionally, whether they are homophobic or not. "Some of my best friends...." and all that aside, we need some degree of restraint and higher standards. We need to get past all the homophobia and accept the fact that we are all here and need to live together in harmony and peace.

5 Women's Best Friend

"An orgasm a day keeps the doctor away."

Mae West

I feel confident talking about women and orgasms. They were openly and regularly discussed during the feminist movement, so it's hard to believe reports that some women still don't have orgasms 50 years later. Some studies report that about 26% of women rarely or sometimes have orgasms. And, it appears that faking it until you make it is operable. Out of 1500 women polled, 45% said they never fake it, leaving 55% that do. Over 60% of females experience their first orgasm between the ages of 14 and 24. Only 29% of women have orgasms every time they have sex in comparison to 75% of men. Most women do not have orgasms during their first sexual intercourse or during intercourse, but instead are more likely to reach it through masturbation.

Orgasm is very similar for both men and women. It starts with a series of 6-15 contractions of high intensity over a 20-30 second period; some may have regular and then irregular contractions for another 30-90 seconds. Two studies conducted reported the intensity, frequency, and duration of muscle contractions during masturbation is the same for men and women. Others say the average duration of an orgasm is longer and number of orgasmic contractions is greater for women than men. A measurement of "theta waves" as a criteria shows that women experience 10 times stronger orgasms than men when they climax. It's believed that if men experienced the same orgasmic intensity as women, the shock to their systems would kill them. Death by orgasm.

Yet, orgasmic contractions are similar in both males and females. This is because during the first trimester of fetal development we are genitally female. Then in the third prenatal month, male fetuses begin to produce more testosterone, which signals the genes to begin creating the structures for male genitals. How about saying it in the feminist way: We all start out as a female; when more testosterone is produced in the third month – we have a male. Whew – we are finally first!

But, as usual, women take longer than men to get to where they want to be and where they are going. I guess we could say we take time to think with our brains rather than our vaginas, while males think with their penises. Intercourse is a harder way to achieve an orgasm and takes a woman a lot longer (10-20 minutes) than through masturbation (under 4 minutes). For some women, it sounds a lot like Thanksgiving dinner – takes forever to prepare and it's over in a few minutes. Over 30% of women also experience multiple orgasms (compound, sequential and serial multiples), but only 10% do so regularly. For whatever reason, it is believed that most men aren't supposed to have a clue when their partner is having an orgasm. Are they kidding? These must be the premature ejaculators or they're dead already. Reasons why women don't have orgasms include: there was not enough foreplay, she just wasn't in the mood, and she was just too stressed out. How about she's bored already and "been there, done that?"

Of course, there is not only a pay gap, but an orgasm gap between men and women. Women are said to have only one orgasm to every three of men. Wonder who's counting? In a study of 15,000 heterosexual college students, the longer the "hook up," the more the gap decreases until it shrinks for women, so they have 7 times as many orgasms after the fourth or more hookups. In other words, the one-night stands or lack of a viable relationship impacts on orgasms for women, not men. We could have told them that! Not surprisingly, on the first "hook up" or sexual encounter, women were more likely to please the man and concerned with him achieving a climax than they were at having an orgasm themselves.

Old Sigmund Freud weighed in on this too, saying that a woman should have an orgasm during intercourse and if she couldn't, something was fundamentally wrong with her. He was wrong again. Reaching an orgasm during intercourse is difficult and only 25% of women will routinely experience it, so it's not us – it's just hard to do.

Oral sex usually settles that problem. We learned from lesbian partners that they have many more orgasms than heterosexual women, almost as many as heterosexual men, and it takes the same amount of time to orgasm during masturbation for women as it takes for men during intercourse (4 minutes). It's all in the mind and method.

Intercourse is supposed to strongly correlate with climax for men, counting as "real sex," while other sexual activities more likely to produce orgasm in women are considered optional foreplay. As always, the brain comes into play, so scientists using MRIs were able to show the similarities and differences between male and female orgasms. The preliminary results showed that both men and women experience significant activation of the frontal pole that feeds back to another lobule responsible for processing sensation. But, while there were slightly different activation patterns for males, females, and individuals, there was an indication that qualitative and quantitative differences may exist for individuals. How about more research? Any volunteers?

Men also need a rest period after the big ejaculatory event before they can get up or get "it" up and go again. Women can have multiple orgasms without a break and the rest period is shorter for them than men. Actually, women usually want to go shopping immediately afterwards. Not just kidding. We just need that research to determine whether women spend more or less money on purchases after orgasm(s).

Women can have orgasms at a very young age that can continue into their old age. They are still impacted more by social forces and dynamics that place men's needs and satisfaction over their own. Orgasms for women can be achieved if they want them and masturbation is the easiest way to have them. Orgasms take the edge off and often settle your nerves. It fits into the old adage for women that "if you don't use it, you lose it," because women who don't use it often shut down their sexual drives and systems.

So, orgasms make your skin glow, your eyes bright, and keep you younger longer; they rev up your system so you use more calories and take some weight off. Under these circumstances, there should no longer be non-orgasmic women out there, unless they have a physical or emotional problem. There is nothing wrong with having orgasms, so women need to just relax and take it one orgasm at a time – or go crazy and have multiple ones. We are in charge of our own minds and bodies.

CHAPTER IV

1 Misogyny

"No one can feel inferior without your consent."

Eleanor Roosevelt

Men's distrust of women causes them to slight and dismiss us. Joan Smith in her book *Misogynies* brilliantly covers how fear and hatred of women permeates every sector of society, by even the "best intentioned people." Freud said we are limited because of our anatomy, Smith says the misogyny women face is rooted in the idea that we are defined and limited by our gender in a way that men aren't, so that men feel we can't be trusted.

Smith came to this conclusion after she examined the Yorkshire Ripper murders in England. She thought the case "seemed to be a pure manifestation of misogyny... and dislike for women whom I saw all around me." She said the underlying assumptions of the police about the Ripper were similar to something I've noticed for years. Many men will say that one of their buddies is a good guy, when he's really a complete shithead and bad news, capable of all sorts of depravity. This was the same case with the Ripper. He went unnoticed to kill again because the cops decided that he didn't stand out as a killer and looked like a normal male.

The famous 1992 case of Lorena Bobbitt points to something similar. Lorena cut off her husband John Wayne Bobbitt's penis with a knife, fled their apartment with it stuffed in a sock, got in her car, rolled down the car window, and threw the penis into a field. Obviously, it's wrong to cut off a man's penis, no matter what's going on. After an exhaustive search for John Wayne Bobbitt's penis, it was found, packed in ice, and later reattached, in a 9-1/2-hour operation. At the same time this was happening, many murdered prostitutes were buried along a Virginia highway where they remained for years. In other words, they could find a man's little sock with a shriveled-up penis in a field, yet they couldn't find women's entire bodies. The missing women were "prostitutes," therefore, not as important as Bobbitt's penis. Dead prostitutes are just not sexy or useful anymore.

Charlotte Bunch, the founding director of the Center for Women's Global Leadership at Rutgers College in New Brunswick, said, "If you want to have a world in which human rights are respected and social development proceeds, you can't have half the population subjugated." She says the epidemic of violence against women claims millions of victims, irrespective of race, class, age, education, ethnicity or culture. It covers domestic violence, rape, sexual abuse, sex trafficking, genital mutilation and honor killings, along with abortion of female fetuses and killing of infant girls.

Female infanticide and gendercide continues throughout the world. Female trafficking is on the rise all over the world and in the U.S. The war on baby girls killed, aborted or neglected from 2012-2014 is over 100 million. And, the "Feminization of Poverty" and wholesale destruction of women over the past 40 years may continue unless we can reduce the gap of gross under-representation of women in the national political governing bodies and take dramatic action. What reason is there for allowing our sisters in the U.S. and throughout the world to be disregarded and discarded because of misogyny, distrust and subjugation?

The great French feminist Simone-Lucie-Ernestine-Marie Bertrand de Beauvoir, known as Simone de Beauvoir, writer, intellectual, political activist and philosopher, said women's oppression comes from men's treatment of us as a minority or "other." In her classic treatise *The Second Sex*, she wrote "One is not born a woman, one becomes one." She also said that another important aspect of white women's lives is that they are dispersed and attach themselves more firmly to white men than to other women:

Women lack concrete means of organizing themselves into a unit which can stand face to face with the correlative unit... They live dispersed among the males, attached through residence, house-work, economic condition, and social standing to certain men....Father or husbands – more firmly than they are to other women....If they are white, their allegiance is to white men, not Negro women.

Black women threw off their chains after slavery. They were separated from their men and often their children, and left alone to fend for themselves against the slave masters. Many of their boys and men were killed and imprisoned, which is still the case in the U.S. This is while white women were being protected and supported by white men -- the "Stepford Wives" dispersed, and standing with and by their men.

Men do not attach themselves to women in the same way, but instead herd and band together for what they want as men. They make decisions for their mutual benefit - compete, play sports, hang out in bars, and in their new man-caves. They congregate in clubs. Bachelor parties thrown for soon-to-be married men have a common theme: bemoaning the man's imminent loss of independence and falling into domesticity. Men organize themselves to fight against the "correlative unit" – women. Their allegiance is to what is good for men. They make their marriages work for them to retain their power and control over their lives, while proscribing the woman's.

Someone has to be the top dog making those tough decisions for the benefit of the herd – the family – so men know where they fit in the hierarchy and learn to push their policies and positions. On a larger scale, they push political agendas; they work together to pass laws; and move toward their common goals. Their goals may be as major as reversing a national law or as simple as a touchdown at the end of a football field. They decide what's important to them, and learn to reap the enormous benefits of being in power and control.

As women, we have to learn to stand firmly with other women for the benefit of our gender -- and for the future of the United States, which is floundering under the weight of the Greedy Old Bastards and their progeny.

2 Men's Brains

"Men's brains are like the prison system:
not enough cells per man."

Anonymous

Men's brains tend to work in a simpler, more limited fashion than women's brains. It's a "Keep It Simple Stupid" (KISS) way of thinking – don't overwork or overcomplicate it. Men are much quicker to abort thinking or stop gathering information and press for a final decision, or to throw a punch, shoot off a gun -- or launch an invasion. Women seem to understand how few problems are truly solved quickly or by violence, punches, gunshots and invasions.

Research has been done in the last decade about the differences between male and female brains, showing that women tend to have many more connections across the two hemispheres of the brain, while men's brains tend to work more vertically within each hemisphere. It's important not to oversimplify the findings of brain research, but it's quite possible that the brooding quality of many men, their tendency to fixate on negative and violent thoughts, is built right into the architecture of their brains, with testosterone leading the way. The violence taking place by men throughout the world is indicative of these violent tendencies.

Women are just as smart as men and, in some cases, much smarter if their avoidance of slaughtering others is an indicator. Intelligence quotients ("IQ's") are a score derived from several standardized intelligence tests. Looking at a bell curve with the hump in the middle at 100 and going down on each side 15 points at a time, or what's called a standard deviation, about 95% of the population has an IQ of between 70 and 130 or two standard deviations from the center. Two-thirds of the people are within one standard deviation of the mean or between 85 and 115. As you go higher, you will find many of the geniuses, and going down the other way, there are those who can't grasp things readily. Many intelligent people with high IQs try to outsmart the rest of us.

Just ask high IQ former President Bill Clinton. During Clinton's testimony to the Grand Jury, he quibbled over the definition of sexual relations and whether the word is 'is', or 'is' ain't. In response to questions posed to him, he said: "It depends upon what the meaning of the word "is" - if 'is' means is, and never has been, that's one thing. If it means, 'there is none,' that was a completely true statement." He later said, "....ask me a question in the present tense." Okay - is perjury and obstruction of justice illegal and an impeachable offense? So, in this case 'is' 'is' 'is'. Whew – high IQ people can be exhausting for us mere mortals! My mother loved Bill Clinton, and I think it would be fun to be with him because he's interesting, entertaining and has soul. He has a sort-of stuffy-nose like me too.

IQ results can be skewed by various factors, such as social status, heredity, and other variables. A test on the Stanford-Binet Intelligence Scale measures an individual's cognitive ability, compared to his or her peers, by dividing the subject's tested mental age by their chronological age, times 100. Genetics and environmental factors clearly play a role in determining a person's IQ. Studies have been conducted to gauge the impact on IQ of family environment, genes, socioeconomic status, and education. One study found that music and musical training correlated with a higher-than-average IQ. I don't think some of the current music counts.

There is no question that people have different reasons for not doing well on tests. If you are undernourished, mentally and physically, how well would you fare on a test? Some of the brightest people I've ever known were Blacks, Hispanics and Asians, all of whom had better than average home environments, upbringing and educations. Health and good nutrition offsets negative effects on testing, along with other factors, such as a pupil's interest in school, willingness to study, and his or her persistence. A more recent finding is that students who lived in disadvantaged areas, unlike more advantaged youth, did not receive additional training and conditioning during summer breaks to prepare them for the start of the next school year, so their white peers did better when they returned after the break.

And a high IQ doesn't always mean that a person will do better than someone around the middle of the pack. Various studies have shown a correlation between IQ and crime, and IQ with conservatism or liberalism. The results probably have a lot to do with who prepared and gave the tests. Generally, criminals are not too bright; our jails are filled with them. People who consider themselves "very liberal" had mean intelligence scores of 106.4 in adolescence and those who identified themselves as very conservative scored 94.8. Listening to some of these conservatives on television spewing their nonsense, there may be some merit to this.

Generally, doctors score above 125, college graduates 115, high school graduates 100, and elementary school 85; professionals and technical groups 112, managers 104, semi-skilled 92 and unskilled 87. There's a lot of controversy about IQ and race that continues without merit. Test scores are impacted by background, upbringing and the environment. When racial, gender, backgrounds, and bias are eliminated, there will be no major differences.

One of my favorite game shows is *Jeopardy*. Invariably there are categories on *Jeopardy* related to male interests, such as sports, athletes and scores. These male-oriented questions are biased, so it stands to reason that men should win the game more often than women. In 2011, 90% of the winners were men and only 1 in 10 women won. One women's opinion why this occurred was this: "Cause women raise kids, have jobs and take care of their lazy-ass husbands. That doesn't leave much time to compete on a game show." I like her reason better than mine.

There are other things I noted between women and men contestants on *Jeopardy* that may create significant differences. Women appear less likely to push the buzzer if they don't know the answer, and they are more conservative in their betting. The male contestants are a select group with huge egos, hubris and the will to win – that's the way the game's played. The selected females are just as smart as the males, but won't win as often until all bias in the game is eliminated and they become more aggressive and ego-driven.

Actually, over the last several decades, women are more likely to go to college and outperform men academically. Girls start school with better social and behavioral skills than boys, so they have higher average grades; in middle school girls are more likely to enjoy school and get good grades from studying more. In high school, when students concentrate in major areas of study, women begin to lose interest, particularly in science and technology because most schools do not emphasize these subjects. By college, women have broader educational goals than the young men who are focusing on science, technology, engineering and mathematics (STEM). Also, boys and men believe that rules and hard work don't necessarily apply to them. Teacher/instructor bias has tilted towards the boys over the girls also.

I always wondered why my girlfriends went from being very smart and savvy, then took nose-dives as we got older, so that the boys and men outshined them. Young girls of high school age become enamored with boys until they marry. Puberty sets in and menstruation begins, then they seem to shift gears into all things associated with ensuring the continuation of the species. They either kowtow down more or smarten up again. Once they get all that love, sex and lust out of their systems, they go back to using their brains full-time.

There's hope for our brains as we get older. Since there's money to be made, the private sector is moving into creating new brain centers to help the "Baby Boomers" retain their memories – good or bad. They say the hippocampus shrinks 0.5 percent each year after 50. Stretching, walking, dancing, and crossword puzzles are supposed to reverse some of the shrinkage, and masturbation. I just threw that last one in.

3 Equal Pay for More Work

"If you say, I'm for equal pay, that's a reform.
But if you say I'm a feminist, that's a transformation of society."

Gloria Steinem

Let's not get equal – let's get even! That's my motto. Women are used to working hard, so if we do more, why should be strive to get the same as the men? They've been making so much more for so long that it should be payback time. Reparations are for making amends for wrongs or injuries done, and rather than take goods, we'll take money.

We should be paid from when Eve was tricked by the lying serpent (probably a male), naively ate the forbidden fruit, and gave some to Adam, making God mad. American women hoped to do better when 29 of them landed with 73 men in Plymouth to help build a new nation, so we should at least be compensated for all those years of injustice and suffering. The Good Old Boys have discriminated historically against almost every racial and ethnic group in the U.S., but women, the largest group at 51% of the population, have been systematically discriminated against based on their gender.

Why should we make up the 23-cent disparity for comparable positions? The difference of 77 cents women get for every $1.00 earned by men is for comparable positions, which is nonsense. Men are in the top positions now and have been for over two centuries. Women are still at the bottom of the organizational hierarchy earning much less, often putting in more time and doing more work for more people. And we should be tired by now of hearing about a "glass ceiling." It's not a glass ceiling – it's cement!

Women are last into jobs, so they are often the first to go when things get tight and the unemployment rate goes up. Women in part-time positions are the first to go; women in mid-level positions or softer positions, such as personnel, are the first out as non-essential during a recession, layoff, or cutback. Pregnant women are often forced out. Secretaries in the typewriter age were replaced by Administrative Assistants in the computer age, but they are at the bottom, and are the first to be purged. Two clerical jobs can pay for a higher-paying job for a male.

A 2013 *Washington Post* article reported that women's wages were actually falling further behind men's and, while the economy was doing better, the gap between men and women's wages was growing. In 2012, full-time women workers earned less than the year before. Yet, women are outpacing men in education, so the fault for the earnings gap is being placed squarely on women's shoulders and their childbearing bodies. The excuses include: Women take time off for family reasons, such as pregnancy, or child care; they work more often part-time to care for children or elderly parents; they work in soft and support positions given less value in our society; they're clustered in lower-paying clerical positions; and they're less likely to invest in market-based formal education and on-the-job training that increases skills and earning power. There is a grain of truth in each of those points -- but they don't account for what's really taking place. Women are being punished for being women.

There are only 20 women (4.4%) at the top of Fortune 500 companies and there are still few CEOs of Fortune 100 companies. Women are also in the lowest paying positions in retail sales occupations. Out of 20 positions examined by the Institute for Policy Research, the 12 most common occupations for women have a "median weekly earnings that will leave a household of four at or near poverty." Women's lower pay will follow them throughout their lives into retirement.

Even women with degrees are paid less than males: Male physicians earn over $12,000 more than female doctors; males with doctoral degrees earn $1,734 compared to $1,387 for females; Master's degrees, it was $1,515 for males, compared to $1,123 for women; Bachelor's degrees, $1199 for males, $930 for females; High School graduates, $720 for males, $554 for females. Clearly, it's women's fault for being paid less!

Current articles say we women can have it all -- striking a nice balance between a successful career and a fulfilling home life. I don't know who's pushing this stuff because I see no balance, only a slide toward exhaustion. One article bemoaned the fact that women for the first time in U.S. history were the "dominant" gender because they are now more than half the workforce. Further, they glorified this position by theorizing that women in higher-paid positions can participate in Reaganomics by "trickling-down" part of their salaries to lower-paid women who provide them with assistance, such as those doing domestic work.

At least there is an admission that the wage gap is caused by discrimination: "Yes, women still do most of the child care. And yes, the upper reaches of society are still dominated by men." And, yes, we're sick of this crap! Supposedly there is also a "last gasp of a dying age of patriarchy." For some reason this reminds me of a smashed dying cockroach. One older man remarked, "Guys...are the new ball and chain," and the long view of the economy is a place where women "hold the cards." He appears to be saying guys may start to resent and restrict women as they become their balls and chains, instead of the other way around because they will be controlling the economy. I had a hard time wrapping my head around this.

The *Urban Dictionary* defines "Ball and Chain" as someone who won't let you do or go anywhere without them or someone who is holding you back by putting a ball and chain on you, the physical restraint historically used on prisoners. They also listed words related to ball and chain as: wife, pussy-whipped, girlfriend, old lady, bitch, married, no balls, slave, spouse and woman. This is nothing but pure and unadulterated misogyny. I don't believe most women will ever stoop this low or hold the economic cards in my lifetime. The only cards women are holding are in bridge, hearts, spades, whist and mah-jongg. Women are at the bottom of the game and will remain there for a long time to come unless they do something dramatic to change it.

The higher up you go, the fewer women you find. It's still a man's world even if some of them are sleeping on the job. Does that mean that a sleeping man is worth more than a pregnant woman? Surveys and polls say that most women know they can't have it all – a full-time successful career and a positive home life. Sheryl Sandberg, author of *Lean In,* said she believes women need to balance their careers and home life, but common sense says that women have to make concessions because "On average, it appears 'having it all' is still little more than a dream for many women."

I believe that any average senior female professional who "leans in" will just fall on her face unless she has all the criteria for being selected for success by a Good Old Boy. This excludes any woman who is older, plain, fat, wrinkled, or has bad feet or bad teeth. You get the picture. Ms. Sandberg's photo is on her book because she isn't old or ugly. She's another well-off, white, nice-looking young career woman, wife and mother, working for *Facebook*. But, she is doing something to improve women's lives at work, so her heart and attitude are in the right place.

Women's work has not only been undervalued in the workplace, but also in our society. Many things women do – such as crafting, crocheting, knitting, quilting, and decoupage, are devalued and considered "cute." My grandmother made a gorgeous "Crazy Quilt" after the war when cigarette packs had silk pieces inserted for improving sales. The Smithsonian has a number of these wonderful artistic pieces, and I have always cherished mine as a family heirloom. Throughout our home we have beautiful pieces made by my mother and grandmother that we treasure. The amount of work that went into these works of art is astounding and they help remind me of my roots. Over the winter, I take time out to crochet or knit scarves out of our alpaca animals' fleece for our friends. It's unfortunate that some of these mainly women's skills are undervalued and becoming lost arts.

In the workplace, I found that women's management style is also underrated because it differs from the WASP style of "management-by-objectives." Women's style appears to be more similar to Asians, who are interested in group dynamics and the team approach to decision-making. This is diametrically opposite of punching the clock, starting on time, putting in eight or more hours, and micromanagement. Some surveys have found that women are generally more supportive and have better team-building skills, while men are better at delegating and managing up. This means men are better at "brown nosing" and kissing ass than women and getting other people to do the work. Women are able to gauge situations better than a man, which increases their ability to persuade others. So what! How about persuading someone to give them a raise or promotion?

Men are more likely to ask for what they want and to show their competitive natures and strengths in negotiating. Even when unprepared, they tend to "fake it until they make it." And according to a *Harvard Business Review* paper, men are more likely to be mentored by senior employees because those employees are mainly males and both genders tend to mentor their own gender. For over 35 years, I supervised employees in various administrative, professional and management functions. During that time, I watched as men pretended they knew something they didn't, while women tended to remain silent when they were unprepared; men tended to goof off more than women, yet wanted to be rewarded simply because they were males.

On one occasion, my boss and I admitted we'd made a terrible selection for the Comptroller position. The man's incompetence was unbelievable. We worried because he was scheduled to brief a top Fortune 500 company executive and his senior staff, including their comptroller. There was nothing we could do, but grin and bear it, hoping we could get through it without being totally humiliated and thrown out the door. We prepared for a disaster.

Steve was a large, white Good Old Boy with a massive ego. He went to the meeting confident, scaring us to death. When his time came to brief, he stood tall, took control of the room, moved up to the charts with his pointer and began his discussion of the budget. He talked numbers with *savoir-faire*, pointing here and there, saying why this was planned, committed, and obligated. Nothing he said added up – it was all theater, as if he were in a play starring Pythagoras or Isaac Newton. When Steve finished, he thanked everyone for their attention. We were hoping for inattention or daydreaming about sex, which occurs in many meetings every day. He then asked if there were any questions – God forbid, we prayed. The company executive then boldly proclaimed: "This is one of the best budget briefings I've ever received in all my years as an executive." What the hell! Those Good Old Boys are really good.

Women usually do a lot of work and a lot of gossiping, which should be considered part of their team-building. Unfortunately, it's considered a tremendous defect instead of a benefit. Yet, gossip actually creates and maintains an effective, informal communication system for the organization, just as the American Indian code talkers did. The only way a woman gets recognized is if she has something "special" to offer or fills some basic need for a male supervisor. You can work as hard as you want but, as we all know, it's who you know and who supports you that is the key to your selection, hiring, and promotion. I received a lot more when I was called "legs" and "blue eyes," than I ever got when the years started to pile on, and my few women supervisors tried to do me in rather than assist me.

Either people in the U.S. are becoming lazier or I'm just noticing it more. I thought that standards were as low as they could go in our society and the Federal government until I came to Washington, D.C. and I don't think we've hit bottom yet. The Pareto Principle, known as the 80-20 rule or law of the vital few, says that roughly 80% of the effects come from 20% of the causes. So, 20% of the population controls 80% of the world's income; 20% of the clients represent 80% of sales; and 20% of the employees do 80% of the work, while the rest coast or try to take credit.

But, that's only a small part of the larger problem. Too many people are brought into the government by nepotism and favoritism – family members, children, aunts, uncles, wives, husbands, babysitters, church members, on and on. Most of these people have no concept of giving a day's work for a day's pay. They're living high off the taxpayer – the middle-class. It's a form of the Good Old Boy union system that goes down the family line, mainly for males – only there are a lot more jobs in the public service.

Then we have all kinds of violations that go on, from having sex on their desks or in stairwells, to stealing supplies, watching pornography, driving government cars for private business, doing private work on government time, and squandering funds. So, there is really no reason to pay women less than men or to keep us at the bottom of these broken organizations, under a cement ceiling. A new pay system is needed: Equal pay for the men and women doing 20% of the work, and less pay for the other 80%, male or female, consisting of incompetents, goof offs, and scammers.

I have also been privileged to work with some of the most amazingly talented people in government, who are dedicated, committed and hard-working. Many of these people are underpaid, under-appreciated and under-rewarded for their efforts because of politics, with incompetents and nonperformers sucking out their share. The "Peter Principle" is also operational in that many employees are promoted until they reach their "position of incompetence." I've had to report to a few horribly incompetent and lazy supervisors that were there every day on time, so they could bask in their daily ineptitude.

The gender gap in salaries is just one small indicator of the inequality that goes on. Telling the victims to "do something" is the same as telling those in poverty to pick themselves up by their bootstraps, when they have none or they are under someone with big boots determined to keep them where they supposedly belong.

4 Abuse, Rape & Murder

"Life is hard. After all, it kills you."

Katharine Hepburn

Two-thirds of all marriages turn violent at some point, so if you're an abused married woman, you're not alone. On average, every 9 seconds, a woman is battered or subjected to violence -- 4 million times a year in the U.S. One quarter of all women in emergency rooms are there because of violence. Children see and come to accept this violence, so the seeds are sown for the cycle to be repeated. Daughters of abused women expect to be abused themselves. Sons who witness their fathers' acts of violence are ten times more likely to become abusers. Just as you were reading those last few sentences, a woman was violated or beaten and the odds were that it was happening in her own home. Even a single abuse is horribly wrong -- and many of us don't realize how incredibly common it is.

Women are kicked in the head, punched in the face, given black eyes, and have their bones broken. Women have acid thrown in their faces and are burned beyond recognition. Women are raped, both inside and outside of marriage; over 22 million women in the U.S. have been raped – 22 million! About 20% of those raped were under 12 years of age! Violence against women often leads to murder. And, although we'd like to think this violence is perpetrated by strangers, at night, in a seedy part of town, the fact is that most women are abused by men they know well, often in broad daylight, often on college campuses, and in other "enlightened" settings. Where is our outrage about this?

Almost 65% of women over 18 are victimized by men whom they trusted: husbands, boyfriends, or partners. Only half of domestic violence incidents are reported to police. Here are just a few recent examples of domestic violence that led to the death of the victim and those around her:

A man enraged at how his wife cooked eggs, took a shotgun and killed her, his stepdaughter and three neighbors, before shooting himself.

A husband in Miami killed his wife, and then posted a graphic photo of her dead body on Facebook with a chilling confession.

A husband who said he loved his wife and wanted to reconcile with her was so enraged by her refusal to reconcile that he shot her and then himself.

A jealous husband walked into the beauty salon of his beautician wife and killed her execution-style in front of her colleagues and customers.

Another ex-husband thought his wife was having an affair, so he beat her, sprayed acid in her face and set her on fire. She is now legally blind and grateful to have a new face donated and attached to where her face used to be. Her scars will never heal; he got 30 years in prison with his face and body intact. Sick bastard!

We women are attacked daily —on our streets; in the parks when we jog; in colleges and universities where we get our educations; on dates; in the military as we try to defend our country; in our homes and in our marriages; we are also raped incestuously by fathers, brothers and uncles. Rape, rape, rape…and unfortunately, the fear must be instilled in all girls and women or they may become another statistic.

The media tries to put a "new twist" on the story of rape with elaborate coverage of the very occasional rape of men, the female rapist, or the fabricated rape accusations. One of the more renowned cases was that of 15-year-old Tawana Brawley. She claimed she'd been raped, thrown in a trash bag, with the words "nigger" and "bitch" scrawled on her body in feces. Her charges raised a firestorm across the nation because of the racist nature of the attack, with TV yelling Al Sharpton leading the way. I won't defend his or her actions, except to say that she was a psychologically-troubled young woman. The fact remains that for every rape allegation there are about 20 unreported rapes. The problem is that the attention given to cases like Tawana Brawley's makes it harder for women who are raped to come forward and be believed.

Women are 91% of the rape victims in this country - only 9% are men. Men are 99% of the rapists - only 1% of women rape. When unreported rapes are factored in, only 6% of rapists ever serve a single day in jail, leaving them out looking for their next victim. Women are no safer in their homes than they are outside. We have no "safe haven." Over two-thirds of all rapes occur in someone's home: 31% in the perpetrators' homes; 27% in the victims' homes; and 10% in homes shared by the victim and perpetrator. Over 20% of rapes are outside: 7% at parties, 7% in vehicles, 4% outdoors and 2% in bars. Of course, these are probably low estimates because so many rapes go unreported. And our current judicial system contributes to this national disgrace. The following are examples:

CHERICE

Cherice Moralez was a smart, lovely 14-year-old girl in Montana who had her whole life in front of her. She also had a 54-year-old male teacher named Stacey Rambold, who raped her and then intimidated her so she would keep it quiet. Rambold had no arrest record – but had repeatedly been warned to stay away from young girls after their families had made numerous complaints against him. Two years after being raped, Cherice Moralez killed herself. Her mother said that Cherice had never been able to get over the rape, so it led to her suicide.

Stacey Rambold was tried for rape and convicted by Judge G. Todd Baugh, a bearded, bald-headed Good Old Boy. He sentenced Rambold to 15 years in jail, but suspended all but 31 days, and even gave him one day served. Yet, sexual intercourse without consent carries a 2-year minimum jail sentence in Montana. So, why did Judge Baugh let Rampold go after 31 days? The judge wrote in his ruling that Cherice was partly to blame for her own rape. After all, he said, she was "older than her chronological age" and "as much in control of the situation as the defendant." This judge needs to be put in an insane asylum.

The Judge was not the only male involved in this travesty. The prosecutors were either stupid or not doing their jobs when they admitted that the minimum mandatory sentence was 2 years, not 30-days. After public outrage, the Judge tried to reverse his 31-day sentence, but the Montana Supreme Court added insult to Cherice's rape and death. They refused to allow the Judge to reverse his decision because it would "cause gross injustice to an orderly appeal." These idiots actually decided that "an orderly appeal" was more important than justice for this young girl. Cases like this happen all the time – the Good Old Boys are either protecting each other, themselves or "the system." Protecting a 14-year-old Hispanic girl from rape and death doesn't count for much.

DAISY

Another recent case involves a beautiful 15-year-old, Daisy Coleman from Missouri, who tried to commit suicide because she was bullied after reporting that she was raped by a 17-year high school senior football player. This is one of those "he said, she said" cases in which the boy's word will be believed over the girl's. Daisy's mother said that her daughter and girlfriend were plied with alcohol (in "bitch cups") at the athlete's home, incapacitated and then sexually assaulted. After they were finished with her, "out of it" Daisy was tossed on her front lawn like a bag of garbage in 22-degree weather. A felony charge of rape against the 17-year-old athlete was dismissed because "there was not enough evidence." Instead, he was found guilty of a misdemeanor for throwing Daisy on her front lawn because it was cold enough to kill her.

The athletes were supported, so where were all the women who should have been supporting Daisy? They probably joined in with the other "my son, my son" women. Daisy managed to survive, and then described her ordeal: "I was called a skank and a liar and people encouraged me to kill myself. Twice, I did try to take my own life." She also said the whole experience made her feel ugly and worthless, and her young girlfriend who was also involved, said she doesn't go out anymore. Two young women's lives were destroyed and they paid dearly for drinking too much and trusting young males.

Jameis Winston, a star college football player, was alleged to have raped a young woman somewhere off campus after she left a Tallahassee bar. There was evidence that included bruises, semen on her underwear and a videotape by a witness. After identifying the perpetrator, the local prosecutor, William Meggs, said he lacked the evidence to charge Winston, admitting the investigation was flawed. Do you think so, Mr. Meggs? Former National Football League (NFL) safety and NFL Network analyst Darren Sharper was arrested in Los Angeles on suspicion of sexual assault. Sharper was also linked to previous sexual assaults in October 2013 and January 2014, and another one in September 2013 that was being investigated by police in New Orleans. The pro-athlete mindset was evident when articles cited the cases and made his football career more important. He was reported as playing for the Green Bay Packers, Minnesota Vikings and New Orleans Saints; he'd led the NFL with 9 interceptions; he'd returned 3 for touchdowns; and the season culminated perfectly in a Saints victory in Super Bowl XLIV.

Sports represent big money that trumps any other considerations. Comedian extraordinaire Groucho Marx in the movie *Horse Feathers* summed it up when he said: "*Have we got a college? Have we got a football team? ....Well we can't afford both. Tomorrow we start tearing down the college.*"

Male athletes are the money-makers who count for other men, fans and owners. The GOB's think women in college should be sideliners, cheerleaders and groupies. Good Old Boy Donald Sterling, previous owner of the NBA franchise the Los Angeles Clippers, was banned for life and lost his ownership for racist remarks he made about Blacks. Listening to the audio, it appeared he was set up by the younger woman and prodded until he said what she expected him to say. He was going down and did. Just as this has caught the public's attention and ire, so should the cases of rape of women by athletes. But the former has to do with wealth, control and power; whereas women are not moneymakers, so they are unimportant and expendable.

Reports are that almost a half a million rape kits are sitting on dusty shelves in police stations throughout the U.S., backlogged and untested. We are allowing evidence from these rapes to be treated as trash instead of spending only $500 and $1500 to process them, possibly preventing another rape. Women can't count on their representatives to handle the problem either. The Tennessee state Senate Republicans voted against an amendment to allocate $2 million to clean up their 12,000 untested rape kit backlog (some since 1980s) saying they want a "full accounting" first. Can you imagine the gall of these idiots? And $1.2 billion allocated by the U.S. Justice Department since 2004 to expand DNA testing and clean up rape-kit backlogs has "gone toward broader purposes." Women are often called "broads," but that's not where the money went. Yet, in 2009 authorities tested 2000 kits and identified 127 serial rapists and matched almost 500 known convicts or unknown rapists. This is a problem that has to enrage women in order for it to be fixed.

Did you know that some of the quotes in Ian Fleming's James Bond 007 series include: "All women love semi-rape. They love to be taken. It was his sweet brutality against my bruised body that made his act of love so piercingly wonderful (*The Spy Who Loved Me*). She explained to me later that she must have been possessed by a subconscious desire to be raped. Well, she found me in the mountains and she was raped – by me." (*In Her Majesty's Secret Service*). Let's not forget *Goldfinger*'s "Pussy Galore."

5   Rape of Our Soldiers

"I lived through this horror, and no one can tell me I have to stay quiet."

Erin Merryn

Rape of our female soldiers is a national disgrace. Last year, after hearings on sexual misconduct by basic training instructors at Lackland Air Force Base in San Antonio, Texas, the current Secretary of Defense Leon Panetta said the ban on women serving in combat roles would be lifted. What was he saying? Sending women into combat is supposed to alleviate the scandalous rapes and sexual assaults? Enlisted women (and men) were being raped during their basic training, but it often went unreported because of the victim's fear of retaliation and a climate that winks at the assailants.

Almost 20 years ago there was a scandal at Aberdeen Proving Ground of male soldiers sexually abusing and assaulting female recruits and trainees. After things died down, the men in charge said the problem had been handled well enough to stop the abuse. Two decades later, we are again witnessing the same assaults on women only in greater numbers because more young women are enlisting. How would you feel if you were raped then testified about this disgrace before an almost empty hearing room? That's exactly what happened.

The misogynistic mindset is what allowed our representatives to simply not show up – it just wasn't important enough for them to take the time. They can spend days on nonsense, profiling and pontificating -- but the rape of women is insignificant, not worthy of their time. Their behavior is despicable. When women who defend our country can't even count on these idiots to listen to what they have to say at a hearing, they should go home and not come back. Women in the U.S. can always count on being raped -- then raped a second time by the system.

The message for female soldiers: 'We give you permission to go get yourself killed, but don't expect us to protect you from being assaulted by your own fellow soldiers. You are just collateral damage.' This is the same message often given to our veterans who return home sick from chemical exposure. It's outrageous. Yet anyone who has ever worked for the military knows that there is an easy fix.

When the Commander says 'Jump!' everyone asks 'How high?' That is standard operating procedure (SOP). The military has SOPs and SOBs for everything. Almost every minute of every day is programmed by rules and regulations for the soldiers and civilians. When the Commander enters a room, everyone, military and civilians, stands at attention until he tells you 'At ease.' When he decides you will have meetings every morning standing at attention, you comply. He tells you what time to meet, and you never keep him waiting. It goes on and on. You follow orders -- or pay the consequences.

If and when the military wants to stop the mass abuse and rape of our female soldiers, all they have to do is to tell the Commander, who tells his other leaders, and down the chain of command. When a rape is reported, if strong and immediate action is taken and an example made of the perpetrator – just as they do with others who step outside their system – rape may not stop completely, but it will be greatly reduced. According to the Pentagon's own records, on average 52 military women are raped *every day*. The Pentagon published another report that sexual assaults rose sharply, up to 70 per day. This calculates to three rapes per hour, all day and night, 24/7. And those are just the reported rapes; many more unreported. Once a Commander fails to get his troops under control, his authority should be stripped. Tear off those stars! That would get everyone's attention.

But instead, the usual excuses prevail. The first is the "he said, she said" problem and we know what she says counts less than what he says. In some Muslim countries, a man's word is worth twice as much as a woman's. Is it any different in our country or are we just pretending to be different?

The second problem is that no one seems to care enough to stop it – as in "We have more important things to do." That's why we get empty hearing rooms. This is all happening while ignoramuses with low IQs spew out that there is "legitimate" rape, and raped women who conceive must still carry and deliver the baby of their rapist.

The third problem is that the Commanders, some of whom were negligent, don't want to relinquish any of their power – so they insist they can handle cases, which they haven't effectively handled to date. What the hell do they want, another medal?

As Commander in Chief, President Obama told Secretary of Defense Chuck Hagel, "*to step up our game exponentially*" to prevent these sexual crimes. We know what he meant, but the use of the word "game" referring to stopping rape and sexual assault against women in the military was extremely poor. Many believe the military cannot fix their problems from the inside because leaders have to cover up the crimes rather than expose them if they want their next promotion. It's a military system that gets whistle blowers jailed for espionage and lets rapists get off scot free.

The prosecuting of rapists takes a circuitous route. Women just can't be trusted to tell the truth – right? She may just be promiscuous and trying to get a man in trouble. She may have asked for it. She was probably somewhere she was not supposed to be – in the barracks or on the Fort. In the end, she probably has to leave the service, while he carries on. I guess it's better than sending her to the front lines to be killed. Of course, the decision to handle and prosecute or take proper action will be left to Commanders "on the ground," as it always has been.

What have they been doing up to now, sitting on their stars? I reported to some magnificent Generals and Commanders who deserve their stars and medals. I've also been supervised by some idiots. One 3-star General didn't like conflict – What! Another 2-star General was more interested in the Civil Rights Director's big ass than his troops. These guys put their socks on one foot at a time just like everyone else – but they have more money and power than most states. So, for a period of time, extra emphasis will be placed by Commanders on these "sexual problems" until they disappear from public attention and criticism. All those that occurred before will fall under a "grandfathering" process as "not on my watch."

As an animal rights advocate, it's hard for me to believe that our military slaughtered thousands of military-trained dogs that served in Iraq, and tossed them into piles as if they were garbage – just another case of collateral damage or euphemistically euthanized animals that served us well only to be discarded as so much trash. Where are our moral compasses – Oh, I'll have to ask the Navy or Coast Guard – they have the compasses.

6 Sexual Predators

"As long as there is rape ... there is not going to be any peace or justice or equality or freedom."

Andrea Dworkin

Gang rapes and trafficking are on the rise in the U.S. For no justifiable reason, separate data is not kept on gang rapes, but it's estimated that 14% to 20% of the rapes in the U.S. are by gangs. An analysis of 739 gang rapes by the U.S. and U.K found that 20% of the victims died of their injuries. And their deaths must have been horrendous. Recent reported cases include: 5 men out of 18 arrested for gang-raping an 11-year-old girl in Texas; a U.S. Naval Academy victim being called a "ho" by prosecutors and saying that because her mouth was open, she was participating; two women gang-raped in Delaware; and five males and females arrested for beating and raping a 16-year-old in Florida. A woman was raped by two men as she jogged in the park in the Washington, D.C. metropolitan area.

Those of you sending your daughters away to college for an education are putting her in harm's way. It's been reported that hundreds of "prosecuted gang rape cases" occur on college and university campuses, which are above the number of individual rapes that take place. These institutions of higher learning charge parents exorbitant tuition, yet gloss over how dangerous it is for girls on college campuses. What are they doing with all that money? Certainly not taking proactive steps to protect female students. Campus drugs and alcohol, date drugs and "bitch cups" are prevalent. Danger lurks around every building, with or without ivy, and in every room and fraternity house. None of this information is part of their recruitment brochures or covered in orientation sessions. Estimates vary widely with surveys that say it's either 1 in 50 college women or 1 in 4 raped. We could count accurately if we really wanted to – but we don't. That would be too much knowledge.

There are about 2 million "working" women (prostitutes) in the U.S. and 15-20% of American men visit them or use high-class "escorts." This data doesn't include those putridly sick men who, wanting to have sex with children, travel to Asia, where about a million children have been sold into the sex trade. They should have an airline called "U.S. Deviants Airline" for those creeps.

The Los Angeles Police Department set up roving teams and went into areas with high numbers of prostitutes and pimps. They said pimps are changing their mode of operation by trolling for younger victims -- girls as young as 12 years old. The media's glamorization of hookers, pole dancers, and prostitutes seems to make girls believe these are acceptable "professions," as portrayed by actress Julia Roberts in the movie *Pretty Woman*.

There's nothing pretty about the oldest "profession" in the world. Cornell University Law School published a paper on the "Relationship between Pimps and Prostitutes," which defined a prostitute as "one who exchanges sexual favors for money, drugs and other commodities, while a pimp is one who controls the action and lives off the proceeds of one or more prostitutes." One organization said that 90% of the prostitutes were pimp-controlled, while the U.S. Department of Justice said it was only half. Some of the data presented showed that "sophisticated" pimps travel the intercity with 10 to 40 girls working for them; recruits are usually vulnerable girls, often runaways abused or neglected by their families.

Pimps often set up competition among their prostitutes, treating those who earn the most with affection, and beating those who underperform. The pimps use the money on drugs, automobiles, clothes and jewelry, and anything else that shows off their status as "the man." The relationship ends when the prostitute is pregnant, goes on welfare, turns to more serious crimes, commits suicide, or is murdered by a customer or pimp. I guess they are then buried along major highways, not to be found for decades. These women are the real "throw-aways" in our society, used by men then discarded as so much human trash.

Generally, prostitutes and call girls are rounded up and jailed, while the "johns" using their services go free. "I have a wife at home," is a refrain heard from johns dragged in wanting to be released for the good of the family. Would legalizing prostitution cut down on abuse of these women and young girls? Perhaps. Taking the profit out of the oldest "profession" should be considered -- just as it has for marijuana users.

Women are the "most numerous victims of the global sex trade with 2 million women trafficked annually and 2 million children, mostly girls, sold, coerced, or kidnapped into sexual slavery." It's estimated that 17,500 are trafficked by being sexually exploited and forced into sexual labor in the U.S. annually. This "human trafficking" is actually inhumane and destroys its victims. While articles include men and boys as victims, most who are sex-trafficked are women and girls. Male pimps, johns, traffickers, rapists and other abusers of women and girls are allowed to continue because we allow it. Many men in the systems that could stop this are part of the problem.

The most vulnerable in our society are targeted by "abuse, threats, lies, false promises, debt bondage and other forms of control and manipulation" to keep them in the sex trade. Women and children are sold online every day and in residential brothels, hostess clubs, massage parlors and businesses, strip clubs and areas of prostitution, all there to meet men's needs, many who are sick, depraved and diseased. As long as women and girls are treated as sex objects, this dangerous and brutal exploitation will continue. As women, we need to become enraged by these criminal acts against our gender. We need to take a stand if this is ever going to stop.

7 Mass Murders & Shooters

"I have a very strict gun control policy: if there's a gun around, I want to be in control of it."

Clint Eastwood

The media portrays women as worse than they are in order to make men look better. For example, an article on 16 murders had a short summary of each; the first large photograph was of a young, bedraggled, brown-skinned woman stating she got life in prison for murder. The list shifts back and forth so you can't tell if you are reading about the victim or perpetrator. The more gruesome the woman's murder, the more descriptive, such as "chopping up his body with a chainsaw and hiding his parts…" Of the 16 murderers listed, 13 were men and only 3 were women – not the perception given to a casual reader.

This depiction of women as being as bad as men is quite deliberate. Over the past 30 years, there have been at least 62 mass shootings in the U.S. and most of the killers got their guns illegally. Only one on the list of shooters was a female; the other 61 were males. *Mother Jones* published a list of mass shootings in an article advocating gun control. The list was said to be all-inclusive and one of the most comprehensive available on mass shootings to date. There have been more since, but using their data, it still constitutes only a small fraction of the people killed annually in the U.S. by guns.

An analysis of the list shows that 98.0% of the mass shooters were men; 71% were White males; 40% were work-related; and ages ranged from 19 to 55 years old. Out of the 25 work-related mass shootings, 76% of the shooters were near 40 years of age, and only 6 (24%) were between 19 years of age and their early 30's. The sole woman was a former postal worker, Jennifer San Marco, who shot her neighbor, drove to the mail-processing plant and killed 6 employees, injured 2 and then committed suicide.

And, the number of mass shootings is on the rise. From about one to two a year, it rose to seven in 2012 and continues to rise.

The U.S. has the highest number of serial killers (76%) – who kill three or more people. The Federal Bureau of Investigation (FBI) has estimated there are 30-50 serial killers active in the U.S. at any one time. Others believe the number is closer to 100. These killers move around, stay hidden and bury their victims. The FBI set up a "Highway Serial Killer Initiative" because they had a 'matrix of more than 600 victims and potential suspects in excess of 275,' with many bodies found off major highways across the country. They reported that serial killers are generally intelligent and clever; intelligent no, deviously clever yes. Further, they wrongly said serial killers are racially mixed and "not limited to any specific demographic group, such as their sex, age, race, or religion."

Reports are clear: 90% of serial killers are male, 81% white males, 19% Black and the remainder mixed. Only 10% of serial killers are female. So, what's going on at the FBI? Writer Lynette Holloway said she contacted them at Quantico to get statistics on Black and White serial killers. She was told they do not maintain statistics for serial killers or track them by race or other factors. So then, how can they say that they are "racially mixed?" This is nonsense! Ms. Holloway also found that these sick killers are not geniuses or more intelligent. Instead, most of them are just your average or below average "Sickos."

I've seen more horrendous pictures of people's guts, brains and severed parts than I ever wanted to see on television between *Criminal Minds* and other such programs. These gruesome pictures only add to the problems we have in our highly diverse and unstable society. Just imagine how this impacts on our youth, particularly young men, along with the destructive and violent games.

8   Pure Evil

"The world is a dangerous place to live; not because of the people who are evil, but because of the people who don't do anything about it."

Albert Einstein

Men head the list of evil criminals. Yet, the mindset remains the same and women get top billing in this category too, no matter where or when it occurs. Ten major crimes to shock the nation listed five women first, then the first male. The six women started with Elizabeth Short, nicknamed "The Black Dahlia," whose remains were found in 1947 in a vacant LA lot (still unsolved); continuing with Lizzie Borden of nursery rhyme fame who took an axe to her parents for 40 whacks (she was found not guilty) and then on to the Amy Fisher, Joey Buttafuoco's 16-year girlfriend who shot his wife in the face at their front door.

After the six women were listed, crazy maniac killer Richard Speck, called the "Born to Raise Hell" murderer, was listed. He slaughtered 8 nurses in a dormitory in 1966 (found guilty and died in prison). Then Charles Manson, who manipulated the slaughter of four people with a blood-filled scene left behind; and of course, O.J. Simpson of the "If the glove doesn't fit, you must acquit," slaughter of his wife and her male friend for which he was acquitted. The Good Old Boys didn't like what he did and got away with, so at the first opportunity, they threw him in jail to rot.

A list of the 25 most evil people in history had just one woman on the list, but it was reversed so she could be listed first. Then they listed the 24 evil men, 5 of them Nazis. The first (or last) woman was Countess Dracula, Elizabeth Bathory, who was purported to have killed over 650 young women. Busy, crazy woman! Modern scholars now believe she was a powerful, educated widow whose evil family wanted to put her in the tower so they could control her assets after her husband died. So they created these stories for public consumption. Sounds right to me! Elizabeth spent three years in the tower before she died.

One article authored by a male listed only the most evil women. He said he had to do it because we all tend to focus on evil men in the world, so he wanted to point out some utterly despicable women. Thanks, and join the crowd! He just couldn't seem to stand the fact that men are in fact the most evil and destructive people on earth. The women listed were all small-timers in comparison to the men, who slaughtered millions of people and heinously tortured them. Most of the women were more specific as to whom they killed and their methods were as grotesque, but differed because they related more to the home front, their jobs, or survival as a monarch, as was the case with the three Queens, Mary, Elizabeth and Isabella. Madness, rampant in sovereigns because of inbreeding, makes one think of the wife-murdering madman King Henry VIII, a handsome and stately man, who ruled the English monarchy for almost 38 years under the Tudor dynasty after succeeding his father.

Henry went through six wives: Catherine of Aragon, Anne Boleyn, Jane Seymour, Anne of Cleves, Catherine Howard, and Catherine Parr. He had affairs and discarded wives who "failed" to give him an heir and spare. He beheaded those who displeased him and remarried. Two were smart enough to get what they wanted from Henry. Remember this. Anne agreed to allow the dissolution of her marriage to Henry, so he rewarded her with two houses, a generous allowance, and the title "The King's Sister." She definitely kept her head about the entire situation. So many wives and so little time for Henry. Thankfully, he died at 55 from medical problems before more women's heads could roll. He will always be remembered for beheading his wives. Just thinking about it can make your neck itch.

Slaughters and atrocities by men continue today. The United Nations estimates that more than 100,000 Syrians have been slaughtered in the country's civil war and another 1,500 from chemical weapons. The consideration of the U.S. to strike against leader Basher al-Assad was based on the use of chemical weapons, not concern for the over 100,000 killed. Is it U.S. policy that if you slaughter your own people or commit genocide or gendercide by traditional means, we won't intervene? But if you use warfare that could spread to our shores, we won't approve of the massacres. What the hell is wrong with these killers? Is it testosterone that drives them to slaughter? Is it brain rot? This is when even I believe there is a case to be made for assassination.

9 Bad Men Come in All Sizes

"Bad men are full of repentance."

Aristotle

So many little evil men have caused so many inhumane deaths. They use their gift of persuasion to seize more power and destroy others. Some people believe that short maniacs have been the scourge of civilization because they have a big chip on their shoulder. What these creatures have done takes more than a chip on the shoulder. They have committed atrocities such as genocide, mass executions, torture, murder, and, of course, rape. A list of garden-gnome beasts go back to Genghis Khan (5'1") and include Napoleon Bonaparte (5'6"), Josef Stalin (5'6"), Francisco Franco (5'4"), and Kim Jong-Il (5'3"). These men were given or took power then destroyed everything in sight.

Shortness is not a barometer for evil, though. After all, Saddam Hussein was 6'2", Idi Amin and Osama bin Laden were both 6'4". The worst of the bunch was Adolf Hitler, an average-size man, between 5'8" – 5'10" and 155 pounds. These men could not have done their evil deeds alone – they needed to persuade others. Hitler was able to rouse the German people, particularly the men, by their mutual enmity and hatred, particularly of Jews. They slaughtered over 20 million people: Homosexuals, Gypsies, Jews and Slavs (Eastern). Those and others who accumulated wealth and power had to be eliminated because they had "undermined" Germany and did not belong to the "Master Race."

This little malevolent hypocritical monster was a horrible-looking man. Hitler was said to have a "...low receding forehead, ugly nose, broad cheekbones, small eyes..." and dark, fine hair. He was a vegetarian who loved chocolate; his dentist later revealed he had "terribly bad breath, abscesses and gum disease." He considered women insignificant, except in meeting men's needs. Yet German women were enamored by him and his power. As with so many short, powerful and wealthy men, he always had a woman by his side providing him with support as he engaged in wholesale slaughter, genocide and atrocities. Eva Braun stood by her man. She met Hitler when she was 17 and he was 40; she remained his mistress for 12 years, marrying him the day before they committed suicide in April 1945 rather than face the consequences.

No man, or group of men, should be allowed to engage in wholesale slaughter and destruction simply because they hold power. As a pacifist (if not provoked), I feel that eliminating one man is better than allowing the destruction and annihilation of many. Americans, particularly women, need to learn the tricks of these powerful men and understand that we are not immune from being lulled to sleep by their rhetoric and charisma. Women cannot afford to join the Greedy Old Bastards, either. If we do, we give up all hope of ever changing the world into a better place for ourselves, our children, especially the girls, and people all over the world who are suffering from sadistic maniacs.

CHAPTER V

1 Coping with Fear

"Love is what we were born with. Fear is what we learned here."

Marianne Williamson

As women, we must be constantly vigilant because our environment is sick and unsafe. We must find ways to protect ourselves and our children in order to cope in today's fearful and male-dominated society. One coping mechanism we use is to stay in confined, secure areas.

When this becomes more irrational, it's called agoraphobia, the unrelenting "fear of a situation, activity, or thing that causes one to want to avoid it and from which one either cannot escape or escaping would be difficult or humiliating." Most of us can relate to it when it comes to the fear of flying or the fear of public speaking. One estimate is that agoraphobia develops in up to 7% of the people in response to "repeated exposure to anxiety-provoking events." That statistic is probably too low and there are degrees of the illness. Phobias tend to run in families, but genetics may be less important than family environment.

Years ago in the U.S., children were told to come home before dark, or when the street lights went on. Other countries, particularly those in warmer climates, do not have the same restrictions and people are out and about late into the night. This may be why Hispanics, African Americans and Asians suffer less from agoraphobia. People with one phobia often develop others. So agoraphobia is often combined with phobias such as acrophobia (heights) and claustrophobia (confined spaces).

Most of us have phobias - I am claustrophobic and mageirocophobic (fear of cooking) – only kidding. Although it really isn't a joke when a person fears being burned when cooking or afraid to cook food. Agoraphobic sufferers have panic attacks, along with intense fear, disorientation, rapid heartbeat, dizziness and diarrhea. They try to avoid situations that provoke these symptoms. The phobia usually starts by adolescence and affects mainly girls and women, particularly those widowed and separated. Not surprisingly, it also affects the poor more often, possibly because the poor often have real problems to fear. In other words, just because I'm paranoid doesn't mean someone isn't out to get me. I believe any of us programmed to come in the house to safety and security may have a form of agoraphobia. Fears can be so severe that they can trap the victim in his or her own home.

One of the more interesting cases is that of wealthy Huguette Clark, who died at age 104 leaving behind a $300 million inherited fortune. The biography on her life, *Empty Mansions,* takes us through her shyness, wealth, fear and suffering. It winds its way from her family's lives during the robber baron period. Thorsten Veblen's "Theory of the Leisure Class," coined the term "conspicuous consumption" to cover that period, but it could just as well pertain to the current 1% or leisure class in the U.S., conspicuously consuming and flaunting their wealth and toys.

Huguette was a shy girl, who inherited great wealth, but didn't seek or use the power that she got from it. Instead, she withdrew into her own make-believe world of dolls and doll houses. Her one marriage ended mysteriously right after the honeymoon. Eventually without family surrounding her, she locked herself away in her mansion, communicating mainly by telegraph, telephone and letters. She was finally found, dehydrated, with her lip and cheek destroyed by cancer, and spent the next 20 years in a hospital room.

Reading her biography, it was clear to me that she suffered from a severe case of agoraphobia. She felt secure by keeping order and structure in her life and remaining in a small close space, first her mansion, then a hospital room. Charlatans took advantage of her illnesses and phobias, just as they do with other wealthy people.

Women suffer more from phobias than men and are three times more likely to have agoraphobia, and twice as likely to suffer from panic disorders and social phobias. They are also at higher risk to develop specific phobias (a particular object or situation) and suffer more from Post-Traumatic Stress Disorder (PTSD) than men (10-14% v 5-6%). Yet, illness phobias are more common in men. Reasons for the higher number of women suffering from phobias have been attributed to physical and mental abuse, sex hormone differences, and anxiety. But besides phobias, there are many more problems from which women suffer that are just as devastating to their well-being.

I have girlfriends who have some form of agoraphobia and have to be dragged out of their homes. When they agree to go to lunch, dinner or shopping, they are fidgety and nervous, eager to go home. Going out after dark is another whole scene to endure with them. I have a girlfriend who won't get on an elevator, so she walks up countless flights of stairs to go to work or visit people. She is also afraid to fly (aviatophobia) and has claustrophobia. Another girlfriend can't drive over bridges, trapping her on her side of the waterway unless someone else drives. Phobias drain a person's energy, life and relationships.

Women also don't do as well as men with breakups and divorces. They spend time blaming themselves and grieving over the loss of a man. Many people, especially women, have autophobia, the fear of being alone, so they rather suffer through a bad relationship. Many books tell women how to get over a failed relationship, while men more easily move on to the next chapter in their life.

CARRIE

My friend Carrie was married to a successful professional, and everyone thought they made a great couple. Then her husband dumped her, and all hell broke loose. She begged him to take her back. He refused. In a cry for help, Carrie drove her car at high speed right into a huge block of cement, just outside the entrance to the company where her husband worked. She wanted to get his attention, but instead she totaled her car, and landed in the hospital with broken bones and her jaw wired shut. She was then portrayed as an unbalanced female lunatic, and people felt sorry for her jerk of a husband, and told him 'No wonder you left her.'

Two years after her recovery, Carrie invited me to her apartment in the boondocks of New Jersey. She had a post-graduate student lover. I guess she'd also lost all of her inhibitions… As I entered the downstairs foyer of her two-story abode, I saw at least 15 photos of Carrie, naked except for a hat. It now reminds me of the great Joe Cocker song "Leave Your Hat On" ("Just take off your coat, real slow, take off your shoes, take off your dress, yes, yes…and leave your hat on."). Getting nude pictures taken was just part of Carrie's recovery. She was also having an affair with a local doctor, while her post-grad boyfriend was at school. When I was there, he came home from studying and they began to drink. Suddenly, they started screwing, so I ran out of there laughing before they could try to lure me into a threesome.

What happened to Carrie happens to many women. A pampered "Daddy's little girl," she didn't get an education past high school, then married a college-educated, selfish man who had a great job and was riding high (and his girlfriend), while Carrie was doing wifely things. Part of Carrie's self-destruction was because she thought their situation was more complex. She thought he left her because she had been unable to conceive a child, when the truth was he was having an affair with a colleague.

Over the years, I've seen so many workplace affairs that they became the norm. They are common because men and women spend long hours together, working in the same places, sharing lunches, and company cars. They often travel together, sharing ups and downs in the same hotels and beds. Current estimates are that 30-40% of women and 50-60% of men will have an affair during their marriage and those are only the ones admitting it or caught. Workplace affairs head the list for infidelity and should increase with more women are in the workforce. Carrie, and many women like her, must be given credit for a safe landing when her whole life was pulled out from under her and she crashed. Carrie and I drifted apart – but I often think of her – and not as a failure, but as a survivor in a man's world – managing to keep her hat on.

2 Hormonal Imbalances

"If any organism fails to fulfill its potentialities, it becomes sick."

William James

Medical research has been designed by men, carried out by men, in the service of men, and to deal with men's specific problems. Researchers are finally studying the special problems of women and the proper treatment of those problems -- but it's a little late for countless women. Sadly, because of our celebrity worship in this country, many women's issues are dismissed until a celebrity talks about them – but it's better than nothing, so we need to thank those celebrity women for coming forward.

Postpartum depression became more newsworthy because of celebrities like Brooke Shields, Gwyneth Paltrow, Angelina Jolie and Britney Spears. That didn't stop actor Tom Cruise, the Scientology apologist, couch-jumping small guy, from ripping into Brooke Shields for seeing a psychiatrist and taking anti-depressants to treat her severe depression after giving birth.

I won't dignify what Mr. Cruise had to say about chemical imbalances in women due to childbirth by quoting him at length. Let's just say he seems to feel that all Brooke needed was some vitamins. He did warn about taking anti-depressants, saying they are hard to put down and let go. And they often are. But when a woman's life and the life of her newborn are at risk, she should go on medications first, and worry later about when and how to get off them. Tom Cruise should stick to something he knows something about -- acting.

No woman is alone giving birth because there are over four million births each year in the U.S. *ChoiceWords* had an article in 2013 about post-partum depression and the strains on the mother from childbirth. The writer asked why we have this binary view of mothers: the "good mother" who loves and nurtures; and the "bad mother" who is evil, or "Mommy Dearest." The writer said it's possible for new mothers to love their children, but hate their lives. Pre- and post-partum, women are awash in powerful hormones that wreck havoc on our systems. So we need to understand the huge changes that take place in our bodies during pregnancy and childbirth. Failing to understand this could be fatal.

There are two types of postpartum illnesses, not one. There is Postpartum Depression (PPD) with symptoms of sadness, hopelessness, low self-esteem, guilt, exhaustion, low energy levels, decreased sex drive, and inadequacy. Then there is Postpartum Psychosis (PPP) with symptoms, which are less prevalent but of greater concern, such as delusions and hallucinations. And, these two serious illnesses are exacerbated if the woman is bipolar or schizophrenic.

Studies estimate that PPD is prevalent in 5% to 25% of the cases, which is another statistic that shows how uninformed we are about the problem. The more serious disorder PPP involves the onset of psychotic symptoms and psychoses affecting 4,000 to 8,000 women a year. And their chances of being treated adequately, or at all, are extremely poor. Following are two tragic examples of young women who couldn't cope after their pregnancies.

BERTA

Berta Estrada, a 25-year- old Mexican immigrant, didn't show up for her shift at Wendy's fast-food restaurant. Her sister stopped by her trailer in Texas to check on her. When no one answered, she forced her way in, and found Berta's 8-month-old niece, baby Evelyn, dangling by her neck from a sweater sleeve and the other three children, 5-year-old Maria, 3-year-old Yaneth, and 21-month-old Magaly, already dead. Berta Estrada gave birth eight months prior to this and she was without adequate support or hope.

Berta left her common-law husband, Gregorio Rodriguez, after accusing him of "raping her, strangling her, and threatening to kill her with a knife." She first moved to a battered women's shelter, then into a trailer with her children, struggling to live on $900 a month. A University of Pennsylvania physician said that Berta might have been suffering from lingering postpartum depression. It was probably PPP, not PPD. The tragedy was ruled a murder-suicide with bogus statements that it was 'unfathomable.' It's not even all that rare; there were reports of seven other "mommy murders" that had already been in the headlines in Texas. We should never forget Berta or her children.

MIRIAM

Miriam Carey, a 34-year-old Black female from Connecticut, was shot to death in Washington, D.C. First reports were that she had tried to ram her Infiniti into the White House fence, when she was actually stopped at concrete barriers that prevent cars from entering a large span in front of the White House. The blocked section was barricaded off years ago from 15th Street across to 16th Street. Videos of the tragedy show Miriam's car surrounded by armed police, their guns drawn. She quickly backed up and fled down Pennsylvania Avenue toward the Capitol building, about a mile and a half from the White House, coming to a stop outside the Hart Senate Office Building.

A Washington, D.C. Wild West shootout took place -- but it was an unfair fight because only one side was armed. Miriam couldn't do anything but flee for her life and the life of her daughter who was in the back seat of the car. Just imagine if she had put her baby in the front seat next to her. She was shot to death in a hail of bullets hitting her body 17 times! As I watched this play out across the news media, I wondered what the hell this country was coming to when an unarmed woman can be slaughtered in the nation's capital by a bunch of armed men because she drove her car to the wrong place. Just learning about PPP, I also wondered if Miriam could be suffering from it because she was said to be hallucinating.

Recently, Miriam's family said they were suing and told news reporters that Miriam suffered serious problems that were exacerbated by the birth of her baby. She fell down a staircase, sustaining a head injury four months before giving birth. Her boyfriend had left her, saying she was mentally unstable and delusional. She was fired from her job at a dental clinic, supposedly for using a handicapped parking space. Then she started hearing voices about President Barack Obama, among other things. Finally, she was on medication for bipolar and schizophrenic patients, which may lead to Post-partum Psychoses after giving birth.

Let's compare these police actions against an unarmed woman to what the cops did to a man who was *actually* climbing the White House fence after Miriam's death. He was arrested, but not shot to death. Another comparison is that of sports star O.J. Simpson in his white Bronco with his friend Al Cowlings driving down the highway in Los Angeles. O.J. was alleged to have viciously slaughtered his ex-wife and her friend, after which 20 police cars joined the chase as we all watched, glued to our TV sets. O.J. was armed, Miriam was unarmed; O.J. was a football star, Miriam was a dental hygienist; O.J. was a male, Miriam a female; O.J. had probably killed two people, Miriam had killed no one. And now O.J. is alive, and Miriam is dead. We are watching a monumental crisis in Missouri because police gunned down two Black males. Unfortunately, there were not many people out protesting Miriam's slaughter. All of these deaths were unnecessary and the U.S. "police state" mentality has to end. We have nonlethal methods, such as Tazers, that could have been used to prevent these human beings – Black Americans -- from being gunned down in a barrage of bullets.

Berta and Miriam, probably suffering from PPD or PPP, died because of their illness. But there are many other illnesses that women and girls suffer from in this country that are not adequately addressed or researched. We women must insist that money be funded or granted so we don't have similar occurrences in the future. We owe it to our daughters -- and to other girls, almost all of whom will be having babies sometime in their lives.

3 This is Sick

"I've been on a diet for two weeks and all I've lost is two weeks."

Totie Fields

I can't think of any of my girlfriends who are not on a diet. Emaciated-bone-sticking-out thin is in today. So we have all types of illnesses associated with women and young girls trying to resist nature by being ultra-thin. Anorexic women refuse to eat; exercise compulsively and may starve to death. Bulimic women eat excessive amounts of food then use laxatives, enemas, diuretics, or vomiting to empty their stomachs; 90% of bulimics are women. Binge-eating women gorge themselves, then regurgitate, grossly spewing up the chewed food. All this happens because of low self-esteem, constant attention focused on women's appearances, and women's dissatisfaction with their own faces and bodies.

My maternal grandmother, who sang opera on the radio, was what I would now consider large. Her pleasantly "plump" body type was "in" at the time, as depicted by the great singer Kate Smith of "God Bless America" fame. As my dear Hungarian friend Laszlo says, "Stronger women are coming into focus." He means fatter women. Body-types change, just as clothing fashions do, so we become programmed and adapt to what is in vogue rather than what is best for us. Our feet are getting larger, so why not expect our bodies to be larger too? I was fortunate not to have a weight problem when I was younger. I've started to gain weight as I've gotten older and more sedentary, and married a husband who loves to cook. I also have good feet.

My father insisted everyone in the family wear shoes that did not crimp our toes. When I cried about it, he crafted a pair of Japanese sandals out of wood for me. After clopping around loudly for a week in the house, my mother outlawed them. I hated my father's many restrictions: no short pants, no smoking, no drinking, and no high-heeled shoes. He said that someday I would thank him for those rules. Too bad someday was so far away, but it did eventually come. I don't want to sound as if I was too obedient. I wasn't. I often wore short pants under long pants, smoked with my girlfriends in out-of-the-way places, kissed boys, and helped my cousin Linda get a bra when she developed sooner than her mother allowed one. But, in the end, I survived intact and without corns or bunions.

It's bad enough that people have to put up with smelly feet – but deformed feet are awful. I didn't know how many women had ruined feet and twisted toes until I supervised two women who had to take time off from work to get their huge bunions removed or sawed off. Since then, I have observed many more women with bad feet because they wore shoes that were too small for them. They stuffed their square feet into pointy-toed shoes, and then tried to walk in high heels. Some of the problems of poor-fitting shoes, besides horrible bunions, are sciatic nerve damage, herniated discs, stress fractures, ankle pain and extremely ugly, misaligned toes.

Who doesn't like high heels? They make your calves look fabulous; you can dangle your delicate foot, cross your legs and look positively smashing and sexy. So, what's not to like? Your ugly corns, bunions, and fungus – that's what. The damage to your feet is multiplied by the amount of time you stand and walk in those stilettos. They often cause calf muscles to shorten, so that when your heels finally come down, the Achilles tendon and other muscles in your legs start screaming 'Take me up again - please!'

Then we have the ballerina slippers without any support, causing the extremely painful plantar fasciitis or "jogger's heel." Finally, there are the women walking around hiding those disgusting heels, all cracked up and horrible. An executive female at one of our meetings forgot we were guests sitting behind her, took off her shoes, pointed her heels at us, and we almost dropped dead!

Leave it to capitalism and the private sector again. The U.S. shoe industry rakes in $68 billion, while creating more fashion victims with bunions and hammer toes. Over 85% of foot surgeries result from bad shoes. We, along with our feet, are growing larger. According to reports, our feet have grown two sizes larger since the 1970s. Almost half of all women say they admit to not buying shoes that fit well, probably because of that nasty "toe box" smashing their toes to smithereens. Instead of designing more wearable, comfortable shoes for women's feet, as they did in designing condoms for male's penises, manufacturers are just scaling down men's shoes, creating more problems for women's feet. Men have always thought they should decide what's best for us women and they're still doing or sticking it to us.

Years ago, when I worked in Manhattan, smart women decided that sneakers and low shoes were made for walking throughout the city. We all carried bags with our spares; it was intelligent and freeing. Men's feet have always been free as they slide them into flat well-designed shoes made specifically for their comfort and endurance. What are we – guinea pigs wearing shoes?

Women have had their feet destroyed for centuries by men. China had the popular feet-binding practice called "Lotus Feet" for young girls to prevent their feet from growing. No young woman in her right mind would have suggested this disfiguring practice. At first it was used on upper-class women, who could be carried to their destinations and served, but later it was fashionably extended to the lower classes. This horrible practice did not die out until the early 20th century, after many women were permanently and horribly disabled and disfigured.

4 Body Prisoners

"Fashions have done more harm than revolutions."

Victor Hugo

Many garments and shoes designed by the fashion industry are for tethering and restricting women, making them body prisoners. The fashion industry is a multi-billion dollar industry and global enterprise that has made many designers rich and famous. My mother always said that men who designed some of the more restrictive and outrageously hideous fashions hated women or had misogynistic mindsets. The industry introduces new fashions on a regular basis in order to increase sales. The industry uses celebrities to model their clothes and jewelry, and make us wish we had them. One of my favorite fashion shows is *Project Runway* with gorgeous body-perfect Heidi Klum and sweet Tim Gunn at Parsons, New York. It's an advertising megahit because women love fashion.

Diane Von Furstenberg, a guest speaker whom I invited to one of my programs, became famous for her wrap dress. Spanx made Sara Blakely extremely wealthy by pushing in our fat fashionably – a new version of the old girdle. And we know all the names of the 10 top fashion famous: Yves Saint Laurent for power dressing women, Pierre Cardin for space-age designs, Tom Ford for international design, Christian Dior for his distinctive couture designs, the Versace's, Gianni and Donatella, for celebrity fashions, Calvin Klein, Giorgio Armani, Donna Karan, and, of course, Coco Chanel and Ralph Lauren who is worth $7.5 billion.

Around and around, fashion goes! We love it, we buy it, we wear it, we store it, we love it, we dump it, and we buy it again and again. Women pay more for their clothes, even if they are identical to men's. For women to go out on the town, or on a first date, it takes expensive underwear and clothes, expensive makeup and perfume, expensive shoes and bag, expensive jewelry – it's exhausting. There's no way for women to dress as fast and easily as men can in their basic underwear, socks, shoes, pants, shirt, jacket, tie, wallet and condoms. I just added that last one.

Men have developed uniforms for all occasions: their jobs, sports, and their male-bastion clubs. The business white-collar world requires conservative attire of shirts, suits, ties, and wing-tipped shoes, overcoats, hats, gloves, umbrellas and briefcases. It hasn't changed in centuries! Blue-collar men have dungarees and "Wife beater" T-shirts. Don't you just love the name – Wife Beater?! A group of women and I would often count the number of days some of the men in the office wore the same pair of smelly, dark-colored pants, matching their stained ties and dirty shirt cuffs. They'd sit in meetings in chairs others would soon have to sit in and in restaurant seats after low-standard, untrained workers wiped the seats with the same cloth used for our table. It is pitiful and disgusting.

Uniforms clearly identify roles, responsibility and authority. Men have hats to go with their uniforms, badges, and emblems. They have logos and mascots, insignias, awards and decorations. These identifiers separate them from the nonmembers and auxiliaries. The uniforms meant for "men only" must be worn by "token" women who look ridiculous or "butch" in the same attire. Men are more comfortable with women in uniforms at "Hooters" or the Playboy Club. But, if women want to be one of them – then, by God, let them wear what we do and say is appropriate. But who wants to date that!

The U.S. Army created strict standards in its dress code for soldiers. Not too long ago, they changed their hats to the new cocked beret style. Females are not allowed to wear their hair in a ponytail during Physical Training (PT), can wear makeup only "conservatively," without such extras as fake eyelashes. They can wear nail polish in their mess and dress uniforms only, with their fingernail length a quarter of an inch, but fake nails, add-ons and extensions are banned. Black females are now allowed to have cornrows or braids. I recently met a young female soldier in the nail salon, who was laughing about all the restrictions placed on her in the military. She told us she couldn't wait to retire because "Enough is enough; I'm getting out shortly, then taking orders from no one!"

With the death of the "don't tell" policy for gays in the military, and many minority men enlisting, there are also standards for them. Men are not allowed to wear makeup, as in the hit television series *Mash* with Max Klinger posing as a transvestite in order to get a Section 8 discharge for being crazy. Men are also not allowed to wear nail polish, and definitely can't have gold teeth; this might alert the enemy when they smiled and the sun hit the gold. But this is all minor compared to the fact that women are still earning less and paying more, no matter how they dress or conform.

Thanks to Hillary Clinton, women were able to put the mandatory conservative skirt, blouse and jacket or dress aside for pants and pant suits. Before that change, corporate rules required blouses and skirts, appropriate heeled shoes, with minimal jewelry and makeup. Women are now wearing more comfortable shoes and stores like "Comfort Shoes" are popular throughout the country. Things are changing for the better, but many of our young girls are headed back again into fashion chains and bindings. After seeing some of the messes that walk the streets and go to restaurants these days, we need to come up with something more appealing.

5 Your Ass is Too Small

"Life is all about Ass. You're either covering it, laughing it off, kicking it, kissing it, bursting it, or trying to get a piece of it."

Unknown

Everyone says Black women have bigger asses than White women. But, my sister and I have big asses inherited from our mother's side of the family. And I have Black female friends with flat little asses. Asses are in and the joke's on us, the women, so try not to laugh off whatever ass you were born with. What's new with someone deciding what's best for us anyway? If you're thin, your ass is probably too small.

Throughout history fasting or starving has been done based on religious beliefs, but the ritual lasted for only a few days to prepare for something sacred. From the 14th to the 16th Century, Christianity believed that women who starved themselves were closer to God. After the 16th Century, this practice was no longer accepted so the Catholic Church said anorexics were witches and burned them at the stake. No surprise – it's all cut from the same religious cloth. We're damned if we do – and damned if we don't. Today, many religions continue to practice fasting.

Just as alcohol does to the human brain when drunk constantly in large amounts, I believe that there is a built-in magic line or cell in the brain that, once crossed or damaged, becomes programmed so whatever control mechanisms were there before are gone. Then social drinkers become alcoholics and normal eaters become addicted to either overeating or starving themselves to death. Women are conditioned to believe they are too short or too tall, too fat or too skinny, or not pretty enough. We obsess about our appearances: our skin is blemished, our noses are too big, and our breasts and asses are too small, or too flat. It's as if we were glued together without all the right-sized body parts. Big breasts and big asses are currently in vogue, so if you don't have them, you'll have to come up with something to compensate.

Straight flowing hair is also in and if you haven't watched the documentary *Good Hair* by Chris Rock you're missing something about Black women and their hair. The film focuses on African-American women's obsession with their hair and the price they pay to get it straightened. The film has received its share of criticism, but, not to worry, white women and women of other races are just as entangled in the money-making hair situation and industry. Personally, I think no one knows or cares what the chemicals are doing to us. Look who's talking… I haven't had my real hair color since I was a teenager, but more companies are at least taking the harsh chemicals out of their products.

I am extremely allergic and makeup is a serious problem for many of us, especially around our eyes. More non-allergenic cosmetics are on the market, but the costs to women are staggering when compared to production costs, especially for the high-named brands. One estimate is that Americans are spending $33.3 billion dollars a year on cosmetics. Another is that when you add in hair and nails to the mix, women are spending $426 billion a year. Imagine how many kids could be fed on that. Women spend an average of $15,000 a year on makeup. I can attest to this just by opening a few drawers that are filled with new and unused products. It's really annoying because reports are that most men don't use a single product in the morning – we can tell though. These are the low-maintenance men. Haircuts for women in the D.C. metropolitan area are as high as $120, yet my husband gets his hair cut for $12.00. He shaves himself and looks good to me.

Adolescent girls are confused enough without making them more bewildered by all this nonsense. They are especially perplexed through puberty, vulnerable to self-loathing and undue concern about their bodies. So we need to assure them that what they have is not only good, but beautiful. If you have a flat ass and that's not in vogue this year, maybe you have beautiful teeth, a great smile, gorgeous eyes, nice ankles, great hair… Put it out there and love it! How about being smart? As was said in the 60s, "Black is beautiful." We're all beautiful, in our own way.

Even our most gorgeous women are forced to wonder how long their beauty will last before aging takes over, with wrinkles, jowls and age spots. Many are not growing old gracefully either as they nip, suck and tuck until they're almost unrecognizable.

6 Growing Old Gracefully

"Old age is no place for sissies."
Bette Davis

"Men-O-Pause" is not a misnomer. Menopausal women just don't like having sex very much, especially if they're having hot flashes and dry vaginas. We've got hormonal imbalances and a long list of problems. No wonder dear old Sigmund Freud thought women were hysterical. You would be, too, if you had all this happen to you just when you were getting some peace and quiet after raising the kids.

Menopausal symptoms sound like a television ad for drugs outlining the myriad of side effects. The list includes: anxiety attacks, discomfort during sex, brain fog, bloating, body odor, depression, trouble concentrating, disorientation and dizziness, feelings of doom and gloom, forgetfulness, headaches, hair loss, joint pain, hot flashes, lethargy and tiredness, moodiness, night sweats, osteoporosis, panic disorder, sleep disorders, sudden tears, and weight gain. Fortunately, I appear to have had only eight of the symptoms in spite of taking vitamins, and other natural remedies that didn't work. Finally, I resorted to medications so I could sleep, go to work and deal with others without maiming someone. One for us – one against Vitamin-Master Tom Cruise!

New aging signs seem to appear almost daily during and after menopause. Wrinkles, jowls, frown-lines, brown spots, drooping eyelids, poor eyesight, hearing problems, sagging body parts, falling arches, and arthritis, if we live long enough. Osteoporosis, back operations and knee and hip replacements are on the way. How about cataract operations and hearing aids? Don't even talk about forgetting – what was I thinking or saying?

So why weren't our mothers howling about this stuff? I was told to enjoy my youth, but the indignities of aging as a woman were missing from the dialogue. Wrinkled old women have no place to go. Wrinkled old men with money are still in vogue! Check the television programs with all the old wrinkled men still being paid, and then look at the dearth of wrinkled old women. Barbara Walters and Betty White did us all a service. A male friend of mine told me years ago: "Enjoy your body while you're young, firm and shapely, because at a certain age men won't even notice you." Another said, "Don't let your body go as you get older."

Hell – I'm not letting it go, it's going by itself. And, those disloyal men stopped their sincere compliments to me somewhere in middle-age, reserving them for tighter-skinned younger women. I should have maximized my days of youthful glory, but like most young women, I didn't think much about it until it left. Many women my age have decided to turn back the clock to their less-saggy days by getting plastic surgery. This is a serious, very costly proposition that doesn't always work out - physically, emotionally or financially.

Staying-young-at-any-cost is another boon -- for plastic surgeons. Americans, 90% women, spend over $11 billion a year for about 10 million surgical and nonsurgical cosmetic procedures, which continue to rise. The top five surgical procedures are: breast augmentation, liposuction, tummy tucks, eyelid surgery, and rhinoplasty (nose jobs). Nonsurgical cosmetic procedures include over 3 million Botox injections, followed by laser hair removal, micro-dermabrasion and chemical peels. We all want to look good, but whatever happened to growing old gracefully, without our faces stretched beyond recognition, and the bodies God and our parents gave us? Growing old gracefully seems to be a thing of the past.

Any foreign body (that penis Steve talked about) or product put in the body causes a reaction. Many women do suffer from urinary tract and other infections. So women should think carefully before they decide to mutilate their bodies by sucking out fat or inserting foreign objects into their breasts. Saline and silicone breast implants may cause scar tissue to distort the shape of the breast implant, and cause pain, infection, nipple changes, and leaks or ruptures. Implant ruptures may cause siliconomas or gel bleeds, and only the Lord knows what else. Reports say that the leaking gel is not thought to have systemic and long-term health problems, such as breast cancer, reproductive problems or connective tissue disease, such as rheumatoid arthritis. "Thought" is the operative word. Women have reported serious complications, such as muscle spasm and pain, swollen and painful joints, rashes, changes in eye and saliva fluid, and hair loss.

Large breasts but no hair... Nice!

7   Wonder Women Makeovers

"After all those years as a woman hearing 'not thin enough, not pretty enough, not smart enough, not this enough, not that enough,' almost overnight I woke up one morning and thought, 'I'm enough.'"

Anna Quindlen

The Plastic Surgery Industrial Complex is an enormous cash cow. Surgeons need more and more faces and bodies to fill their offices and tables. Pull them in, stretch them, fill them up, suck it out, carve them up and push them out! And, as usual, addiction to cosmetic surgery is happening. A horrible example is Hang Mioku, a 48-year-old former model, who was refused further surgery so she resorted to injecting cooking oil in her face. Her surgery started when she was 28-years old, continuing for 20 years, until her entire face became permanently disfigured.

Good Old Boy Dr. David Matlock, a plastic surgeon, went a step further. He married Veronica then began his "Wonder Woman Makeover" on her, creating his view of the "perfect wife." Did Veronica ever wonder if he married her because she was lacking and he was going to use her for marketing his business? Then there is Lacey Wildd with 22 surgeries, known for having the world's biggest breast size as a triple LLL, so she looks like a circus sideshow performer. One of the scariest looking women with an addiction is New York socialite Jocelyn Wildenstein, often called the "Bride of Wildenstein" or "the Cat Woman." She spent $4 million on various procedures after her 20-year marriage ended. It would have ended sooner if she'd had the procedures while she was married.

U.S. spending on plastic surgery was reported by Reuters to have dipped by 3% to $10 billion because of the recession. A list of things to watch out for included: Less formally trained physicians, discomfort that really is extreme pain and oozing, bargain-hunting treatments, unknown long-term effects, serious mistakes being made, more surgery needed, and treatment by self-regulated board certified physicians. Only 9% of cosmetic surgeries are for men, the other 91% are on women; women also get cosmetic surgery 10 years earlier than males, on average, and even younger females are doing it.

Many celebrities get addicted to cosmetic surgery. Donatella Versace of the Versace fashion empire, once a decent-looking woman, is ghastly after numerous cosmetic surgeries. La Toya Jackson seems to have stopped just short of her brother Michael's serious addiction. She now has a pointy Caucasian nose instead of the one she was born with as an African American, but at least it's not caving in. The list goes on and on with celebrity men joining the "ranks of the distorted," the worst three: Kenny Rogers, Mickey Rourke, and Bruce Jenner. Billions of dollars are at stake, so companies are cashing in on our obsession to stay young as the baby boomers age.

The trademark of a national facial cosmetic surgery company "Lifestyle Lift" has infomercials showing "before and after" photos. They promise minimally invasive surgery and mini-lifts, which are possible only when the jowls are the most significant problem. Doctors hungry for supplemental income sign up to perform the surgery. Reputable, seasoned plastic surgeons charge between $10,000 and $15,000 for full face/neck lifts; a "Lifestyle Lift" often costs half that amount. Women have forgotten that you get what you pay for. Most women are unaware that there have been two major suits against the company into their marketing practices. The "revolutionary" procedures they advertised were actually the older, more outdated ones. The company settled and now uses "a new approach to a well-established procedure" for its marketing. In other words, it's a fast, cheaper, older procedure done by surgeons who want to supplement their income -- and women are their major target.

As far as I'm concerned, liposuction is just paying someone to suck the fat out of your body with a toilet plunger. It's disgusting and the risks include skin and nerve damage, infection, fat and blood clots, thermal burns, scarring, bleeding, asymmetry, persistent pain, damage to nerves, blood vessels, muscles, lungs, and abdominal organs, swelling of the legs, deep vein thrombosis, and cardiac/pulmonary complications. Many women have died from liposuction, alone or when it was combined with other surgeries. For example, a 61-year-old woman died after a 10-hour liposuction operation; a mother of two died after paying $3,600 for a standard lipo-sculpting procedure requiring 22 incisions. One of the better-known losses was the musician Kanye West's 58-year-old mother, Donda, who died from uncontrolled bleeding after a combined breast reduction and tummy tuck.

The body can only take so much before it gives in and out, so these surgeries should never be taken lightly. It appears that when you double the surgery, you double the trauma, double the pain, double the risk and, likely, double the cost for you and the income for the surgeon.

"White Hairs" are what the media is now calling the older generation. I don't know about anyone else, but I could never imagine my maternal or fraternal grandparents going under the knife to look younger. They worked hard for those wrinkles and white hairs! And they lived long enough for us to enjoy them. Orson Welles, a brilliant film director and man, but dysfunctional, talks through a marvelous song entitled,

**"I Know What It Is to Be Young,
But You Don't Know What It Is to Be Old"**

And, that's the beauty of it all!

CHAPTER VI

1 Her Story, Not His

*"If particular care and attention is not paid to the ladies, we are
determined to foment a rebellion, and will not hold ourselves
bound by any laws in which we have no voice or representation."*

Abigail Adams

If women would only band together, they could make needed changes for themselves and their children. They can go even further by stopping some of the atrocities against women and children throughout the world. Rather than sitting on the sidelines observing, they can become movers and shakers against the status quo and man's destruction against humanity. I think we're ready!

The first thing to know is that American women have been agitators against inequality and our own subordination for a long, long time. In the 1780's, Abigail Adams told her husband, John Adams, that if there were no women in the Continental Congress, the women of the United States shouldn't have to follow any of the laws laid down by that Congress. So much of women's history has been lost because the gatekeepers and historians have been male. But let's start by raising a toast to the Suffragettes, who agitated enough to win us the vote in 1920. Can you imagine sitting at home on Election Day, while your man went to the polls to cast his vote?

Let's also toast all of their allies, females and males, the agitators, the boisterous ones, and those who did the right thing to openly stand up for equality in the world's greatest democracy. It was a tumultuous time, and history could have gone in another direction. In 1920, the forces of basic fairness and progressive thinking got together and the 19th Amendment to the U.S. Constitution was passed -- an amendment stating that the voting rights could no longer be denied or abridged "on account of sex." It may have been 150 years late – but, again, it's better late than never.

In the flush of that enormous victory, after women were willing to go to jail to gain their right to vote, many women and progressive men thought the world had been remade. The assumptions were that gender inequality was behind them and from that point on the genders would live side by side in equality. This was understandable, but naïve. The great feminist Alice Paul suggested an Equal Rights Amendment (ERA) in 1923. Why not? The ERA was very much in line with the guaranteed right of women to vote. But, the ERA stalled in Congress and was quietly, and underhandedly, put aside.

History then took another direction. Women were told their place was in the home, bearing and raising children. They were told they were pure, innocent and nurturing; they were skilled in child-rearing and had household duties to cook, clean, decorate; skills men didn't have. Therefore, women should do what they were best at - repetitive domestic work and caring for others. They were told they were much better off than their mothers and grandmothers with new "labor-saving devices" for making domestic chores easier, so what could possibly be better?

It took awhile, but women -- especially white women in suburbia -- were seething about inequality and dissatisfied with their roles as homemakers. In 1963, along came Betty Friedan's book *The Feminine Mystique,* which woke up many sleeping women to their unidentified malaise. We'd been told to be grateful for our wonderful lives in powerful post-war America. But Friedan said our dissatisfaction was a normal reaction to a false and unfair labor arrangement that was inherently restricting and isolating. It led women to be totally dependent on their husbands, and their intellects unused and unappreciated, except by other women in similar situations. Friedan said that women needed to feel they were living for a purpose – a purpose greater than changing diapers, cleaning the house and vacuuming the rugs. Many women joined her and the modern feminist movement emerged.

Betty was joined by other strong females like Gloria Steinem, Shirley Chisholm, and Bella Abzug. The National Organization for Women (NOW) was formed; women held mass meetings, planned marches and took to the streets. We worked for progressive political candidates, and banded together to discuss what we wanted and needed. We took off our bras and openly discussed sex and orgasms. We left our homes and insisted on full partnerships with men.

Feminism was seen as a white, middle-class women's movement even though there were many black women who joined in the fight. Black women were still struggling with their own problems -- problems that were worse than those of white women. Today, there is still a separation on what is important to women based on their race, national origin, age, and religion. But, as an extremely heterogenic and diverse country, in order to be effective, the majority of women have to stand together or we will continue to fall together. And, as Caroline Kennedy said, "*It is not easy to stand up against your constituents or your friends or colleagues or your community and take a tough stand for something you believe is right...*"

Remember – a man is a man, no matter what race or national origin he is, so he comes first in the minds of men. The right to vote was being given to black males first, not women. Once sex was added to the 19th Amendment, the controversy drove the right of women to vote – as a fluke – that eventually passed both the House and Senate. This is continuing today as we vote in the first African-American President, when Black males represent only 6% of the population and women 51%. Why haven't we elected a woman President yet - because males are considered first, irrespective of demographics?

2 Bring in the Tokens

"Women who seek to be equal with men lack ambition."

Timothy Leary

What did the sly little testosterone-fueled devils do to blunt the feminist movement? They brought out a Good Old Girl (GOG) token white female Phyllis Schlafly. As in Harriett Beecher Stowe's 1852 novel, *Uncle Tom's Cabin*, these women are the "Uncle Toms" or "Aunt Tomasinas," Uncle Tom's twin. They are subservient to white males and join in the oppression of their own gender. They personally do well -- while their sisters suffer.

Phyllis Schlafly, a lawyer, Catholic and conservative Republican, spearheaded the opposition to the feminist movement and the Equal Rights Amendment (ERA). Her motto was "Stop Taking Our Privileges" or STOP ERA. A year after Betty Friedan's *Feminist Mystique*, she authored and self-published a book for women about choices, then later a book on the flipside of the movement for conservative women. An effective political activist and strategist, Schlafly tried to scare women by saying they'd be drafted as soldiers if the ERA was passed into law. This hypocrite lived the life of a well-to-do wife, mother, and educated careerist, who traveled constantly, preaching her gospel that women should stay in the home.

In her attempt to make herself more appealing, Schlafly said she cancelled speeches whenever her husband thought she'd been away from home too much, and women's lives were improved by such things as paper diapers for babies and clothes dryers. Schlafly fought against *Roe v Wade* because she said it killed millions of unborn babies and the ERA because it would bring about same-sex marriage and deny women social security benefits. Her scare tactics must have worked because the ERA never passed.

I thought Schlafly was dead politically, if not in reality, until she was dragged out in 2011 to support Republicans Michele Bachmann and

Rick Santorum as part of the conservative right wing. She was lending her support to a broken, splintered, and anachronistic Republican Party that needed someone who appeared to have a modicum of intelligence. The Republican "National Crier" John Boehner, who often looks as if he's about to burst into tears, and nice-guy George W. Bush were not bringing the necessary sense of confidence to the party. They apparently needed "a woman's touch."

I don't want to be too downbeat on the Republican Party, because all Republicans are not alike. If truth be told, in this country of certified liars, the Republicans and Democrats are often hard to tell apart. However, the Republicans do need to change their strategy because their anachronistic views are out of sync with our present-day society and norms, particularly those of the younger generation. The Reverend Dr. Martin Luther King, Jr. said:

> *"Change does not roll in on the wheels of inevitability, but comes through continuous struggle. And so we must straighten our backs and work for our freedom. A man can't ride you unless your back is bent."*

Women allowed Schlafly and her ilk to stand on their bent backs, so they lost their struggle to have the ERA passed. As usually occurs during a struggle for women, name-calling became prevalent, and the terms "feminist" and "feminism" became toxic. Many women are still afraid of those words.

There were still great and impressive gains made by women during the feminist movement, but we have to admit that, in 2014, women are largely stuck again. The President of Barnard College, Debora L. Spar, a mother of three, said: *"I thought these issues were heard and dead."* Understand, nothing is ever dead until the Good Old Boys say so or until they are dead and buried themselves – their policies and practices along with them.

This reminds me of a recent dinner I had with two male gay friends. None of us had children, so we would have to decide to whom we are leaving our assets. We noticed some buzzards circling us, wondering when we were going to kick up our heels so they could get their piece of flesh. After a few glasses of wine, we thought it was hilarious that they were probably asking each other, "Are They Dead Yet?" This has now become our mantra for the childless among us with assets. Well -- the same can be said to the old buzzards and Greedy Old Bastards who are keeping this country from moving into the next century without destroying it. Are they dead yet?

Sadly, they can count on their male progeny (GOBlins) to carry on the good fight of retaining their power bases and controlling almost everyone around them. They believe women cannot make effective decisions for themselves and others. These men think they are so powerful, intelligent and privileged that they can control and lead the country without any help from the rest of us. I don't believe most of what they spout daily. I think our financial institutions are on the verge of collapse if we continue down the road they have set out for us – mortgaging us and our futures for greed. They are bankrupt and so is our economy, if anyone looks closely enough.

Maybe women need to come out swinging every four decades in order for things to improve. The right to vote took place in the 1920s and the feminist movement in the 1960s. Here we are again – but we're late! We also need a major cause to get behind. How about tearing down the Greedy Old Bastard's systems that are in place?

If we know and understand anything about the Greedy Old Bastards, it's that they will not cede their power or wealth without an earth-shattering fight. Strong, intelligent women gave us wonderful and popular role models that we can learn from to forge ahead for future generations. And the female agitators and feminists are abhorrent to the GOBs' values and beliefs.

For example, President George W. on a trip to China on food production couldn't help knocking feminist leader and Congresswoman Bella Abzug, who was there at the same time. He said, "*I feel somewhat sorry for the Chinese, having Bella Abzug running around. Bella Abzug is one who has always represented the extremes of the women's movement.*"

When told of the President's remark, Bella, 75 and wheel-chair bound, retorted: "*He was addressing a fertilizer group? That's appropriate.*"

In 1917, there was a lone woman serving as the first U.S. Representative. Almost 100 years later, there are still only 82 (18.8%) Congresswomen out of 435 and 20 (20%) female Senators out of 100. And, there is a striking difference in the House between the Democrats and Republicans. The Democrats have 62 women (76%) out of the 82 elected, and the Republicans 20 (24%). It appears that many Republican women aren't interested in getting their little white gloves dirtied in the political game, one in which their males thrive. But who can blame them? It's a dirty, mud-slinging game, but that's the way it's played by the boys. And we can't win if we don't play!

3 Dirty Political Underwear

*"Power is not something that can be assumed or discarded
at will like underwear."*
John Kenneth Galbraith

Males don't mind rolling around in the dirt and mud to get what they want. After all, they have been called pigs and dogs. The political system has been devised by and for men, and they have no shame. Who wants their crappy laundry or underwear hung out and aired throughout the nation in order to be a public servant? I know I don't and many of my female friends don't either because women are already torn apart by our society. But we cannot continue to stand on the sidelines while laws are promulgated against us -- or things will only get worse. We have to devise a way to enter politics and win without being destroyed in the process.

The United States is the richest country in the world, with resources beyond compare. Yet, our wealth is distributed so that we also have hungry and homeless people; we have sick and abused children; we have lonely and discarded elderly; we have the insane housed in prisons; we have shootings in our schools; we have pollution of our land, air and water; and we have the Greedy Old Bastards in charge. Women have no alternative but to step into the dirty fray of politics if we hope there will ever be positive change or before we fail miserably. The Great Depression happened before and it can happen again. As long as women politicians are willing to take us in new directions, we must elect them to fight the political Good Old Boys.

In 1984, Congresswoman Geraldine Ferraro, an attorney and Democrat, was the first female vice presidential candidate for a major political party in U.S. history. She was on the Mondale-Ferraro ticket. Her credentials were outstanding, but her experience and ability were questioned. Polls showed that while 22% of women were happy about her candidacy, 18% were not. Questions began to surface on her finances and her pro-choice position. Even former First Lady Barbara Bush jumped in to add a sexist comment referring to Ferraro as a $4 million dollar "rhymes with 'rich.' What could that possibly be? Not nice, Mrs. Bush. Later when Ferraro was asked if it was all worth it, she said she wished she had done things differently, but felt that she'd opened the door for other women to run. The door is still being slammed in our faces, so how long does it take?

Women have been running for President since Victoria Woodhull ran in 1872 as an Equal Rights Party candidate. At least 35 women have run for president, all without success. Yet at least 26 less-progressive countries than the U.S. have put women into their highest office. Hillary Clinton is expected to throw her pant suit in for 2016, so the sharks are already circling the waters. Good Old Boy Karl Rove hit the first low blow by bringing up Hillary's health, suggesting she may have brain damage. He needs to have his brain checked out. Hillary's fashion sense has been a topic of discussion because she's just not into it and male candidates have their standard uniforms. But, with her money, she should take someone with her to put her together on the campaign trail and pick up some fashion sense. A hairdresser would be good too – my sister, a cosmetologist, and I will volunteer.

Karl Rove was playing dirty politics because he knows no one wants a president with brain damage. We know we don't want anyone with Alzheimer's disease, either, but we had one while in office. We don't want one that dies right away, but that happened, too. We don't want one shot to death and we've had several of those. We don't want womanizers, drunks, sexists, racists, and perverts either, but I'm sure we've had lots of them. Hillary is smart and anticipating that Benghazi and 'standing by her man' will be issues. Do we think that Monica Lewinsky's recent coming out was accidental? That's just naïve. The Good Old Boys are strategizing because they are not about to relinquish their power base without a truly nasty fight and certainly not to a woman even if she is smart and qualified. And the time is right for a female President. Or isn't 142 years long enough since Victoria Woodhull threw her hat in?

Ms. Magazine pointed out recently that conservatives and those opposed to the liberation of women may try to repeal, or to "reform" progressive laws beyond recognition: The Social Security Act of 1935; the Equal Pay Act of 1963; the 1994 Violence Against Women Act; Medicare and Medicaid (1965); and the 2010 Lilly Ledbetter Fair Pay Act. These statutes also impact on men and the elderly, but women are the most affected.

We should remember the ERA was crafted by Alice Paul in 1923, and resurrected in the early 1970's. It passed both houses of Congress in 1972, but it had to be ratified by at least 38 state legislatures by 1982. That never happened. A coalition of southern whites, evangelical Christians, Mormons, Catholics and Orthodox Jews joined with political conservatives to oppose it. Those in the anti-ERA coalition made no bones about their position that men were the proper lords and masters in religion, the workplace and home. In public, when addressing moderate or liberal groups, they made clever and cynical arguments against the amendment. They will say and do anything to get their way - little boys grown tall and powerful.

The States are filled with those who are engaging in conservatism and trying to turn back the clock. Cases such as *Roe v Wade* are being challenged. The 1973 decision dealt with the constitutionality of Texas criminal abortion laws. Single and pregnant, a woman code-named "Jane Roe" brought a class action suit challenging the Texas law that prevented abortions except for the purpose of saving the mother's life. Forty years later, the conservatives are at it again moving to decide against a woman's right to make decisions regarding her own body even in horrible cases of rape and incest. Who is going to take care of this unwanted baby after it's born and for the next 18 years? Not them. It's been said this is a white woman's fight because it's really not about babies of other races – it's about the Caucasian population. We need more white babies in this country if we are going to remain in the majority.

They have even gone further by throwing in the fetus' heartbeat. Good Old Boy North Dakota Republic Governor Dalrymple signed a bill, submitted by the Republican-controlled legislature, forbidding abortions once a fetal heartbeat is "detectable." A woman will be required to get a trans-vaginal ultrasound whether she wants one or not. The media said the conservatives are pushing this question so that they get a review and decision from a conservative Supreme Court because they believe the majority of them are against women's right to choose what happens inside and outside of her body.

While we should be proud of what women have achieved over the past 50 years, we have fallen short and apart. Even if we manage to protect the legacy of progressive legislation, women still face the great problem of misogyny and the systemic war against them, or what Gloria Steinem calls "a cult of masculinity."

We cannot allow the GOB's to turn back the clock to the "Good Old Days." When my girlfriend Mary hears this refrain, she invariably asks: "Good old days for whom?" We also can't allow ourselves to be lulled to sleep or tricked by charismatic and charming orators, like Ronald Reagan, Bill Clinton, or Barrack Obama, while we continue to lose many of our rights. Republican or Democrat, white-skinned or dark-skinned, all these guys are Good Old Boys.

4 Toothless Equal Rights

"Listen to the wisdom of the toothless ones."

Fijian Proverb

Would you believe President Ronald Reagan would do anything to hurt women? After all, he had Nancy in the Red Dress, and they were an adoration team made in heaven and the movies. He would say, "I believe in the 'E' and 'R' – but not the 'A'" – as if he wanted equal rights for women; he just didn't want to paper the sacred U.S. Constitution with "radical" amendments.

After he was elected President, Reagan applied the economic policies called "Reaganomics," fostered the tearing down of the Berlin Wall, and defeating communism. He took dramatic actions to reduce the Federal government and regulations. He took drastic action to destroy unions. Ronnie, as Nancy called him, was really a big money man and leader for the Greedy Old Bastards in this country.

In 1981, President Reagan fired over 11,000 air traffic controllers after a 2-day strike to show them they could not control the sky or mess with national security. Have we ever recuperated from that wholesale purge? I certainly don't feel safer in the skies. Some say this was one of the most important foreign policy decisions he ever made as President because it showed he could make tough decisions and not allow one segment of the workforce to harm the rest of us. I think he was just showing everyone he was boss.

I met Ronald Reagan at California State, Long Beach in the 1960's. He had just gotten started on his move from "B" movies into politics. He was light-hearted and charismatic – a typical Irishman, with English-Scottish roots. Reagan had a gift, a charm and a drawing power that was admired by many so he became a heroic figure. Most Americans believed he could solve America's problems; the ability to take care of us and change things for the better. He was a gifted orator; he could touch people's emotions; he remained focused on his positions; and, he knew himself. He said what he meant and meant what he said, as only a member of the Good Old Boys can. Highly likeable, he enjoyed being center-stage and in charge; he used his honeyed voice, his quips and ever-present smile to soft-peddle his conservatism.

Reagan's legacy lives on in spite of liberal administrations in office since. Republicans march in and take charge, while the Democrats piddle around trying to prove they are for everybody and everything. I told my husband that President Obama would be visiting us soon since we live just across the bridge from D.C., he flies by us in his helicopter, and we are an inter-racial couple. He has verbally been for everybody and everything – so we're probably next. Unfortunately, if you try to be everything to everybody, you may become nothing to anybody.

Historically, Americans prefer the "wild west shoot'em up" type decision-making that was Reagan's forte. He combined hubris with demands on countries abroad so we were not seen as "sissies" or weak, without the backbone or enough power to say what we mean and do it. Even the prime minister of England, the Iron Lady Margaret Thatcher, joined Reagan in fostering conservative and uncompromising politics that are not hurting that country today.

American women outnumber men, so even though we don't hold enough political offices, we have the votes. Women helped to propel Barack Obama into the Presidency in 2012 and into his second term. They were joined by the majority of Blacks and lots of young people. This is probably why states, such as the Good Old Boy state of Texas, are instituting new voter requirements making it mandatory that voter's ID's be exact. This is often more difficult for women who generally change their names upon marriage. The new rules state that when there is a difference encountered between the ID and the voter information, the individual will be given six days to straighten out the inconsistency. The Republicans probably believe that many women will just go home and forget it. It's a new GOB game, along with redistricting, and other strategies to curb the new power of women and minorities who are impacting on elections when they care enough. Women, particularly those in states like Texas, need to stay alert to these tactical and strategic moves by those men in their 10-gallon hats with their guns at their sides. Unfortunately, they are probably riding the same horses.

As a civil rights professional, I can say categorically that the civil rights process and systems in the U.S. are a joke! Don't count on them to stop discrimination or retaliation. An "Un-civil Rights Act" would now be more appropriate thanks to all the lawyers having their hands in the pot, inside and outside agencies and Departments. Speaking of lawyers....

5 Old Farts

"I never said most of the things I said."

Yogi Berra

"Old farts" may fade away, but their stink sometimes lasts for decades! And with the number of old farts on the Supreme Court we can expect more of the same. Today, the conservative Good Old Lawyers for Life – ruled 6-2 that Michigan voters have the right to change their constitution to prohibit race-based admissions to public universities. GOB Justice Anthony Kennedy wrote the majority opinion that there is no authority to commit this policy determination (to reverse historic discrimination under affirmative action) to the voters. He was joined by his fellow GOBs: Roberts, Alito, Scalia, Breyer and Thomas, who all said they'd go even further by banning racial preferences. Does Clarence Thomas really believe he would be a Supreme Court Justice for life, as a Black male with a scandalous pubic-hair history, without affirmative action? He has no shame.

Of course, recent female Hispanic Justice Sonia Sotomayor dissented and was joined by Justice Ruth Bader Ginsburg. Justice

Elena Kagan did not take part in the decision. Justice Sotomayor is like a breath of fresh air in a stodgy old, cigar-filled room of old guys. She was said to have disagreed so much with the decision that she read her dissent from the bench. President Lyndon Johnson put "Affirmative Action" in place to help reverse the centuries of slavery, racism and discrimination. Most believe it's on its way out at a time in our nation when our ethnically diverse country is suffering from discrimination and retaliation. I believe the Civil Rights Act and Federal organizations to protect employees, such as the Equal Employment Opportunity Commission (EEOC), Merit Systems Protection Board (MSPB), and Office of Special Counsel (OSC), have been so distorted that they have become disincentives to employees' protection and equal rights.

I was willing to give President Obama every chance to succeed for us and his people, Black and White, and women. A mixed-race Good Old Boy himself, who likes sports, and all things manly including flirting, he used the "War on Women" as a slogan. He signed an Executive Order for Federal agencies to create a "Council on Women and Girls" that did nothing. He said he would defend and protect whistle blowers, but the opposite has taken place. He said he would improve things for the downtrodden and the poor, but they are still at the bottom of society trying to survive. Many of his political appointees have been totally ineffective.

Obama's logorrhea hasn't stopped since he took office, and his talk doesn't match up with his political appointee's walks. Even Blacks who said they would never criticize him for anything while he was in office came out to do just that. He threatened to veto the "Working Families Flexibility Act." The Act would allow more flexible work schedules in the workplace for the private sector in line with government family-friendly policies. It would have given parents more freedom in juggling their at-home and work requirements. Americans are tired. Mr. Obama was said to have vetoed the bill on behalf of unions, so that his party could duck behind his veto before it passed the House 223-204. I asked a friend of mine what was wrong and his only reply was: "He's a lawyer."

Is it any surprise that women are afraid to use their entitled maternity leave? One article said the U.S. is the "only modern, industrialized country that does not offer paid maternity leave to new mothers." My girlfriend Alice said women in Hungary are given two years off after the birth of a child. Only about 17% of U.S. companies allow paid leave and this drops even farther as jobs become scarcer. Pregnancy discrimination is prevalent, and on the rise, according to government data. Many of those with maternity leave return to work early because they're afraid of being fired or removed from their jobs. Competition for jobs and high work environment demands discourage women from using their benefits.

So, the U.S. is basically punishing women for propagating the race and doing two jobs instead of one. With a downturn in the economy, causing men to look for jobs, all jobs, especially professional jobs held by women, are up for grabs. They'll grab you by your milk-filled breasts if they have to and toss you out on your pregnant belly. Whatever it takes! And some of these guys are the ones who got them pregnant in the first place.

An Internet blogger decided that the reason European countries are going bankrupt is because of their long paid maternity, parental leave policies, and government supported day care, public transportation and great schools. This idiot also asked if the male boss should be expected to do the job for these "absent women" himself. Hell no – let's just go to war and use the money for the military instead, or let's bail out more banks so their executives can become even richer, or let's have Congress travel more, or send our money to foreign countries that hate us.

The Supreme Court old farts can't help themselves. They recently ruled that U.S. companies can exclude birth control from their insurance coverage for employees on religious grounds. Conestoga Wood Specialties and Hobby Lobby, "closely held" corporations controlled by members of a single family, argued that the Affordable Care Act (Obamacare) violates the First Amendment and other federal laws protecting religious freedom. Justice Samuel Alito wrote the opinion and was joined by the Good Old Boys Roberts, Scalia, Thomas and Kennedy.

The three female Justices (Ginsburg, Kagan, and Sotomayor) and Justice Breyer opposed the ruling as a possible intrusion into further religious-based moves that would limit individual choice and rights. Justice Ruth Bader Ginsburg said the ruling would disadvantage employees who did not share the employer's religious beliefs and it may open the question of allowing companies to "opt out of any law" they decide is incompatible with their religious beliefs. Since when do corporations have religious beliefs and whatever happened to the separation of church and state? This is the first time that the Supreme Court has allowed companies to declare religious beliefs. Are these religious corporations required to still pay taxes? Do we get to overturn the Supreme Court for being stupid?

Many people believe that the "brain drain" in the U.S. has to do with the movement of women into the workplace. We women have to even be smarter than all the dummies in this country making laws or not. I believe the brain drain is because the Greedy Old Bastards are draining our resources. Even our schools have suffered. My generation always had paper and pens or anything we needed to get our educations - so with all the new money, where is it going if not to our schools? What's happening to all the gambling money that was supposed to go to our educational systems? Many kids can't do math, compose or write a sentence. Would we rather have people "home schooling" their children when some of them don't appear to have the minimum credentials? Some religious groups are schooling children and providing day care, along with conservative indoctrination. Education is being reserved for those in power and with wealth.

A recent look at how far we have gone down as a country intellectually is scary, but that doesn't stop the U.S. from cutting more areas related to the family and education. My girlfriend says, "The masses are in a mess and many of them are morons." Is this what we want?

6 A Medal or Monument?

"Monuments and archaeological pieces serve as testimonies of man's greatness and establish a dialogue between civilizations showing the extent to which human beings are linked."

Vincente Fox

Nefertiti and Cleopatra did better than U.S. women today – where is our greatness being recorded? Whenever I brag about something, my practical sister asks me whether I want a medal or monument. I have two medals and tons of awards that haven't done me much good in my life or career as a woman, so I usually say "I'll take the monument."

Men have monuments, memorials and other similarly visible honors essential to affirming their belief in their own superiority. It's not that we women haven't questioned the dearth of monuments and statues honoring us in the United States. It would be easy to say that, as women, we just haven't achieved enough. But, as NOW said: "Women are just put in the footnotes of history, which represents separate and unequal treatment. I don't know about you, but I hate being a footnote!

There are over 5,000 outdoor sculptures of individuals throughout the U.S. and only 394 or 8% are of women, probably shoved in a corner. In our nation's capital there are statues of men everywhere, every circle, and in front of thousands of buildings. They say, a picture (or statue) is worth a thousand words and it's believed that we can't be what we can't see. If you've never seen something, describing it is sometimes impossible. So this sends a clear, nonverbal, subliminal message to young girls and boys as to who is important in this country and who is not.

None of our 44 national park memorials are focused on women or their achievements. And it will continue unless women make some noise on behalf of their own, just as the men do. When Maryland tried to drop a "long-forgotten war hero" in favor of a woman's statute, one male said men have defended this country and women already have

— 143

the Statue of Liberty and the Virgin Mary. A statue given to the U.S. by France and a religious symbol are enough.

There are 109 protected areas designated as national monuments. They are established by the President and Congress, under the 1906 Antiquities Act and Executive Order. Three Presidents who did not designate national monuments were Republicans Richard Nixon, Ronald Reagan, and George H.W. Bush. So, it is not surprisingly that in 2014, the House voted on a new bill to amend the Antiquities Act that would strip presidential authority to unilaterally designate national monuments. Instead, it requires them to consult with and get participation and comment from the public, local stakeholders and the congressional delegation. Kate Sheppard of *Huffington Post* said it all by the headline of her article: "Obama Plans to Designate New Monument, Republicans Plan to Freak Out."

President Theodore Roosevelt established the first national monument -- and created a total of 18 of them during his administration; Jimmy Carter created 15 and protected areas in Alaska; Bill Clinton created the most at 19; President George W. designated 5; and President Obama has designated 10 sites with a new monument named for African-American abolitionist Harriet Tubman.

Many of our national memorials and buildings have been renamed after male Presidents. For example, the Washington International Airport was named after Ronald Reagan; the Central Intelligence Agency was renamed the George Bush Center for Intelligence (an oxymoron); the Ariel Rios Buildings housing the U.S. Environmental Protection Agency were renamed the William Clinton buildings – which many employees nicknamed "Bubba North and Bubba South." Why weren't the EPA buildings named for Rachel Carson, the well-known environmentalist?

Now that President Clinton has his name-sake buildings, he needs to go inside and view the Native American paintings done by an artist during Roosevelt's New Deal Works Progress Administration (WPA). The huge paintings are visible when you get off the elevators.

They depict Native Americans as raving-maniac savages, slaughtering white men and naked white women running towards them from their covered wagons. EPA has a higher than usual number of American Indians and women employees, yet their protests were ignored, which is similar to the Washington Redskins controversy.

After employees protested and filed complaints about the offensive murals, I found a federally-workable solution to the problem. Since the murals were considered historic works of art, I located a statute that said when the purpose (or mission) of a building changes, art work can be moved to another more appropriate location. Prior to the EPA occupying the building, it was used by the U.S. Postal Service (USPS). Therefore, these murals about the USPS delivering the mail could be moved to another building or the Post Office Museum.

The mucky-mucks or Good Old Boys called me in and told me to "back off," they were handling the matter. I finally realized why they are called "mucky-mucks," because they "Muck" up everything around them. As the controversy raged on, the artist's son went to Congress to protest saying his father's murals should stay right where they were even though they offended employees. That would be about 9,000 against 1 little GOBlin. But he had all the GOB's with him. In all their stupidity, they decided to ignore the law, me, women, and American Indians for their fellow GOB's, father and son.

If you visit the William Clinton buildings housing EPA in downtown Washington, D.C. on Pennsylvania right next door to the Old Post Office, soon to become a Trump hotel (we sell everything for a dollar), make sure to ask to see the offensive Native American murals in Bubba's main building. You will have to peer around huge screens on two of the floors that were erected to cover the racially-offensive and sexist murals with a sign telling you why they are covered. Then you can pick up some Washington Redskins football souvenirs to take home with you. Another idiot white male refusing to budge even though the name of the team is offensive to American Indians. He'll be going down - if not now – then "is he dead yet?"

My friends and I have decided that the "Washington Redskins" name should be changed to the "Washington Warriors," which would fit the brave American Indian warriors who fought valiantly for their rights, land and people. It would also allow the GOBs to keep the logos and other things that help to make them rich without besmirching our proud American Indians that they all put destroyed. I don't know about anyone else, but I'm also sick of the continuous renaming of everything in this country by the private sector – such as the Verizon Center, and advertising us to death. We need to rename them after women. I'd like one.

A bird's eye view of the nation's capital includes the huge Washington, Lincoln, and Jefferson Memorials, the John F. Kennedy Center for the Performing Arts, and at least 38 others throughout D.C. Arlington Cemetery has John F. Kennedy's perpetual flame and there is a new Air Force Memorial in Arlington, Virginia. More recently, the Rev. Dr. Martin Luther King, Jr. Memorial was added, with African-American memorials and monuments appearing to be more politically correct than those for women. There are also 13 Presidential libraries throughout the country recognizing our male Presidents.

My girlfriend Alice recently took exception to the new Obama Library the state of Illinois wants to fund for $100 million as a tourist lure. She said, "Forget the library, and use the money for the poor people who have lost everything in the recent mudslides, hurricanes, and tornadoes. People don't need another Presidential library, they need help!" The President said he wanted a library, so states are fighting for it; Chicago at the forefront. What's the matter with his childhood home of Hawaii? We all know where Donald Trump would suggest - Africa.

7 Still No Roses

---

*"This is rather different from the receptions I used to get fifty years
ago. They threw things at me then but they were not roses."*

Susan B. Anthony

Reach in your pocketbook and pull out some money. If women and
girls don't consider highly-visible male monuments and memorials
important, they can just look at their spending money. U.S. paper
currency has all men printed on it, from George Washington on the
$1 dollar bill to the James Madison $5,000 dollar bill. A $1,000
Cleveland bill was discontinued and there are 336 known-to-exist
$10,000 Salmon P. Chase bills, named after Lincoln's Secretary of
Treasury.

If you have some change, it could range from the Abraham
Lincoln cent to the George Washington quarter. Of course, there
is the Sacagawea Golden Dollar and the Susan B. Anthony Dollar,
minted from 1979 to 1981, and again in 1999. Intentional or not, the
Susan B. was considered one of the most unpopular coins in American
history. Why?

Vending machines were not outfitted for the coin and its size and
color looked a lot like the quarter. This dollar received its share of
female name-calling by being referred to as "Suzie Bucks, the Anthony
quarter, and Carter quarter." Poor President Carter couldn't even get
this right. Did anyone tell him that in 1875 a failed 20-cent piece was
rejected by the public because it was confused with the quarter? The
2005 Presidential $1 Coin Act proposed that Suzie Bucks be taken out
of circulation. So we finally had a woman on the currency -- and they
tried to kill her off!

Instead of dealing with the question, Congress told the Secretary
of Treasury to review the issue and get back to them in a year -- after
the elections. We never give up, either, so be sure to collect those
Susan B. Anthony coins in case they go out of circulation; at least

Suzie Bucks may be worth something. But don't forget to demand more bills, and more coins, with pictures of women on them. The girls of America are watching. We'll take more medals, monuments and money – remember, we're not trying to get even. As they say, "We want more, we want more!"

This Susan B scenario may appear to be accidental or unusual. It's not. Years ago when the military wanted a new statue to distribute and sell, I recommended one with a female soldier on it along with the males. I thought it was a brilliant way to recognize all the women who have served and died for our country. The men thought I had lost my mind. A new statue came out with only male soldiers. So – it's nothing new for women to be among the missing.

8 Intellectual Property Thieves

"Nothing's more disgusting than a guy who steals another person's ideas and tries to claim them as his own."

Joe Rogan

Male thieves have stolen and taken credit for women's work, along with their inventions for centuries. I inherited my father's inventive spirit and he helped me develop many of my prototypes. I proudly submitted a patent and applied for trademarks. My drive to invent has driven me crazy. I'm always dreaming up new products, but I've never found the time to market them because that's not my talent and I've always worked full-time.

So, instead, I used my creative and organizational abilities to develop innovative plans and programs for women and minorities. Various supervisors and employees tried to purloin my policy papers and ideas, but I didn't allow it. Other women haven't been so feisty and I'm amazed -- and appalled -- to learn how many women have had their inventions stolen by men -- or were denied credit for them.

Males took credit for the computer programmer and mathematical genius Ada Lovelace Day's description of how computing machines could solve problems. Instead she was called "mad as a hatter…a manic depressive… with delusions of her own talents." Male colleagues of DNA double helix discoverer Rosalind Franklin buried her role and took credit. The two creeps went on to win the Nobel Prize four years after she died. It sounds crazy to call two Nobel Prize winners creeps, but they were! It took 40 years for Rosalind Franklin to be properly recognized.

Margaret Knight invented the paper bag, but her patent designs were stolen by a man who said no woman could have made such a breakthrough. She sued and won after three years. Elizabeth Magie invented "The Landlord's Game" for which she received $500 from Parker Brothers, which they renamed "Monopoly." On and on, males took or got credit for women's genius and inventions that included the hypertext fiction database system, the idea of nuclear fission, and the opioid receptor. One male's comment on the thefts was: "That's the way the game is played."

Candace Pert discovered a group of G protein-coupled receptors in the brain that allow opiates to lock there. It was an amazing discovery! It means there may be other receptors in the brain that lock in drugs other than opiates. It has huge implications for smoking, drinking and eating disorders. My aversion to dissection never allowed me to do what I really wanted to do: study the brain. But I certainly understand that the brain is where our instincts and addictions come from and are stored.

There are many more items that most people don't know were invented by women. Here are a few: Antifungal antibiotic, the car heater, the circular saw, the cooking stove, the dishwasher, the engine muffler, the disposable cell phone, fire escapes, globes, the life raft, medical syringes, the oil burner, the refrigerator, the rotary engine, the washing machine, windshield wipers, alphabet blocks, diapers, and school desks.

Only 10% of all patents are awarded to women and few receive credit as the creators. A patent in 1715 for a corn mill had to be taken out under the name of Sybilla Masters's husband; the legal system at that time could not imagine a woman inventing anything worth patenting. The inventor of the circular saw, a Shaker named Tabitha Babbitt, never applied for a patent because Shakers did not believe in patenting their work.

Chocolate chip cookie inventor Ruth Wakefield took free chocolate for life from Nestles for her recipe. Typist Bette Graham, who invented liquid paper, got fired for spending too much time on her invention. Female prodigy and genius Margaret Knight created the square-bottom paper bag, invented the machine to cut, fold and glue them -- and 20 other inventions.

Josephine Cochrane invented and received a patent for the dishwasher in 1886 because her servants were breaking her heirloom china. Every time it rains or snows and your windshield wipers start, think of Mary Anderson, who received a patent for her squeegee with a handle on it. What if you had to put your arm out of the car to wipe away the elements?

Then we have to thank those who received patents, such as Sarah Mather for the telescope and lamp; actress Hedy Lamarr for a system of frequency-hopping that allowed radios to guide torpedoes without interference. Stephanie Kwolek, who died just as this book was going to press, was the daughter of Polish immigrants. She worked at DuPont and invented Kevlar, which is used to strengthen skis, radial tires, brake pads, suspension bridge cables and helmets. Kevlar has made bulletproof vests much stronger yet lighter and easier for military and law enforcement personnel to wear. She worked 15 years at DuPont without a promotion yet made several billion dollars for the company -- and saved thousands of lives. Added to these inventions are the foot-pedal trash can, the retractable dog leash, the folding cabinet or "Murphy" bed, the solar house, scotch guard, and invisible glass...

If you've never heard of these wonderful inventions and inventor-esses, your education has been biased and incomplete. Our history books need to be revised and updated so that women's achievements are included or we are only receiving half of an education. How about some monuments or memorials?

9 Missing for 200 Years

"By all means let's be open-minded, but not so open-minded that our brains drop out."
Richard Dawkins

Men in this country believe they own 52% of the population - the females, particularly the white females. This can be traced all the way back to the Charters of Freedom when our country was throwing off the yoke of British domination. The U.S. Declaration of Independence of 1776 didn't include women in, "We hold these truths to be self-evident, that all men are created equal..." No one adheres to this today by saying when the gender male is mentioned, it includes women, too. That's crap. Abigail Adams knew it and so do we. If it's not so important – how about reversing it and saying "All women are created equal" and then saying 'Oh, we mean you men are included, too.'

If we go along with the male-female premise, women are also "endowed by their Creator with certain unalienable Rights, that among these are Life, Liberty and the pursuit of Happiness." And, as a transcript of the Declaration states in throwing off oppression, we women can say,

"We have warned them from time to time of attempts by their legislature to extend an unwarranted jurisdiction over us.

We have appealed to their native justice and magnanimity, and we have conjured them by the ties of our common kindred to disavow these usurpations, which, would inevitably interrupt our connections and correspondence.

They too have been deaf to the voice of justice and of consanguinity...."

White Anglo Saxon Protestants (WASPs) believe they built this country single-handedly with some rift-raff assisting them. An 8-hour, 4-part miniseries on the History Channel is entitled: "Men Who Built America." The half-assed (male only) program profiles all-white male Robber Barons Cornelius Vanderbilt, John D. Rockefeller, Andrew Carnegie, and J. P. Morgan. The series was written by men: Stephen, Patrick, Keith, Randy, Ed and David.

These "Robber" barons were innovators, but they didn't build this country. They can be credited with bringing about revolutionary change -- but so did Thomas Edison and Alexander Graham Bell. White men controlled the country, enslaving, killing, and subordinating others - leaving no room for anyone else to compete with them. We will never know what others could have achieved if given half a chance. This is again a glorification of white males to the exception of others, and without the majority, even these men wouldn't have succeeded.

Ignoramus Pat Buchanan had to add his two cents. He said America was "built by white folks," and "folks" in this case means men. The view of white women was of them at home gathering moss and Black women as enslaved. All the other non-white immigrants were just taking up space: African slaves, Chinese railroad builders, American Indian bridge builders, Mexicans, Japanese, and all the other ethnic groups.

White men built this country on the hard work and backs of others. They enslaved people, broke treaties, slaughtered, and subordinated various groups. They stole land from the native people, brought diseases, destroyed animals; they caused the dust bowl and the Great Depression; they created homeliness and poverty. They caused environmental disasters and pollution of our air, water and land. Recent "Occupy" groups protesting against Wall Street, big business, environmental pollution, corruption, and the International Monetary Fund were strategically silenced by the Good Old Boys breaking up their encampments. Just looking around us, we have to appreciate the enormous and enduring contributions made by white males to this country – but, they didn't do it alone and it's time they made some room for others.

Finally, I've always loved the 1976 movie *Network* in which Howard Beale says:

> "*I don't have to tell you things are bad. Everyone knows things are bad. It's a depression. Everybody's out of work or scared of losing their job. ....We know the air is unfit to breathe and our food is unfit to eat, and we sit watching our TV's while some local newscaster tells us that today we had fifteen homicides and sixty-three violent crimes.*"

Then in response to, "*Please, at least leave us alone in our living rooms....,*" Howard says:

> *Well, I'm not going to leave you alone. I want you to get mad! ...I want all of you to get up out of your chairs. I want you to get up right now and go to the window. Open it, stick your head out, and yell,*

> *I'M MAD AS HELL, AND I'M NOT GOING TO TAKE THIS ANYMORE!*"

Maybe Howard Beale was right. Maybe that's what we need to do – tell President Obama that we want September designated as "I'm Mad as Hell and I'm Not Going to Take This Anymore" Month. We can use one day to open our windows and yell. Do women, minorities and the middle-class believe it would change any behavior of the Greedy Old Bastards?

I don't think it would. The GOB's would probably let us scream our heads off until we got weary, then jail some of us for disturbing their peace, and then get the U.S. Supreme Court to ban yelling from windows. That's how the game is played in the Good Ole U.S. of A.

CHAPTER VII

1 Poverty

*"You better cut the pizza in four pieces because I'm not
hungry enough to eat six."*
Yogi Berra

**Women represent about half of the 8 million people living in
poverty in this country.** Over 28% of women are living without a
husband present. Poverty for a family of four is $20,614/year; a family
of three is $16,079; and a family of two is $13,167. As a wealthy
nation, we should be ashamed! There are numerous articles stating that
"Women are the Poorest of the Poor." And, it's as true today as it ever
was that women – and the children they care for -- are the poorest,
making up 80% of the world's impoverished, with two-thirds, mainly
female, illiterate out of 800 million worldwide.

In order to survive at the poverty level in the U.S., the poor receive
Federal food stamps under a program called Supplemental Nutrition
Assistance Program (SNAP). The program allows $4.00 per person a
day for food. Always one to appreciate the military acronym fetish,
I believe it should be renamed: Citizen's Relief Assistance Program
(CRAP). Because $4 a day is crap and the fat-cats in Washington,
D.C. know it. There is a mean spirit permeating our country, especially
toward the poor, elderly, disabled and disadvantaged.

Republican Congressman Stephen Fincher uses God to bolster his
view that there should be drastic cuts in SNAP. He forgot that "God
doesn't like ugly." He quoted the Book of Thessalonians, "The one who
is unwilling to work shall not eat," and from Matthew, "The poor will
always be with us." Fincher supports a rider on a farm bill that would
effectively cut 2 million people from SNAP, mainly for children and the

elderly. This is while he and his family received cotton farm subsidies for a decade of over $8.9 million from taxpayers. Another Greedy Old Bastard reaping money, while sowing starvation and poverty for others. Did he vote on the farm bill for himself -- or did his pals do it for him?

Blonde-Tressed Airhead Ann Coulter is carrying the banner saying, "Then there are the 22 million (sic) Americans on food stamps. And, of course, there are the 39 million greedy geezers collecting Social Security. The greatest generation rewarded itself with a pretty big meal." How stupid are these people? Tea Partiers claim the poor are abusing the program – those lazy shirkers! How would they know about the lives of the poor, as they sip their wine at upscale restaurants on Capitol Hill or elsewhere, after making speeches and spewing out the party line?

An annual report by the U.S. Department of Agriculture said 45% of food stamp benefits went to children under 18, about 20 million young people in all; 9% of recipients were 60 years or older; and almost 10% were disabled. With the major downturn in the economy, job losses, and "bank-induced" homelessness, there are now 47 million getting food stamps with the average monthly amount of about $133 per person. The poor can't use SNAP for paper towels or pets, even though studies show animals improve the well-being of their owners. Many homeless residing on our streets have their faithful companions by their sides willing to starve with them.

After the U.S. designated September as "Hunger Action Month," the wealthy state of Connecticut challenged taxpayers to live on $4.00/day in food stamps as do 11% of their State's recipients. The challenge made headlines, but didn't change the mindset of the fat cats. And even Congressman Fincher knows the Federal travel regulations for "Meals & Incidental Expenses" (M&IE) range from $46 to $71 per day per person plus another $5.00 per day for incidentals – and easily increased with the flip of a pen.

In other words, these hypocrites believe 4 million poor women and their children should live on $4 a day, while 3 million Federal government workers and representatives, already receiving hefty salaries and benefits, get a dollar more for just their incidentals and up to $71 more a day while travelling. We all know that travel is a major item for government employees, particularly those in the Defense sector, both inside and outside of our country. There are millions of Feds living like Kings and Queens on the Federal dole.

How about giving a new jazzy name to Congressional representatives ripping off Americans and call it: Congressional Rip-offs and Pork (CRAP) or Congressional CRAP, so it's not confused with SNAP? They never pay a dime on those "fact finding" trips, which always seem to be in some of the sunniest resorts. A reported 129 lawmakers and their staff spent their month-long recess on junkets to: Israel, Turkey, Tunisia, Portugal, Macedonia, Spain and China. This does not include the "working-vacations" of political appointees in the various cabinet Departments and agencies. And please don't look up all those fabulous conferences paid for by the lobbyists and taxpayers. We should require trips and conferences to be publicly-posted so we can track where everyone is headed on vacation with our tax dollars. It was just announced that our representatives are going on a 5-week break – or vacation, while "Rome" burns.

Recently the public took a fit over the First Lady Michele Obama's junkets to Spain, China and Africa that cost $150 million for her, her mother and daughters. Africa was about $60 to $100 million at a time when Americans are suffering. This was not good for her or her husband's image. Certainly, as the first Black First Lady, she should not be held to a higher standard than all of the White First Ladies, but it's almost as if she is thumbing her nose at someone. She always looks mad at the President, so who knows.

With these trips added to the constant flow of movie stars and other celebrities into the White House, along with the other trappings of wealth and privilege, President Obama looks no different from his pre-decessors or one of the Good Old Boys. "His people" are in dire straits in this country and they will still be there when he leaves office, no matter how loud Al Sharpton screams on his bully-pulpit television show.

2   Child Abuse & Neglect

*"There can be no keener revelation of a society's soul than
the way in which it treats its children."*

Nelson Mandela

**The U.S. has the worst record among industrialized nations,
with child fatalities of 4 to 7 children a day.** We have an epidemic
with over 3 million reports of child abuse involving over 6 million
children. How many do we need to get people's attention? The abuse
ranges from parental to medical neglect and abuses from beatings
to rape. Horror stories abound; over 70% of the children killed by
their abuser are under the age of four. And more than half of child
fatalities due to maltreatment are "not recorded as such on death
certificates." The cycle of abuse repeats itself as the abused become
the abusers. One estimate of the costs for this neglect: $124 billion
dollars a year.

In 2013, there were over 400,000 U.S. children in foster care,
one-quarter of them in relatives' homes and nearly half in non-
relative homes. Each year, about half of the 400,000 children leave
the system and an equal number enter it - a movement of almost a
half million children. The data is often inaccurate and mired by poor
decisions. If our government can keep track of us by surveillance, why
the hell can't we keep better track of these children? It's because they
aren't important or "terror suspects." Stories about "heartwarming"
placements are the exception, not the rule. The most defenseless
children are the most likely to be abused. And, the system is broken.

Children are placed in out-of-home placement settings, group
homes, shelters, residential treatment facilities and other places away
from their parents or guardians. Monetary incentives for taking in
foster children add to the need for effective monitoring. About 60%
of children are returned to their family of origin, often to be abused
again or killed. One example is an 18-month old girl who was already
suffering from a cracked skull and broken ribs at 2 months old being

placed back with her biological parents. The foster care parents wanted to adopt her, but instead she was sent to her birth parents -- and beaten to death. What kind of country allows this to happen?

Only about one-fifth of foster care children are adopted by new families, with older and disabled children less likely to find permanent homes. That means four-fifths are not adopted. The number of children in our foster care system does not include the 16 million in the U.S. who live in poverty and another 32 million in low-income families. That's a lot of children in jeopardy. We are failing our most precious resource – our children! And I consider this to be the responsibility of women who bear these children in the U.S.

Caucasian children are not exempt from poverty, but the largest numbers in low-income families are Black, Hispanic and American Indian. Over 60% of children in poverty are living with immigrant parents; 40% with their native-born parents. Parents with less than a high school diploma are part of the low-income family group and poverty varies by location. The South has the highest number, followed by the West, Midwest and Northeast; rural areas have more poverty than urban areas. And, as with violence in families, poor children are likely to become poor parents of the future. This fixable cycle of poverty costs our country half a trillion dollars a year. Americans also go outside the U.S. to adopt children, even willing to take disabled children from Russia before adopting our own. Clearly, our adoption system doesn't work and needs to be fixed!

Go to an Alpaca farm. Watch how carefully the babies are fed and protected by their mothers, then given extra care and feeding by the farm owners. Why? The Alpaca baby represents a near term return-on-investment. The time horizon for our babies is long and our return isn't immediately clear. We don't seem to recognize that the little hungry toddler, the sulking 6-year-old, will soon be 21-years old and capable of holding a job – or carrying a gun. We get a return on our investment – but it's of a long duration and may not be what we want or expect. Hungry and angry kids will grow up madder and more dysfunctional; they will get and stay in trouble; become under- or un-employed, and hold back themselves and our country. Chances are they'll end up in either in one of our many prisons, foster care, dead or a threat to others.

3   No Head Start for You!

"It is easier to build strong children than to repair broken men."

Frederick Douglass

Instead of increasing funding for the education, care and feeding of our children, let them be illiterate, unloved and hungry. Congress is slashing the highly effective Head Start program by $400 million. It serves a million of the nation's poorest children under the age of five, preparing them for school. About 57,000 children are expected to be denied a place in Head Start and Early Head Start. This is the largest cut in the program in 50 years since President Johnson created it to fight poverty and discrimination.

Let's ask air-head Ann Coulter her opinion. Should we pay about $350 million for one F-22 fighter or give 57,000 children a head start? Should we buy another F/A-18 Hornet for $94 million, the EA-18G Growler for $102 million, the V-22 Osprey for $118 million, the F-35 Lightning II at $122 million and on and on, or take care of our children? I like the military comparison since it's the largest part of our budget, but one critic noted we spend more on Halloween each year. Our greedy little children want to be educated and eat – that's totally unacceptable when our warriors need the money.

The mindset is this: At a Head Start Children's Holiday celebration of 125 children each year I sponsored on an Army base, two white males came to my office to object to the program, griping "These children don't look poor to us." We spent over $8 billion a year on that base for military programs, yet these guys wanted only ragged street urchins out of a Charles Dickens novel to receive a modicum of happiness during the holidays. They didn't even care that many of our noncommissioned soldiers' children were as bad off, so I included them and women's shelters in the program. The message was that we want our poor to look and act poor if they get anything from us.

Even President Jimmy Carter, a very good, hard-working, idealistic man cut two of the best youth programs that existed in the U.S. – the Youth Conservation Corps (YCC) and the Young Adults Conservation Corps (YACC). These programs took at-risk youth and young adults out of the ghettos and put them in state and national parks, on military bases and other sites, helping them to bond with other young people, and to learn useful job and life skills. They built bridges, cleaned waterways, learned blue-collar trades and received much-needed time away from violent, drug-filled inner-cities. For every dollar spent, these programs returned two dollars and helped out with our failing infrastructure. Yet, after five years in start up costs, planning and development, the programs were totally shut down, leaving the Job Corps to struggle along!

Demolishing or decreasing programs that return more than they cost, directly and indirectly, such as YACC, Head Start and SNAP, is part of the GOB process. If there is nothing in a Federal program for them or their children, they want to slash and burn it, and use the money elsewhere. I always wondered where the pittance used for YCC and YACC went when they closed down. Now I wonder where they are moving the SNAP and Head Start money. Maybe they need more money for CRAP – Congressional Rip-offs and Pork.

4 Hand-Outs

"We think sometimes that poverty is only being hungry, naked and homeless. The poverty of being unwanted, unloved and uncared for is the greatest poverty. We must start in our own homes to remedy this kind of poverty".

Mother Teresa

We keep people in poverty, give them hand-outs, and believe they should be grateful for living in one of the richest nations on earth. The psychologist Abraham Maslow developed a very insightful theory about human motivation and development. He theorized that people have a "Hierarchy of Needs" that moves through five levels and stages. Only when the needs are met at one level can a person move to the next.

Level 1 covers our most basic survival needs, such as breathing, food, water, sex, sleep, homeostasis, and excretion. Level 2 covers such things as safety and security, employment, resources, morality, health, the family, and property (40 acres and a mule). Level 3 includes friendship, family, sexual intimacy or love, and belonging. Level 4 includes achievement, self-esteem, confidence, and respect for others. Level 5 is only reached when the person meets all those below and achieves self-actualization, a rarity.

Basically, Maslow's theory says that if you are without food and water, sleep and excretion, you will have to achieve those before you can move to feeling safe, secure and employable at the next level. I believe Level 5 is rarely achieved today because we have divided families; few stable, long-term relationships; less face-to-face communications; too much computer and television connectivity with too little real time connectivity; and, undue concern for material possessions and wealth. Greedy and technological advancement are boundless, and they can't bring us happiness and peace.

In dire poverty, sweet, innocent children, many Black, Hispanic and American Indian, are at the bottom of the Maslow's hierarchy trying desperately to meet their basic needs. They cannot advance to higher levels, and then are accused of being lazy, shiftless, no-accounts with character flaws and genetic deficiencies. Many of the unique cultural traits of the poor are denigrated because they don't fit white society's ideals and values. For example, the strength of minority women, particularly Black women, is unappreciated and undervalued. They have strong church, club and school affiliations. Music, athletic prowess, and education are areas of emphasis in the black community. Yet most have stayed at Level 1 or skipped Level 2 and jumped into Level 3 where they have family, a modicum of safety and security, and other resources.

There is controversy about Maslow's hierarchy, but the model helps us understand that human beings need to move through a positive system that provides the most basic fulfillment of their needs. It shows that constant poverty leaves entire families without the necessary tools to achieve what other communities take for granted. Based on this simple model, it would only take emphasis on Level 1, where many of those in poverty are, to move them up. Just providing minimum necessities of life will not enable them or the next generation to leave the boarded-up, burned-out, drug- and violence-infested ghettos. Some will escape, but most will remain at the bottom, from one generation to the next.

A dear friend of mine, an African American male, owned a sheet metal company in Newark, New Jersey. He was given contracts by the Port Authority -- but at the absolute minimum level so that he could do no more than eke out a living. This is the same case with "entitlement" programs in the U.S. that are designed to keep a person barely alive rather than giving them what they need to succeed. Children are malleable and have a thirst to learn. So we can pay now or we can pay later and run for our lives as they, often understandably, take their anger and aggressions out on us.

We are already paying for our unaddressed mental health problems as more and more mass shootings occur. Struggling to survive in a country filled with millionaires, billionaires and Greedy Old Bastards manipulating, buying-selling, lying, cheating and stealing from the good ole democratic U.S. of A. is criminal.

This leads us to our next chapter.

5 Prison-Industrial Complex

"Nothing can be more abhorrent to democracy than to imprison a person or keep him in prison because he is unpopular. This is really the test of civilization."

Winston Churchill

If you're a Black male in this country, you may as well go directly to jail without passing "Go." That's the game of Monopoly, but it's just as serious as what's going on in the U.S. The private sector **BU**siness **M**en or BUMS, joined by our judicial and justice system, have taken over the prison system, so it's now called the Prison-Industrial Complex (PIC). The prison population in the U.S. went from a low 113 years ago of 56,000 to quadruple since the 1980s. This is a result of mandatory sentencing laws, the war on drugs, and housing the mentally ill. The U.S. loves to decentralize by dumping everyone out of our institutions, then fails to adequately and effectively address where these people are going. We did it with the orphanages and now with the mentally ill and insane.

The deinstitutionalization policies and practices, particularly those transferring homeless and hospitalized mental patients from state hospitals, was a wholesale dumping that can now be readily seen on our streets and in the overcrowded facilities these people are herded into during cold weather. The poor stand on street corners, asking for handouts, like beggars in a Third World country. A long article by Clayton Cramer tells the story of his brother, who served in the U.S. Army, and later was diagnosed with paranoid schizophrenia. Reading Cramer's account shows the tragic costs to his family of our national inability, or refusal, to treat the mentally ill:

"Look around you in any big city, and you will find enormous numbers of people living on the streets, most of them mentally ill. What sane person would spend a single winter night sleeping on a bus bench if they had any alternative? ... We have a crisis going on in this country. It is a crisis that makes us less safe on the streets, and

that degrades mentally ill people to a point where many people can no longer feel human compassion for their suffering."

There is no state or city in the United States without mentally disabled people in their streets. There are the "grate" homeless, who sit and sleep on city grates with blankets over their heads to keep warm in the winter months. There are the "shopping cart" homeless in the suburbs, who drag their lives around in a cart "borrowed" from a commercial store. And, we now have the "prison" homeless.

Europeans have noted our national prison disgrace. The United Kingdom reported the U.S. has "the largest prison population of any nation in the history of the world" with a growth of 790% since 1980. Further, we house the severely mentally ill, with horrific abuses such as rampant rapes, solitary confinement for weeks, many suicides, delayed or denied treatment for cancer and other infections, stabbings, beatings, malnourishment, chronic hunger, serious rat infestations, and filth.

Five years ago, 1 in every 31 adults (7.3 million) in the U.S. was behind bars, or being monitored (probation and parole) and about 93% of prisoners were male, with Blacks making up 40% of the 2.2 million of those in prison, according to the Department of Justice. And not all of these inmates are guilty as portrayed in television programs. One young male refused to give up so that he and the others were freed after 18 years of confinement for a crime they didn't commit. He said it took him 15 years to get documents under our "Freedom of Information Act," which is ludicrous and should be criminal. Taxpayers will be paying for the white male mindset that "all Blacks are guilty until proven innocent" because of their skin color. This is what happens in a corrupt system of justice.

The U.S. has a high number of drug offenders, higher crime rates, and tougher sentencing laws, so we put more prisoners in jail than anywhere else in the world. We are ranked as No. 1 with 2.2 million, followed by China at 1.5 million and Russia at 870,000. But the populations are significantly different: the U.S. has over 318 million people; China has 1.3 billion; and Russia has 142.4 million. So, while the U.S. has only 5% of the world's population, it ranks first in incarcerating its own people at 25%. And we don't just jail more people; we also keep them there longer. About 100,000 women are in prison with increases due to recreational drug use and a lack of proper treatment facilities.

About 19.5 million (8.3%) Americans report they are on illicit drugs; another 54 million are admitted binge drinkers, and 15.9% heavy drinkers. That means over 75 million (37.5%) Americans, in specific age groups, are "out of it" by one means or another. The direct and indirect costs related to drugs and alcohol consumption are enormous. And there are half a million Americans awaiting trials in our laborious and costly system, adding another $9 billion a year to taxpayers, mainly the middle-class. So, what is the Greed Old Bastard solution to all this? Build more prisons!

Again, we can thank capitalism and the private sector. The GOB's privatized the prison system, so PIC now costs Americans $74 billion or about $30,600/inmate. The basic profit-making principle is: "The more prisoners, the richer we get." They publish studies to show PICs are more effective than public-run prisons. The American Civil Liberties Union (ACLU) doesn't agree. They say PICs are filthier, more violent, less accountable and more costly. Assault rates are three times higher and they are "a major contributor to bloated state budgets..."

"Out of sight, out of mind" seems to be what we feel about prisons in the U.S. with most of us gladly never setting foot in one. Our prison system has become an enormous profit-making enterprise and machine. Louisiana, considered the "prison capital of the world," said that most of their inmates are housed in "for-profit facilities" that must be supplied with human beings for their $182 million industry to survive. These PICS could not survive without the assistance of our justice system filled with lawyers and judges. And the amount and type of corruption that occurs in this billion-dollar system is tremendous.

In other words, the U.S. is in a "Prison Feeding Frenzy," with a 40% recidivism rate. Bring'em in, beat'em up, and throw'em out! Repeat and repeat the same old stuff on behalf of industry. The PIC reminds me of the movie, *Little Shop of Horrors*, with the blood-eating plant saying,

> "*Feed Me!*"
>
> "*Does it have to be human?*"
>
> "*Feeeed me! Feed me all night long. Because if you feed me, Seymour, I can grow up big and strong.*"

Then the narrator says:

> "*Subsequent to the events you have just witnessed/Unsuspecting jerks from Maine to California the acquaintance of a new breed of flytrap/And got sweet-talked into feeding it.../Finding jerks who would feed them their fill/And....proceeded to grow, and grow/And began what they came here to do/Which was essentially to/Eat Cleveland/ And Des Moines/And Peoria/And New York/And where you live!*

And eat the mentally ill, Black and Hispanic males, Catholic nuns and Amish men. We are the jerks allowing the Greedy Old Bastards to feed the prison plant our human population so it can grow bigger, stronger and richer. This is the "U.S. Prison Industrial Complex Shop of Horrors!"

6 Charity Begins at Home

"It is justice, not charity that is wanting in the world."

Mary Wollstonecraft

The U.S. gives more foreign aid than any other country in the world. In 2012, the U.S. Agency for International Development (USAID) gave over $50 billion dollars in aid, with President Obama asking for another $5 billion. A Congressional report lists where some of our money goes: Tanzania got $531 million, Ethiopia $580 million, Nigeria $625 million, Kenya $625 million, Jordan $676 million, Egypt $1,557 billion, Iraq $1,683 billion, Pakistan $2,102 billion, Afghanistan $2,327 billion, Israel $3,075 billion. Conflict areas get the most; we pay you to fight.

This huge and endless stream of U.S. money to well-off countries reduces the amount sent to struggling but "less important" countries where women and children are seen fleeing and starving to death. Not to discount political considerations or needs, but many Americans believe charity should begin at home, especially when less than 10% of the billions sent to foreign shores and leaders could solve some of our more serious problems. Our tax money is enriching many Foreign Greedy Old Bastards!

American money is not only used for "foreign aid," but it is thrown around everywhere. Years ago, I attended a wedding in Jamaica where I met a father and daughter who came in by helicopter from Haiti. They were covered in diamonds and gold, bragging that their garbage business, subsidized by the U.S., made them wealthy. I knew garbage was big business for us in the U.S. and New York, but Haiti? I felt like a poor relation to these two non-Americans grown rich off our taxpayer money. Why should we enrich people in other countries, while we work our asses off trying to realize the disappearing American Dream? Garbage in, garbage out – it's big business, as is our constant road construction. We pay road tolls, we pay parking meters, we Federal tax, state tax, sales tax, we pay fees, we pay penalties, we pay tickets, and we pay and pay, so the Greedy Old Bastards can have more, at home and abroad. Let's stop it. Tear down those toll booths and those sneaky speed traps!

Americans are screwed at home as well as by other countries. Charities in the U.S. are no exception to the greed that permeates our daily lives. In all the years of contributions to Goodwill, did you know that Goodwill Industries International rakes in about $4.8 billion of profit a year? Its CEO makes over a million dollars a year, yet pays his disabled employees as little as 22-cents an hour. This is white-collar crime at its worst. But the CEO of Goodwill points out that nothing he is doing is illegal. The Fair Labor Standards Act allows it. The U.S. Department of Labor allows it. *We* allow it.

The catchy name "Goodwill" is worth its weight in gold and makes us feel good. The company's policies are anything but good will and include testing the disabled rather than providing a fair wage and reasonable accommodation. Goodwill's tax returns showed over a hundred stores paid less than minimum wage, while paying over $53.7 million to top executives. The former CEO of the Goodwill of Southern California received more than $1.1 million in total "compensation." Don't you love the word compensation? While we get paychecks, these "fat cats" or "charity pimps" are getting compensated -- as if their lives are so horrendously hard they need to be compensated for it.

After the Goodwill scandal broke, Goodwill Board Chair, Tommy A. Moore, Jr., didn't apologize. Instead, he said, "The board goes through a rigorous process to determine his compensation based on the impact of his leadership, strategic goals and performance." As Jay Leno would say, "Oh, shut up!"

There's a lot of information now on the Internet about our so-called "charities." The CEO of UNICEF was getting $1.2 million a year salary, along with perks; the Red Cross Director made over $650,000 with incredible benefits, some for life. Red Cross' answer was: "This is considered well within the range for executives of large non-profits, like the Red Cross, a $3.3 billion organization." This is a charity, not a Fortune 500 profit-making company. United Way (UW), a "religious-based" charity, pays its head only $375,000 a year, with lifetime perks and benefits. They said, "Well-meaning donors (that's us) sometimes fail to consider that the CEOs are typically running multi-million dollar operations that endeavor to change the world."

So, you "well-meaning" dummies – or donors - read everything you can before you give. Don't believe the reviewers, either, because they don't use a valid system for rating them. Instead, just ask how much money goes to administrative and overhead costs, including salaries and perks, and how much goes to the people in need. Let's make them publish this annually so we can see the abuse firsthand.

CHAPTER VIII

1 The Greedy Old Bastards

"I have a mind to join a Club and beat you over the head with it."

Groucho Marx

The Good Old Boys or Greedy Old Bastards, have an amazing gift for nostalgia and selective memory. They are native to the Deep South of the United States, but you'll find versions of them entrenched everywhere. Let me give you just one example of a true-blue Good Old Boy, Paul Hemphill of Birmingham, Alabama.

Born in 1936, Paul was Harvard-educated and published a number of books. I believe some may still be read. In 1974, he published a memoir of sorts about the South before 1970. You would think, then, that Paul's book would at least attempt to describe the enormous, convulsive changes in gender and race relations taking place in those years: the marches, the sit-ins, the lynchings, the burning of homes and churches. Women were slapped back down into their places; and racial segregation was enforced at gunpoint (similar to what is happening again), except when the Good Old Boys went to visit their black mistresses. Homosexuals were so deep in the closet that they were completely lost in the fray.

Thrown in this tragic period were some gruesome wrecks on back roads, dozens of people dead from drinking bad liquor… thousands of brave soldiers marching off to die in the horrible jungles of Vietnam. This is the real picture of those years. And let's not forget the well-bred white women of that time, standing by their men, wearing gloves and carrying parasols to keep their skin flawlessly white, while all hell was breaking out all around them.

But, what did Paul Hemphill describe in his memoir of the Good Old Boys? The 'vanishing' South of "country music, stock-car racing, moonshine, hard-living and high-power preaching." Paul Hemphill was just in a typical white male mindset. And he's just one Good Old Boy out of millions of them. But the things he describes are all of a kind: markers of southern identity stuck in a time warp and divorced of all consequences. We all know there's a dark side to racing cars much too fast, drinking moonshine, and listening to sermons that ratify the status quo, making people believe the Lord wants it to stay this way. Paul writes at one point about growing up a redneck:

"In an age when all America seems to be traveling down the road to a bland uniformity of styles and commercialized plastic sameness, there still remains one last group of true romantics anchored to their convictions, beliefs and folkways -- the good old boys..."

The Good Old Boys and their clubs have become even more entrenched and sophisticated since the 1970s Hemphill portrayed. Now their power and greed has no boundaries. Their moniker is a misnomer because there is nothing good about an exclusive club, for young or old boys, developed, designed, and maintained strictly for them and excluding others. What we need is to look at the American way of life and how the strong keep the weak in their places all over the world. We think we're different from other countries, but we're often at the top of the heap for abuses. We need to radically change the way we think about the structures and organizations built to maintain the power bases filled with men in the U.S. We need to redefine our relationships. We need to topple the Greedy Old Bastards!

The top of the hierarchy (that 1%) is reserved exclusively for the wealthiest members of the Greedy Old Bastards (GOBs). Women who represent 52% of the population are not allowed, except for the few tokens of Good Old Girls (GOGs). These people separate themselves from everyone else. They have secret Clubs, meetings, and mindsets, pass special laws with loopholes designed especially for their own benefit, and do everything possible to maintain the status quo. Every organization or Club needs its servants. Women are the major servers and supporters as "Auxiliaries." We haven't come far from de Beauvoir's "other" concept. And the women help to birth, nurture, and train Little GOBlins to take over when Daddy dies.

The entire system is like the Mafia; we know it exists, but we pretend it's not there. And we know it's basically malevolent; but we pretend it's benevolent. Both the Greedy Old Boys Club and Mafia have the same *raison d'*être - to get richer, and retain power and control. We will deal with each of the individual Clubs later. Sorry, Mafia boys and girls – I had to say it, so don't come after me either. I'm from New Jersey and I may have met some of your people. Who knows?

2   Let's Hear It for the Boys

"I do not care to belong to a Club that accepts people like me as members."

Groucho Marx

This book is about the Greedy Old Bastards and the systemic War on Women in the U.S. "Blueblood" men are taught to act as if they're in charge. Their power and wealth are handed down to them, from father to son, as from Kennedy to Kennedy, Rockefeller to Rockefeller, and Bush to "Shrub." Things are not be the same for the girls and women in these families.

The Kennedys and Bushes are already lining up the males of their clan to run for political office. Jeb Bush, 43rd Governor of Florida, is chomping at the bit to run against Hillary or Biden in 2016 as the youngest member of the Bush clan. He is a Catholic convert with a pro-life stance, a member of the Knights of Columbus, and married to his first sweetheart, a Hispanic. JEB, the initials of his full name, was the Governor who wouldn't unplug Terri Schiavo based on her husband's wishes after she was on life-support for 15 years. The action was found to be unconstitutional by the state's Supreme Court. Only when the U.S. Supreme Court declined to hear the case was Terri Schiavo able to finally rest in peace.

When my father had a major stroke, my mother was constantly asked by hospital personnel if he had a Living Will. Because they'd been married 52 years, she would reply, "I'm his living will." I thought it was pretty ingenious. But, when we were told he was "brain dead," my mother asked that he be taken off life-support; three doctors refused. Fortunately, the Emergency Room (ER) doctor, who asked to put my father on life-support equipment to stabilize him, honored his agreement to take him off if my mother asked. My father and our family were saved from what Terri Schiavo's husband's had to endure. Why does Jeb Bush believe he has the right to make life and death decisions for others? He can't really have an aversion to killing because he seems to admire our broken justice system.

Jeb oversaw 21 executions from death row and never commuted a single sentence. He passed major reforms putting caps on medical liability damages and the Florida Medicaid system. He is only doing what other good conservative Republicans do because he wants and needs the party's votes. He hopes to get the Hispanic vote based on his wife's race. His "One Florida" policy abolishing affirmative action and the 2000 Florida voting controversy of "Chad-proportions," lost many of his Black votes. He's also appears to be an ingrate and hypocrite, when he says he achieved everything on his own and nothing because he's part of the Bush family "Skull & Bones," Presidential, and CIA clan.

I hate to tell him, but he was a GOBlin from the minute he was born, and needs to read Chapter I of this book. Mommy was a stay-at-home nurturer and Daddy was head of the CIA, then President. Even the family dogs were famous. Jeb got everything most of us didn't, so he could be successful, even if he wanted to be unintelligent, lazy, or off-the-wall. Remember all this when he runs for office. He wants to be famous like Daddy and Brother.

Another major U.S. GOB family is the Kennedys, who have had their share of tragedies and scandals. Known for being major philanderers and womanizers and proud of it, the Kennedys should have a medal, not a monument, for their infidelity, which they consider their due.

Maria Shiver could have had her choice of many men, but she selected another womanizer, Austrian muscle-man and movie star Arnold Schwarzenegger with his ridiculous accent and super-macho arrogance. She is a Kennedy, yet that didn't stop him from humiliating her and the family by having a baby boy with their maid. The jackass didn't even care enough to protect himself during sex. And this "little blip" hasn't stopped the Terminator. He was photographed in front of the new Lamborghini on the market and is trying to have our laws changed to allow foreign-born citizens (him) to run for the Presidency. Our answer: *Hasta la vista*, Arnie.

Then we have "poor" Robert Kennedy, Jr., who had no choice but to continuously stray. He divorced the mother of his children and wife, Mary Kennedy. She's been portrayed as a crazy woman with fists of steel, who created havoc, then committed suicide. Mary's death deserved a better public obituary than the one written by a man for Robert. Instead of portraying her as a beautiful, kind, and talented woman, they belittled her in life and death, all for his benefit.

Robert didn't even take a breath before he became his Cousin Michael Skakel's advocate. Michael was convicted of bludgeoning his neighbor Martha Moxley to death with a golf club. He was found guilty. Robert said that's only because his high-priced attorney did a lousy job. GOB Connecticut Judge Thomas Bishop agreed and granted Skakel a new trial.

The judge said, "…*defense in such a case requires attention to detail, an energetic investigation and a coherent plan of defense*." Did you ever hear more judicial GOBligook than this? Tell it to all those people in jail who had public defenders, so they can get new trials because their defense wasn't energetic, detail-oriented, and without a coherent plan. More guys without shame! This move to free Skakel was timed to be a month before the 50th anniversary of President Kennedy's assassination in Dallas. Put him back in jail for killing that innocent girl and tell Robert that he needs to concentrate on his new wife or paramour. Too many women have died or been destroyed by the Kennedys. Oh dear, another group that is going to hate and come after me!

Senator Elizabeth Warren in her book *A Fighting Chance* covers bankruptcy laws and bank bailouts that resulted in the distribution of $172 billion here and $700 billion there, until hundreds of billions were thrown around to everyone's satisfaction except the American taxpayer and those bankrupted by the banks. She relates how she was on the "outside" and not a member of the Club, "never drinking the club's Kool-Aid." While she includes many good guys, mainly liberal Democrats, she also tells her story of being a woman in the big boy's world of politics. Not surprisingly, she said the games played in government are "rigged to work for those who have money and power." And if something doesn't work the first time out, powerful insiders just wait and bring it out again until it does.

This is what I call the "Pete and Repeat Strategy" (P&RS). In grade school, we told a joke: "Pete and Repeat were out in a boat. Pete fell off. Who was left?" Of course, the answer is "Repeat." So we would repeat the joke all day long, laughing hysterically. But the laugh is on us because this is really a major political strategy used by the Good Old Boys. They repeat something over and over until it becomes a part of everyday rhetoric or mindset. Then they combine it with shock, chaos and confusion if they can. The P&RS includes floating something to see if it will fly or die. Timing is essential, so if it fails the first time out, bring the boat out again until it passes, or everyone involved fell off the side and were drowned. That's why women are asking – didn't we settle that long ago? No – Pete and Repeat are still in that damned boat and if Pete falls off, guess who is left? Clearly, Senator Warren heard the joke too.

There's another strategy that I call the "High Visibility Strategy" (HVS). I learned it years ago from a top union official. A Good Old

Boy, he attended all high-powered meetings, raised his hand, and said the same thing over and over for years, ad nauseam: "What we need are High Visibility Jobs." Those of us at the meetings would just wait for his hand to go up and we knew what was coming next – "High Visibility Jobs." Sometimes ideas get stuck in people's craws, doing a kind of P&RS, by repeating it as if we are all deaf or stupid. The poor guy's message was lost, but he did put forth the idea that repeating and visibility counts! How else could the Tea Partiers (TPers) survive?

3   Secret & Male-Only Clubs

"The very word 'secrecy' is repugnant in a free and open society; and we are as a people inherently and historically opposed to secret societies, to secret oaths, and to secret proceedings."

John F. Kennedy

There are Clubs and Secret Societies throughout the U.S. reserved for those in power; some are shrouded in darkness and evil. Even their membership lists are taboo – Americans are not allowed to know who these "spooks" are hiding under their Club's cloaks, like KKK sheets. What's all the secrecy about? It can't be good.

Best-selling author and famous psychic medium Sylvia Browne divided secret societies into two groups: Political and Religious. In her book *Secret Societies and How They Affect Our Lives Today*, Browne explored the dark side of these secret societies, and how they shape our lives. I had trouble going back and forth between Browne's research findings and Francine the ghost who talks to her about the past. In spite of this, Browne exposes the way these clubs are private reserves of the wealthy and powerful – the U.S. elite and the Greedy Old Bastards – who impact on our daily lives.

Wouldn't you like to be a member of the largest men's club in the world – The Yale Club of New York City? You could be a part of the "intimate oasis in the heart of Manhattan," with a 22-story clubhouse that has 138 guestrooms, three restaurants.... roof-top dining, modern athletic equipment and banquet facilities. Not suffering from the lack of funds, a $10 million capital improvement was completed to ensure that the 11,000 members and their guests could enjoy the most modern amenities available. But you can't become a member and partake in these amenities and privileges, unless you meet the following criteria: Did you get a degree from Yale University? Were you a full-time Yale graduate student completing a degree-granting program? Are you a full-time Yale professor? Are you a Yale-affiliated member's child or grandchild? If not – forget it.

This Club is not the only one in New York, or in other states throughout the country, you probably can't join. Manhattan is filled with private clubs that cater to "old" and "new" money with strict membership guidelines and requirements. A number of clubs with open membership only require that you be among the "rich" families earning over $3 million annually, or the "ultra rich" families earning almost $14 million a year. Not in that tax bracket yet? Sorry, you'll have to network and do business with a different crowd. It takes more than your pin money if you're invited to join the Core Club in NY. The initiation "fee" for admission will cost you only about $50,000, with an annual fee of $15,000. These elitists pay a "fee," a sum charged for a privilege, not "dues," charged for annual membership like the rest of us. Dues sound so bourgeois and fees keep out the rift raft.

Women have been denied membership in many of these "gentlemen's clubs" for decades. Until 1969, the Yale Club barred women from being members. Wives had to enter the club through a separate service entrance. The club's bar, dining room and athletic facilities were not open to women until 1974 and they couldn't use the swimming pool until 1987. But that doesn't mean when these clubs open their doors to women, it means they're ready for mass inclusion. I was a member of the prestigious World Trade Center Club in Manhattan for almost 23 years, joining when I worked in NY. In

1980, there were about 1,700 male members and fewer than 100 females. Twenty years later, the number of men had almost doubled to 3,156, yet the number of women had risen only from 100 to 202 before the Towers were destroyed on 9-11.

Yale University also has one of the most powerful secret societies in the U.S. known by various names: the "Order of the Skull & Bones," "Brotherhood of Death," and "the Order." Skull & Bones' (S&B) logo is a head skull with two crossed arm bones under the number 322. The number is supposed to connote the astrological sign of Aries or "Cardinal Fire" on many monasteries, churches, and Vatican City buildings. Another account is that the society was founded at Yale in 1832, and was the second formation after the first in Germany, hence 322. The S&B symbol was also used by the Nazis.

About 2,500 alumni have been inducted into the secret society since its founding, with about 500-600 members living today. Since 1982, no official rosters have been published of the "power elite" in the club – it's very hush-hush. The chances of your son or daughter belonging if you are an average person are about the same as winning the lottery. There has been a lot written on this club, believed by some to be sinister, satanic and deeply racist. It was founded by the Russell family with money purported to have come from illegal drug operations of the Far East opium trade.

The Russell's joined with the Tafts to form the society and design its logo flag flown on all Russell Trust Company ships. Initiation ceremonies take place annually on an island in the St. Lawrence River owned by the Russell Trust Association. Most of the land on which Yale University stands is owned by the Russell Association. The "Eastern Establishment" families were at the core of this institution and they were later joined by other wealthy families, and intermediaries, to form their rich and powerful clique.

This represents only one of the many clubs, organizations and institutions that foster and maintain a class system of the power-elite within in the U.S. It's not accidental that granddaddy Prescott S. Bush was a Bonesman and his son, George H.W., and grandson George W. were bonesmen and U.S. Presidents. These clandestine organizations, with their initiations and secrets, are part of the Greedy Old Bastard system that needs to be torn down and destroyed. Now I even have to watch out for the George H.W. Bush CIA crowd.

The Bush administration's policies increased divisiveness, reversed environmental strides, mixed church and state, increased surveillance, and reduced taxes for the wealthy, while opposing minimum wages. Lee White, now deceased, Counsel to Presidents Kennedy and Johnson, in his book *Government for the People*, said the Bush good old boys were often "grossly incompetent," yet able to transform our nation through its "super-secretive" policies and spending. There's nothing democratic about the tyranny and oppression these groups can inflict on the American people under the cover of darkness.

4 Shock, Chaos & Confusion

"Chaos is a name for any order that produces confusion in our minds."

George Santayana

Do you think most Americans are dumb and like being "played" for fools and suckers? Strategies are used on us to do just that -- making us one of the largest and wealthiest "Ship of Fools" in the world. People in other countries, while not better off materially, seem to be more sophisticated when it comes to politics than we poor suckers are with our themes of: Liberty, Justice, Democracy, Equality, Freedom.....

The U.S. uses shock for developing new policies and increasing disaster capitalism, as defined by Canadian author Naomi Klein in her book *The Shock Doctrine*. Catastrophic events such as 9-11 and national disasters become opportunities so that policies and practices previously considered illegal or against the rights of the people can be imperceptibly implemented. There is a window of opportunity when those in power must act decisively or the chance will be lost to achieve what they want while people are compliant and in shock.

Then we have the "Chaos and Confusion Strategy" used by members of the Yale Skull & Bones, such as George Bush. Hell - no wonder we were just as confused as George W. was when he was in office. Did he and Condi ever find the weapons of mass destruction? This was all laid out in an interesting white paper written in 1991 for the Japanese. It said that President George W. belonged to the "Order" and promulgated policies that represent a "New World Order."

The Order is an elite group of WASPs that believe they have the moral right to control world affairs. They are being primed and educated for government and intelligence community positions, such as Daddy Bush, throughout the U.S. They use their elite establishments, clubs, societies and networks in government and industry to do the job and keep the minions ignorant and silenced. They said one of their strategies is to plan and create "Constructive Chaos" to keep the masses out of their business by sending mixed messages, and sowing confusion by ambiguity and secrecy. It's a wonder we are not all insane or jailed.

A 2009 book by Russ Baker traces the unlikely climb of the Bush men to their rise in power and ability to keep it, so that their policies can live on through other administrations. It's a damning portrait of them and their connections. It makes Daddy Bush look even trickier than Tricky Dick Nixon. Historian Anthony Sutton and journalist Ron Rosenbaum believe Skull & Bones has degenerated into "more of the occult and ritualistic trappings of the majority of European freemasonic and Illuminati secret societies." Rosenbaum, himself a Yale graduate, claims the society's German origins are "inherently wicked and pre-Nazi," with a core group of no more than 20-30 wealthy families who form the nucleus of the Order. This is just as terrifying as the CIA, NSA and other spook agencies in the U.S. – all controlled by men.

Historically women, Jews, Blacks, Asians and other non-WASPs were excluded from the Yale S&B Club. Requirements restricted most of these groups from admission. Somewhat liberalized for select people, the guiding principles of the Order resemble those of the late Roman Empire – remember - it collapsed.

Clubs were formed in ancient times to help people band together for social, professional, service, or personal reasons. They were designed to unite those with common interests or goals. There have been many "for men only" Clubs that kicked and screamed when they had to finally admit women. Some refused by saying that they wanted to continue their exclusive male bonding. Some will always ask the question, "What's wrong with having a 'men only' or 'women only' club?" The obvious answer of "nothing" is naïve. Club membership allows networking and the formation of long-term alliances. Is there a place in our "democratic" nation for the "spooks" with a S&B Club at Yale and one supposedly in the CIA, or a "Double-Cross System" symbolically represented by the crossbones?

Americans are enamored of the principles formulated by our founding "fathers" even when they are being destroyed under their noses. We are also complacent when it comes to our rights and protecting those who uncover and expose corruption. Whistleblowers are destroyed in our country, as are people who dare to speak out. Our methods of containing them just differ from other countries. I have seen witnesses and whistle blowers sent to jail because they spoke out. I believe one witness in a major discrimination case deserves a pardon, but has only had nervous breakdowns so far. Instead, as major GOB, Mr. Wonderful on the *Sharks* TV show, says, along with our country: "You're dead to me."

5 It's a Hoot!

"I drilled holes in the floor of the club, and it's sinking."

Bobby Darin

As Church Lady on *Saturday Night Live* **would say – "Well, isn't that special?" and "We like ourselves, don't we?"** One of the most exclusive golf clubs in the world, the Augusta National Golf Club (ANGC) in Georgia, opened in 1933 as a private, all-male club built on a former plantation run by slave labor.

About 20 years ago, NOW criticized the ANGC, demanding that Fortune 500 companies suspend their sponsorship until women were admitted. They replied that it was a private club so they could do as they pleased. The Club was also racist in refusing to admit Black males, but requiring all caddies to be Black – an extension of slavery.

In 1990, the men-only policy was changed to admit Black males, but still no women – nothing new here. The ANGC took 70 years after its founding before admitting women. I hope it won't take the U.S. 70 years after voting in the first Black male President before voting in a woman. So who did the ANGC finally admit? Two "acceptable" tokens and Good Old Girls: Condoleezza Rice, George W. Bush's Secretary of State and National Security Advisor, and Darla Moore, a well-connected, well-to-do Atlanta business woman. A Black and White woman works.

The Augustus Club hung tough, their penises rattling, as they gave NOW a hard time and treated NOW's Chair with distain, calling her approach "offensive and coercive." The ANGC Chairman Johnson said it was no different from other clubs across America for Junior Leagues, fraternities and sororities, Boy Scouts and Girl Scouts. Believe it or not, both the ANGC Chair and NOW Chair, Martha Burk, were nicknamed "Hootie," so the whole thing was nothing but a "Hoot." This year's winner of the Masters Golf Tournament at

Augustus is Bubba Watson, who won his second in 3 years. "Bubba," "Hootie" – we get the message.

Hootie Johnson called Hootie Burke a man-hating, anti-family lesbian. Name-calling is a GOB tradition, tactic and strategy; we women become whores, bitches, lesbians, pussies, cunts, and man-haters as soon as we open our mouths or rock the boat. Female Hootie was being denigrated and maligned; male Hootie was being portrayed as a "defender of all things Southern," a gentleman defending the south from these intruders (women) who should know that a woman's place was not on the golf course, but under a parasol or man.

The ANGC gives out a green sports coat with the club's logo to whomever wins the Masters Tournament, but they have to return the jacket after a year to prevent it from being sold to collectors. Hootie Johnson told NOW there might come a day when a woman would wear the green jacket, but not at the "point of a bayonet." The ANGC is just another sexist organization that succumbed only due to political pressure. The next token will probably be Hispanic because that's how the GOB's roll.

Former President and D-Day Commander General Dwight D. Eisenhower was a member of the ANGC. He kept hitting a tree at the club so instead of cutting it down, they just named it after him, along with Ike's Pond and Eisenhower Cabin. The membership of the Club looks like a Who's Who of the Good Old Boys, with over 300 by-invitation-only members, an initiation fee between $10,000 and $30,000, and annual dues around $10,000. Some of the more notable males include: Warren Buffett, Pete Coors, Bill Gates, Sam Nunn, and T. Boone Pickens. The Club's founder, Cliff Roberts, said as long as he was alive, all golfers would be White and all caddies would be Black. I assume he's now dead and turning over in his grave.

6 Good Old Girls

"Good girls go to heaven, bad girls go everywhere."

Mae West

Good Old Girls are tokens and "Aunt Tomasinas" are used by the boys to assist them in carrying out their agenda. So it was no surprise that Shrub Bush's Condoleezza Rice was one of the first two women selected for membership in the Augustus National Golf Club. In 1982, she switched her allegiance from the Democratic Party to the Republicans, purportedly because of former President Jimmy Carter's foreign policies and because the Democrats would not register her father to vote in Jim Crow Alabama -- but the Republicans did.

Frankly, that's a bunch of GOGligook and it's not the first time she has used it on us. The question is whether or not the lying is pathological. In the case of her big switch, her decision was made decades after his father's non-registration by the Democrats. What took her so long? In 2001, Rice headed Chevron's committee on public policy after which Chevron honored her by naming an oil tanker the *SS Condoleezza Rice*. After much "controversy" because she knew the President of Kazakhstan and Chevron was trying to get a $10 billion development project there, they removed her name and renamed the 129,000-ton supertanker. Reagan's Secretary of State George Shultz recommended Rice for the Chevron Board, furthering the incestuous relationship between them and Chevron.

Rice did President Shrub's dirty work by backing the invasion of Iraq in 2003 because Iraq had "weapons of mass destruction," which was said to be really on behalf of Daddy Bush who was insulted by Hussein. When Iraq denied they had the weapons, Condi Rice said Iraq was lying; the U.S. needed to go after Saddam Hussein; and "constructive confusion" ensued. Even when asked about waterboarding, she used the legalese pap that she "could not recall," even though she'd sat in many meetings on the subject. This very smart woman, with a sharp memory for anything which might serve her career, develops very convenient amnesia on certain other subjects. Either that or she is pathologically inclined to deceive.

Fortunately, there are young people out there awake because Rice's history has resulted in campus protests at Boston College and Princeton University. She was again met with protests from faculty and students at Rutgers University when asked to be a 2014 commencement speaker. She cancelled and was unable to receive the $35,000 speaker's fee and an honorary degree. One article said Rice may run for President. She certainly has the credentials of a certified lying GOG and wants to be perceived as "Every woman" or an American mutt. She says her roots are 40% European, 9% Asian and Native American, and 51% African, with her mtDNA being from the Tikar people of Cameroon. But we already know where she comes from and so do many college students.

There are women's clubs throughout the U.S., but their power and influence is limited in comparison to all of the men's clubs. The women's clubs do not have male auxiliaries as do the men's clubs, such as the Shriners and Independent Order of Odd Fellows (IOOF). Women's clubs are generally for social purposes. The Washington, D.C. metropolitan area has many Black females who are successful physicians, dentists, lawyers and other professionals in industry and government. Those with incomes over $100,000 often become members of "The National Coalition of 100 Black Women," which has 7,500 members and chapters in 25 states. The "Girlfriends, Inc." is another social club that allows Black women to network, while contributing to the next generation of Black females through scholarships, mentoring, and other assistance.

Out of all the White women in my circle of friends, not one of us is a member of a women's club. Wonder what that says about us? I guess we don't need clubs because we are attached to the Big White Boys Club even if we are servers, auxiliaries and subordinates.

CHAPTER IX

1 Religion – A Man's Domain

*"Just as a candle cannot burn without fire,
men cannot live without a spiritual life."*

Buddha

**Organized religions try to keep women subordinate based on
dogma and doctrine - for all time.** Faith is necessary for the spiritual
life of individuals and people, in which they place their trust in a deity
or the doctrines of a religion not based on proof. The various religions
have organized systems of beliefs, ceremonies and rules for worship and
activities for individuals and groups. Religious institutions argue that
males and females are equal, but the deity has given them distinctly
different roles and functions -- with the male's role being superior
and women's inferior or the woman protected by the man. I will deal
with only a few religions to stress the inequality of the sexes based on
religious doctrine, starting with the Catholic Church since I was raised
in that religion.

I will also relate how the U.S. Good Old Boy judicial system is
prosecuting and imprisoning Catholic Nuns and Amish men using
statutes related to terrorism and hate crimes.

A Catholics

POPE
BISHOPS - ARCHBISHOPS - CARDINALS
PRIESTS - PRIESTS - PRIESTS - PRIESTS - PRIESTS
NUNS - MONKS

There are 1.1 billion Catholics in the world and more all the time, with young people flocking to the faith. The Catholic Church is wealthy, in cash and property all over the world. The hierarchy is male-dominated, starting at the top with the Pope to the archbishops, bishops, cardinals, priests, and finally down to the lowest level with nuns and monks. The Church is a highly-structured institution with many degrees of freedom and wealth, to vows of poverty, obedience and chastity. "Orders" vary, each readily recognized by its own uniform, garb or habit (religious garb).

There have been 266 Popes listed from St. Peter (32-67) to the current Pope Francis (2013 -). He followed Benedict, who resigned after eight years in 2013 due to "ill health" and the canonized "Blessed John Paul II," who reigned for 27 years (1978 to 2005). The previous two Popes protected pedophiles in the church, which some say led to Pope Benedict's resignation because he could no longer "physically, psychologically and spiritually" handle his duties. The church's position on pedophilia seems to be "conceal, confess, forgive, pay up, and forget."

Pope Francis failed to say why gays would not be marginalized in the church, yet women still would be. In 2012, the Vatican's *Catholic News Service* wrote about the dismissal or "firing from the faith" of priest Roy Bourgeois because he'd helped ordain a woman. This is based on the catechism that only men can receive holy orders because Jesus, a male, chose men as his apostles and the "apostles did the same when they chose collaborators to succeed them in the ministry." The higher roles of Jesus' mother, the Virgin Mary, and Mary of Magdalene, possibly his wife, count for nothing when it comes to church leadership. Many other women traveled with Jesus and his disciples, such as

Salome, Rhoda, Naomi, and Judith, yet the Catholic Church does not consider them collaborators.

Blessed Paul II wrote that women's ordination was not open to debate because "The son of God became flesh, but became flesh not as sexless humanity but as a male…" My son, my son continues because priests are to serve in the image of Christ, so they believe their maleness is essential to that role. The Church proclaims men are "especially suited to the priesthood" because priests love the church in a male way: "yearning to take care of its structure, the roofs of the buildings, and its Bishops conferences." Women's exclusion is because "women are more apt to draw from the mystery of Christ…." and to "convince the male that power is not most important….So women don't need the priesthood, because their mission is so beautiful in the church anyway."

Another exclusionary theme is that women have a special relationship with Jesus related to his maleness. Their access to him is through prayer, which is easier for her than for "us men, because he's male." So the relationship between women and Jesus is one of love and attachment in the subordinate female way. The Last Supper, the 15th century mural by Leonardo da Vinci, depicts Jesus and his disciples, in groups of three. There may well be hidden messages in the painting as to the identity of the person to Jesus' right. Is it Mary Magdalene? Is it John the Apostle? Some scholars believe the painting shows women's involvement with Jesus, and that the Holy Grail cup represents woman's vagina. All agree that women were an integral part of Jesus' pilgrimages and life. How could it be otherwise when a woman gave him life? Yet, the Catholic Church continues its sexist exclusion of women from posts of authority and power, while marginalizing lesbians -- but not gay males.

Resign or Retire Strategy

"It is the public scandal that offends;
To sin in secret is no sin at all."

Moliere

Resignation, retirement and money are strategies used by the Good Old Boys for handling scandals, and the church is no exception. The sins of the men in the Catholic Church resulted in a "Scandal of Historic Proportions" with testimony to a Philadelphia Grand Jury that included:

An estimated 100,000 victims over a 24-year period (1981-2005), far greater if data from Latin America and Africa was included! An 11-year-old girl was raped by a priest, became pregnant and had an abortion; a boy was molested repeatedly in the school auditorium by a priest; two boys were molested at the same time by a priest; a boy was intoxicated, then had oral sex performed on him by a priest while three others watched and masturbated; a 12-year-old boy was repeatedly raped by a priest; on and on, ad nauseam. The Church's cover-up increased the number of victims because the perpetrators were moved around, so they could defile youths again and again.

Pope Francis faulted the church for becoming "obsessed" with gays, abortion and contraception, while ignoring its larger mission to be "home for all." He addressed homosexuality by saying: "*Tell me: when God looks at a gay person, does he endorse the existence of this person with love, or reject and condemn this person? We must always consider the person.*" In response to questions by reporters on homosexuality in the church, he said: "*Who am I to judge a gay person of good will who seeks the Lord? You can't marginalize these people.*" Asked whether or not there is a "Gay Lobby" within the Vatican, the Pope responded that he hasn't seen sexual orientation "*stamped on anyone's ID cards.*" Better not have ID cards for "celibate" men, Your Eminence. This is somewhat like the military's "Don't ask, don't tell" homosexual policy that ended in 2011. If it's not on ID cards, "It ain't happening."

When asked about women's role in the Church, Pope Francis ruled out women's ordination, saying the issue needs more study. Do we need another study – we've been here forever? He said women must be involved in top decision-making matters because, "*The feminine genius is needed wherever we make important decisions*," but said it was a challenge to find just where women fit. When asked about Catholic nuns, the Pope said he was alive because a nun was astute enough to increase his doses of penicillin and streptomycin when he had lung disease in his 20's.

The Catholic Church has tons of dollars to use at their discretion. A small example is that of the Catholic Church in Germany receiving $5.2 billion in 2012, allowing their Good Old Bishops to drive BMWs, Audis and Mercedes. Pope Francis suspended German "Bishop of Bling" Franz-Peter Tebartz-van Elst after he spent $42 million on home renovations. The Vatican issued a statement that the Bishop was suspended "for a period of time." As was said in the 1984 movie *The Terminator:* "He will be back!"

Pope Francis' style, personality and "liberal" positions have made him popular so that Catholics are returning to the church with money in hands, increasing their wealth even after decades of scandal and misuse of their donations. Women remain subordinate in all aspects of church doctrine and yet they donate and support that position. Although I am religious, I cannot belong to an organized religion that clings to sexism and uses enormous amounts of donated money of the faithful to cover up its scandalous behavior of defiling young people.

Nuns Jailed in the U.S.

"JFK used to say the bishops and the cardinals were all Republicans, but the nuns were Democrats! I sort of believe that too."

Kitty Kelley

Catholic nuns were jailed for protesting against nuclear weapons in the U.S. How disgraceful! For protesting against the Y12 Nuclear Weapons Complex in Oak Ridge, Tennessee, Sisters Carol and Ardeth were convicted of misdemeanors for trespassing, even though they were American non-violent anti-war advocates. As Dominicans, they said they were peacefully protesting because *"Democracy is built on these elements, on being able to speak what we believe is truth."* But, they could have been talking to the Berlin Wall or President Putin because the Good Old Boys decided their democratic rights and truths were excuses for terrorism.

GOB Judge H. Bruce Guyton sentenced Sister Carol to 30 months and Sister Ardeth to 41 months in Federal prison. Remember, the filth that raped Cherice, who committed suicide, got 31 days – these nonviolent American nuns got 30-41 months. A photo of the judge shows him sitting at a table filled with white males, one black male, and no women. An article said that over an 18-month period, more judges, including Judge Guyton, took office in the Eastern District of Tennessee than any other year in history. As a Good Old Boy, he can be credited with sending the good Dominican sisters to jail for long terms in order to send the message that you can't come into Tennessee and protest against their money-making nuclear facility, even if it is dangerous.

Another nun, 84-year-old Sister Megan Rice, recently got almost three years in jail for "breaking into" a U.S. nuclear weapons complex and storage bunker. I think to be accused of breaking and entering, the doors can't be open. After her arrest, it was found that security forces needed to be retrained (Can you imagine!) and contractors had to be removed and replaced (Unbelievable!) in a nuclear facility. Sister Rice was found guilty of sabotaging the plant and damaging Federal property with her cohorts, who got five years in prison. The three protesters said "God was using us to raise awareness about nuclear weapons" and they viewed their break-in as a "miracle."

In other words, they didn't expect to break in and couldn't believe security was so lax that they could barge in. The only miracle is that they were not terrorists, but peacefully protesting Americans. Sister Rice asked for no leniency and said remaining in prison for the rest of her life would be "the greatest gift." She was probably thinking this would wake up Americans to Chernobyl-like danger of these facilities being manned and "protected" by outside contractors. She was wrong. Instead of jail, these Americans should be thanked and pardoned for exposing our failed security systems.

Tennessee seems to have other problems in its judicial system. In the U.S. District Court in Chattanooga, they seem to have no problem with conflicts of interest. An interview with the wife of District Court Judge Frank Wilson was unbelievable. She admitted that she sat as a juror in her husband's court and felt strange about it. Her solution? Not to speak much in case it didn't go "so well with him." She said the lawyers didn't ask her questions so it wouldn't be revealed to other jurors that she was the Judge's wife; she wanted them to think she was "just another juror." I guess she thought her last name was not a dead giveaway and these were some really stupid jurors. She was proud to say that the verdicts "went both ways," for plaintiffs and defendants – nothing like Good Ole' Tennessee justice.

Sadly, it only went one way for the nuns sentenced to prison. After being released in 2005, Sister Carol said, "I learned to make it (prison) a meditation, almost a prayer." I guess her prayers didn't reach the Vatican. Where was the Pope's support for these nuns? This is not the same support or punishment given to many of the guilty pedophile priests.

A "terrorist" can be defined as someone who engages in violent acts intended to create fear, such as those involved in 9-11. But, it has taken on a new life, so it can destroy and delegitimize political protesters in the U.S., such as these nuns. The "Nuns on the Bus" and their leaders, Sisters Carol Gilbert and Ardeth Platte, were branded as "terrorists" by Maryland State Police and placed on the national watch list (NWL). This is the list that is used by the FBI and other Federal agencies. Six years ago, there were one million records, and almost 2,000 added daily.

After whistleblower leaks in 2013, it was shown that these statistics were falsely underreported. No surprise. I have no doubt that I, and many of my friends, are on the NWL because we were part of the whistleblower and Occupy protests. Edward Snowden also thought he would have the appreciation and support of Americans as a whistleblower, but he was wrong too. He's been called a traitor and had to seek asylum in Russia, which makes him a "double traitor." Chelsea Manning, formerly Bradley Manning of the Wiki Leaks case, was recently sentenced to 35 years by the military. Are these Americans whistle blowers and protestors or terrorists and traitors? Do you have faith in your government and representatives to do the right thing?

B Amish

"At Motel 6 in Amish Country I wonder if they leave the light on for you?"
Jay London

Don't worry, we're not just jailing "terrorist" female Dominican nuns. We're also imprisoning Amish men for committing "hate crimes." In 2012, there was an internecine struggle between two groups of Amish. Our government got involved and accused 16 Amish men and women in Ohio of "hate crimes and conspiracy" for cutting beards off of members of another Amish group. The leader of the beard-cutting, Samuel Mullet, was given a 15-year sentence in prison, more than some killers receive, with other Amish receiving sentences from 1–7 years. Many were sent to prisons across the country, creating an undue hardship on their families; they can't travel to visit because of their religious beliefs.

This entire episode was "cruel and unusual" punishment, and the U.S. government overstepped its authority. It used the 2009 hate-crime statute to jail Amish men instead of interpreting the beard-cutting as an intergroup struggle. Of course, this reminds me of something....

Friedrich Niemoller's famous poem when the Nazi's rose to power said that if you won't speak out when they come for others – such as the mentally ill, minorities, whistle blowers, nuns and Amish people, then no one will be there when it comes your turn. Just fill in the blanks:

First they came for the Socialists, and I did not speak out –
    Because I was not a Socialist.
Then they came for the Trade Unionists, and I did not speak out –
    Because I was not a Trade Unionist.
Then they came for the Jews, and I did not speak out –
    Because I was not a Jew.
Then they came for me – and there was no one left to speak for me.

Harvard Law School Professor Noah Feldman said: "If you accept the interpretation that this (Amish incident) is a hate crime, then any dispute within a religious group could be called a hate crime... If I think my wife should obey me and my religion teaches me so and I take a swing at her, then I've committed a hate crime," rather than engaging in a domestic dispute. But Professor, who's listening to the injustice in our Good Old Boy system?

The Amish are a small but well-known traditionalist Christian fellowship that forms a subgroup of the Mennonite Churches or Anabaptist religion. In 2014, there were about 281,000 Amish; they speak English, Pennsylvania (Dutch) and Swiss German; 165,000 live in the U.S. and a small number in Canada. They're getting lots of exposure in the U.S. from the new Amish reality television programs. The Church has districts with 20-40 families in each, led by male bishops and several deacons or ministers like those in the Baptist

Church. The Amish believe large families are a blessing from God, and they restrict marrying outside the Church.

Formal education typically stops at the eighth grade, so that the children can be trained for their tasks of working in the fields, building for the boys with their fathers and for the girls, working inside the home and gardens with their mothers. The Amish do not use U.S. entitlement programs like Social Security, and as pacifists, they refuse to take part in any type of military service. They practice shunning, or shame and excommunication for those who refuse to conform to their ways. The Amish average seven children per family, as was the case when the U.S. was largely agricultural and needed many hands to do farm labor. They avoid the mainstream by living in isolated areas.

With their high rates of procreation and intermarriage, Amish populations suffer from Dwarfism and blood-type metabolic and genetic disorders. But their cancer rate is only 56% of the national rate, and they have lower rates of skin cancer. Their lifestyles do not include alcohol, tobacco, or numerous sexual partners. Birth control is thought to be immoral as is abortion or any artificial means of birth. The Amish are not immune to psychological and emotional problems, but they are far less likely than other Americans to commit suicide.

President Obama should take the time to pardon the "terrorist" nuns along with the Amish "criminals" and send them home to their families where they belong – not feeding the U.S. Prison Industrial Complex.

C Muslims

*"I believe very much that the most damning thing you can
say about Muslims is that you're afraid to say anything
because they'll hurt you."*

Penn Jillette

There are 1.6 billion Muslims in the world today. That number will
rise to 2.2 billion in the next 20 years. A list of the demographics of
religion by the CIA's *World Factbook* says the total religious population
is just over 7 billion, with Christian at 33.4%, Muslim at 22.7%,
followed by Hindu 14%, Buddhist 7%, Sikh 0.4%, Jewish 0.2%,
Baha'I 0.1% and other religions 11%. The nonreligious and atheists
represent about 11%.

I won't say too much about the Muslim religion because I want
to respect their beliefs – and I don't want to be hunted down if I say
the wrong thing. Also, I want to make it clear that "some of my best
friends are Muslim." A former employee and now dear friend of mine
is Muslim, and I learned a lot from him. I provided him with a private
office so that he could carry out his prayers without interruption and
he joined with other Muslims on Fridays to pray in the U.S. Capitol
building, in a room set aside for them.

The holy Quran states: "Men and women are equal," yet the
proverbial "but" states that, "Men are the protectors and maintainers
of women." Since women cannot protect themselves, it's up to the men
to arrange for their protection. And, their protection is in any way
the men determine is necessary. The Quran talks of the love between
men and women, asks them to be kind to each other, but permits men
to "…restrain their carnal desires (except with their wives and slave
girls), for these are lawful to them…." and further that the husband
should first "chide or admonish" them, "remove, send, banish, leave,
or refuse to share their beds," and finally to "scourge or beat them
(lightly)." Basically this is no different from the recalcitrant women
in any society, when brute force is used on women who disobey men.

Sunni Muslims are the largest group or sect in North America, representing 75-90%; Shia Muslims represent only 10-20%. The most Muslims reside in Indonesia, Pakistan, Bangladesh and Egypt, and large groups of Muslims are in India, China, Russia, Ethiopia, Australia, Europe, and the U.S.

To maintain modesty, Muslim women cover their hair, their bodies, their heads, neck, shoulders and faces. Memoirist Jean Sasson wrote an enlightening story on behalf of Princess Sultana of Saudi Arabia to bring women's issues in her country to the forefront. She provided a spirited overview, particularly for women in this country, of the various issues facing women in Algeria, Bahrain, Egypt, the Gaza Strip, Jordan, Kuwait, Qatar, United Arab Emirates (UAE), Yemen, and Saudi Arabia.

While there are variations, women still endure arranged marriages, and remain mainly in their own households. Few work outside the home. Some Muslim women may drive cars and enjoy various freedoms -- but many are still circumscribed and totally segregated from men. There are honor killings, self-immolations, and murders. Divorced Muslim women often lose custody of their young sons. Muslim men are within their rights to pressure women to give up their rightful inheritances, and this leaves Muslim women with little property and few assets. Most Muslim countries are strictly patriarchal, often requiring the testimony of two women to equal that of one man.

D Hasidic Jews

"Once is orthodox, twice is puritanical."

Lord Melbourne

In 2014, there were almost 14 million Jews in the world (39% of them in the U.S.). Two million Jews are Orthodox and, of that number, only half a million are Hasidim, meaning "Pious One" in Hebrew. Founded in the mid-18th century by Jewish mystics, it gained popularity among poorer, more persecuted, and less-educated Jews. Those who survived the Holocaust in Russia, Poland, Hungary and Romania fused their practices with mysticism as they moved to America, Israel, and Western Europe. Hasidim now thrives in New York and New Jersey, where Orthodox Jews preserve their religious traditions and Yiddish language, in tight-knit communities.

Hasidic Jews fulfill their religious duties by being fruitful and multiplying as stated in *Genesis*. They typically have 5 or 6 children per household -- many more than non-Hasidic Jews. Recently in the Catskills, a friend of mine and I noticed an Hasidic couple walking down the street pushing a new baby in a carriage with at least four children in tow, and a new one on the way. After observing the group, my Catholic friend asked if I knew that Hasidic males have sex with their wives through a hole in a sheet. I checked and found this is a myth. Hasidic Jews believe they are explicitly commanded by God to get totally naked for sex.

Unfortunately, ancient Jewish traditions are still practiced today, so that women menstruating are considered "unclean" or "impure." The taboo limits who and what a woman may touch during these unclean times, what activities she can join in and how she may relate to her husband. At the first sight of blood to the end of the bleeding, she must have seven clean days, and immerse herself in a ritual purification bath before she can have sex. Of course, impurity lasts longer after the birth of a girl than a boy. Some women say the bathing rituals help to prevent infection at a time when the vagina is vulnerable.

Hasidic women are as devout as their male counterparts, but must remain subordinate. They have limited education and training, yet are often the breadwinners so their husbands can pursue a higher, scholarly calling. But, that still does not make her the head of the household because "He's the man!" She is prohibited from mixing with men at social events, swimming at retreats, or threatening the idea that Hasidic culture must remain a male domain. It's too much to imagine the Super-Hasidic Woman as she tries to be all that she can be, while constantly pregnant, working and yet "contaminated" for a major portion of her life.

On one occasion, I invited an orthodox Jew to speak at an event for Federal employees. As he was escorted and introduced to me, his host, and other staff members, he refused to shake my hand, but instead addressed, shook hands, and talked with male subordinates, ignoring me and the women in the office. I never got used to these and other slights and insults directed at me and other women based on religious doctrine. After all – *si fueris Rōmae, Rōmānō vīvitō mōre; si fueris alibī, vīvitō sicut ibi* or *"if you should be in Rome, live in the Roman manner; if you should be elsewhere, live as they do there."* So, for everyone who comes to this country -- when in America…

But, we have to remember that Rome declined with the causes debated for its dissolution and causality from general malaise to catastrophic collapse. Some historians theorize that it was inevitable because prosperity of the empire decayed it and removed the artificial supports, so that it disintegrated from its own weight. Others have referred to environmental degradation and epidemics that caused population and economic decline, along with high taxes and unsound economic policies. High taxes were needed for the military budget and there was a decline of loyalty away from the government in favor of the popular military commanders. In addition, it was thought that malaise of its people was caused by the intrusion of religious ideas, urbanization, and public disasters. The conclusion is that the gradual collapse of the Roman Empire was the result of a series of events and that no one thing made it happen.

So – we have artificial financial supports, environmental degradation, high taxes, unsound economic policies, a huge military budget, and loyalty away from government – and there is no question that Americans have a growing malaise for catastrophic events and disasters. Religious doctrine has also crept into various areas heretofore determined to be separate and distinct and we are moving towards a police state environment and undue surveillance, shooting and imprisoning of our people.

E   Mormons

"My parents divorced when I was born, and my mother is a political science professor, like a feminist Mormon, which is sort of an oxymoron."
Eliza Dushku

There are perhaps 12 million Mormons in the world with Christ as the center of their belief. Mormonism is the principal branch of the Latter Day Saint (LDS) movement of Restoration Christianity begun by Joseph Smith, Jr. in upstate New York in the 1820s.

In 1831, Smith received a revelation that "plural marriage" should be practiced by men. Thereafter, he and other top Mormon leaders took multiple wives, including Brigham Young, who moved the practice to Utah after Smith was murdered by a mob in Illinois in 1844.

Smith's revelation of polygamy continues today in Utah despite the fact that it's illegal in the U.S. or is it? If polygamy is illegal, why hasn't the Department of Justice put these men in jail, along with those who wed prepubescent girls? The Catholic nuns and Amish men are in jail – so why are these men with all their wives on television shows instead?

Modern countries forbid polygamy, and many developing countries are outlawing the practice. So where are the conservative and Christian forces on this issue?

F   Scientology

"Writing for a penny a word is ridiculous. If a man wants to make a million dollars, the best way would be to start his own religion."

L. Ron Hubbard

And, that's just what L. Ron Hubbard did. He started Scientology, an off-shoot of his self-help, self-healing work called *Dianetics* for which he once griped made him so little money. His visionary body of beliefs, practices and teachings are that people must free themselves from limits by going through counseling and re-experiencing painful and traumatic events in their past.

Hubbard called it a tax-free religion. Many consider it a pseudo-religion and cult. Those who leave are in fear of character assassination and other abuses and, as usual, women's rights are abridged. A former member of Scientology's Sea Org said women understood they were not to have children and were pressured to have abortions. A male member said when his wife became pregnant, she was ordered to have an abortion; the organization denies this.

The Church of Scientology also inflates its membership, ranging anywhere from 8 million to less than 25,000. In order to increase it, Hubbard created a celebrity club or centre with the former silent-screen star Gloria Swanson and jazz pianist Dave Brubeck among the first group, and, more recently, Kirstie Alley, Tom Cruise and John Travolta, as members.

The 2012 movie *The Master* was said to be tangentially about L. Ron Hubbard and Scientology. The film was analyzed by various critics and touted for Hollywood awards. After seeing the movie with a friend, I thought it was the biggest piece of sexist garbage I had seen in years. The film was filled with outrageously repulsive scenes, such as: Joaquin Phoenix "humping" a female-shaped sand hill, fingering it, and then masturbating in the ocean; a woman reading pornography to him that includes using cunt and fuck; and, full-frontal naked women frolicking in all their pubic glory, next to fully-dressed Philip Seymour Hoffman. Unfortunately, my girlfriend noticed everything else about the film, but didn't pick up on the misogynistic mindset and filth until I pointed it out. I wonder what has happened that allows these morally-bankrupt people to prevail, under the guise of excellence in acting and art.

Finally, L. Ron Hubbard died of a stroke in 1986. He was an obese chain-smoker, with a prominent growth on his forehead, and suffered from various injuries and illnesses. His body was cremated and his ashes scattered at sea. Members said his body had become an impediment to his work, so he decided to "drop his body" to continue his research on another planet.

2 Business Clubs

"The superior man understands what is right;
the inferior man understands what will sell."

Confucius

Greed and gouging of Americans by the private sector is a national pastime! The **BU**siness **M**en or BUMs have no consciences or shame when it comes to money or bilking the public.

The *Wall Street Journal* recently featured a dapper man with a slight smile on his face, in a conservative black suit and tie. He was standing in a wood-paneled room, one hand in his pants pocket, the other on the back of his executive chair. Chairman of Occidental Petroleum Ray Irani was departing with "a lump-sum severance of $14 million, plus about $1.3 million annually for security, travel and financial planning," and a life-time parking space at Occidental's offices.

Mr. Irani had wanted $2.8 million more, but the poor guy didn't get his performance bonus for 2013. He was already one of the highest paid executives in the U.S. earning about $1.1 billion in compensation

(1994-2012). In response to this greedy disgrace, a spokesperson for Occidental said they believe in "excellent pay for excellent performance." Oh, shut up!

The overall cost to Occidental was $26 million, which is pocket change for oil executive exits, while Americans are ripped off daily at the oil pumps. Chesapeake Energy Corporation paid $67 million in 2014 for benefits to its former CEO and co-founder, Aubrey McClendon. SandRidge Energy, Inc. is paying ousted CEO Tom Ward about $95 million in severance and an accelerated vesting of his stock awards. These bonuses and exit payments are only possible because Americans are being abused at every turn by capitalism and the private sector. The masses still believe in the "American Dream" and bet on the lottery-type fairy tale of – someone has to win, so if we take or are given a chance, we can win too. But, the deck is seriously stacked, so take a guess at the odds. Sadly, these thieves represent only the tip of the GOB iceberg. Speaking of icebergs....

Maybe Global Warming, that we are told doesn't exist, will fix these guys. I believe we are having natural shifts in the earth or terrestrial globe that is causing major changes to occur, including warming, tsunamis, earthquakes, tornadoes, and other phenomena. Then there are the "unnaturally-caused shifts" that may be occurring due to our continuous fracking, cracking, and gas emissions into the environment and atmosphere. My mother always believed that when we launched rockets, missiles and satellites, it changed our atmosphere, space, and weather patterns. It's as good as anyone else's guess and she didn't get millions or a Nobel Prize.

A recent article in the *Wall Street Journal* listed the top "10 Best-Paid Chief Executive Officers (CEOs)" who raked in $420 million in compensation: Oracle CEO Larry Ellison earned the highest at $76.9 million; CBS Leslie Moonves $65.4 million; Liberty Global Michael Fries $45.5 million; and the remaining seven: Freeport-McMoRan, Viacom, Walt Disney, Time Warner, Aetna, Estee Lauder, and General Electric earned $231.8 million. Median's CEO pay exceeded $10 million in 2013 and increases were over 8%, while U.S. workers averaged a 1.3%, many getting 0%. A picture of the smiling all-white male Greedy Old Bastards appeared in the *Detroit Free Press*. The previous Robber Barons or the so-called men who built America had nothing on these guys.

Someone who could be the poster child for the BUMs is "The Donald." Trump breezes onto his popular television show, *The Apprentice*, with the theme song of "Money, Money, Money." He uses his show to advertise for his cronies and brags about the money collected for charity by the celebrities. He pits one celebrity against the other as if we are all in the Coliseum watching the gladiators rip each other apart for Caesar. No one is supposed to get more exposure and publicity than him and his dynasty, so his older children sit beside him as he gloats on his throne. His trademark hair bouffant may be laughable, but he laughs all the way to the bank with it.

Trump appears to prefer women from other countries. His first wife, Ivana Zelnickova, is a native of Czech Republic. She took her money after 15 years and ran so he could move on to a younger wife –sounds like one of Henry VIII wives. He tried an American by marrying Marla Maples; they divorced in 6 years, after she was accused of cheating. Then he married Slovenian model and socialite Melania Knauss. He has five children to carry on his dynasty, the latest named Barron, with two r's, not to be confused with Baron, the lowest-grade title of English nobility. More likely, Barron was named after the American weekly newspaper of the same name that covers financing and marketing information. His daughter with Marla is named Tiffany after the New York building, so another child could be named Duke or Forbes.

I selected Trump out of all the other BUMs because he seems to hate women, particularly strong ones. So far, he has taken on star Angelina Jolie because she has had sex with "so many guys." He called celebrity Rosie O'Donnell "a big, fat pig." And, he spewed out some nasty stuff on successful Arianna Huffington.

First, he said her husband probably left her for a man, not because he's gay, but because she's "unattractive." A woman's place for him is at home and on the "Ms. America" runway, not creating a successful company. He sounded like a petulant little boy when he said the *Huffington Post* purchase for $315 million by America On Line (AOL) was a stupid deal, making AOL dumber than her husband. He then bragged about teaching Arianna a lesson by raising the rent "especially for her" to $100,000 month so she couldn't move into one of his Trump buildings in New York.

Come on Donald, stop beating up on women - we don't like braggadocios, sexist dinosaurs, or caveman misogynists. In his book on how to get rich, Trump said that the all the women on his TV show flirted with him either consciously or unconsciously. Please… That's nothing to brag about because women do attach themselves to older, fat, bald, impotent, or small-penis men, as long as they have money. The more money, the nastier they can be and worse they can look. This was evident by the Jacqueline Kennedy–Aristotle Onassis merger.

Onassis was short and ugly, but he was a Greek shipping tycoon, with a large ship. She needed a place outside the U.S. to hang out where she could be secure and protected from the Kennedy killings. Aristotle was said to have paid a mere $3 million, negotiated by Teddy Kennedy, for the privilege of marrying her. I thought dowries went the other way. Oh well, the privileged make their own rules.

A Legal Drug Pushers

"Reality is just a crutch for people who can't handle drugs."

Robin Williams

There are seven top U.S. pharmaceutical firms making billions pushing legal drugs. They are: Johnson & Johnson, Pfizer, Abbott Labs, Merck, Wyeth, Bristol-Meyers Squibb and Eli Lilly. Other firms are Schering-Plough, Baxter International, Genentech, and Procter & Gamble. I call them "The Legal Drug Pushers." They rake in billions of dollars and they employ close to half a million employees to do it.

We appreciate and thank the scientists and researchers who have come up with vaccines that cured millions of people of diseases around the world, which were once fatal. But, for every good drug that comes out, there are tons of bad ones. Many current drugs on the market have side effects worse than the diseases they're designed to treat. Their ads include caveats that range from passing gas to dropping dead.

Drug manufacturers and distributors have been responsible for: Thalidomide that caused serious birth defects in the 1950s-60s, withdrawn but returned to the market for use in leprosy; Lysergic acid diethylamide (LSD) marketed as a psychiatric drug, causing numerous problems; Fen-fen which causes heart valve disorders; Phenylpropanolamine (Dexatrim) for weight loss that causes the risk of stroke in women under 50; and the list go on. I found only one drug listed as withdrawn because of poor sales.

In 2013, the U.S. Department of Justice said J&J engaged in, "one of the largest health care fraud settlements in U.S. history." J&J had to pay $2.2 billion to end civil and criminal investigations into kickbacks to pharmacists and marketing of pharmaceuticals for off-label uses. The case covers the marketing of psychotic drugs Risperdal and Invega, and the heart drug Natrecor.

J&J promoted Risperdal for "controlling aggression and anxiety in elderly dementia patients and treating behavioral disturbances in children and individuals with disabilities." It cost the government "hundreds of millions of dollars in uncovered claims," and the huge settlements don't even make a dent in the company's profits.

A book by Jerry Oppenheimer called *Crazy Rich: Power, Scandal and Tragedy Inside the Johnson & Johnson Dynasty* says the poor J&J family is one of the "the most dysfunctional" of the Fortune 500. Their vast fortunes have pitted them against each other over "trust funds, divorce settlements, paternity and other familial issues." There have been murder plots, shootings, tragic accidents, suicides, and other mayhem.

In the 1940s, a block of 100 J&J stock was $3,750; by the end of the 1990's the shares were worth "a whopping $12 million..." Women make 85% of all healthcare decisions, so every time you use a band-aid, baby powder, Tylenol or Modess, think of the grief and misery you are causing the wealthy J&J heirs. It's hard to feel sorry for them, isn't it?

Many doctors have become part of the problem. Not long ago, I saw my own doctor being wined and dined by pharmaceutical salesmen at an upscale D.C. restaurant. A friend of mine who couldn't sleep was prescribed Lorazepam (Ativan) by her physician. The side effects included everything from hives to suicide. It is also highly addictive. When she tried to stop taking the medication, her blood pressure spiked to pre-stroke levels and she spent days in Emergency Rooms with her daughter. None of the doctors she contacted were able to help her either.

One doctor finally told her that since Ativan is a short or intermediate-duration drug, and Valium (Diazepam) is a longer-duration drug, she may be able to wean herself slowly from one onto the other and then quit. It took her a year to do it, but it worked. But, I wonder how many people just had stokes and died when they tried to get off that or other drugs or went on insane rampages? Tom Cruise gets a point for this.

B They're Killing Us

"Sometimes the appropriate response to reality is to go insane."

Philip K. Dick

There are a lot of sick people in the U.S. - shooting people, taking drugs, committing suicide, drinking themselves to death, drunk driving, maiming and killing. There are mental health problems that we are not adequately treating. Some of our mental disorders include: Anxiety Disorders, Obsessive-Compulsive Disorder (OCD), Panic, Post-Traumatic Stress Disorder (PTSD), Social and generalized Phobias, Attention Deficit Disorder (ADD), Bipolar Disorder, Borderline Personality Disorder, Depression, PPD and PPP, Eating Disorders, Schizophrenia, and Autism. In the last 20 years, autism has increased by more than 600% or 1 in every 110 children.

I trained an autistic girl at Douglass Residential College in New Jersey when autism was something new. It's a major undertaking to get these children to focus and communicate, even for those trained to do so. We used behavior modification therapy by withholding something the child wanted until they achieved their task. My beautiful little girl with long pigtails learned to speak after many hours spent in a phone booth-sized space with me. I withheld a piece of her lunch until she repeated a word. We bonded from our daily closeness, so by the time the semester was over she could communicate with me, her parents, and others. It was very rewarding for me and I often think of her beaming face when she spoke to her parents.

The increase in the number of autistic children is being attributed to women bearing children later in life, which is nothing new since women are always blamed if nothing else can be found. That certainly wouldn't count for the enormous increase. Autism is also being counted in the "autism spectrum" along with children having Asperger syndrome and Pervasive Developmental Disorder (PDD). Autism is three times more likely to affect males than females. Other possible causes are a virus, vaccine shots, food sensitivities, and toxins/ pollutants in the environment. I believe we are poisoning our children, while the GOBs pollute and destroy our environment and get rich doing it. Autism is only one outcome.

Years ago, a high cluster of autism was found in a small town in Leominster, Massachusetts. Children in the area remembered what color day it was from the particles in the air spewed downwind from the Foster Grant sunglass factory. The factory also dumped years of liquid toxic wastes in the area. Research suggested genetic damage may have occurred due to chemical exposure and carried in male sperm across generations. U.S. soldiers exposed to Agent Orange (dioxin) and other chemicals during the Vietnam War also reported as siring autistic children.

In 1980, Congress passed a law to clean up hazardous waste sites. An amendment in 1986 added minimum removal and remedial actions under a "Superfund" site designation. Later, President Clinton attempted to strengthen the requirements but couldn't get bipartisan support. In 2010 over 1,200 sites were on the priority list. Over a 5-year period, $1.6 billion was collected from companies for cleaning up their abandoned and uncontrolled waste sites. But, in 1995 the Treasury stopped collecting and the $6.0 billion trust fund balance was exhausted by the end of 2003. So for the last decade, American taxpayers have been paying to clean up these private sites, while profits keep rolling in to the polluters.

The State of New Jersey's air is ranked as one of the worst to breathe, and both New Jersey's land and water are contaminated. The smells from the refineries between Elizabeth and Newark are ghastly. New Jersey has over 50 designated "Superfund" sites ranked and rated by EPA, and has cancer rates higher than average nationally.

NJ women suffer the most from cancer: New Jersey females 54%; U.S. females 38%; New Jersey males 46%, U.S. males 45% - over their lifetimes. There are also clusters throughout the state. Joseph Mangano wrote a piece on the "Geographic Variation in the U.S. Thyroid

Cancer Incidence, and a Cluster Near Nuclear Reactors in New Jersey, New York and Pennsylvania." He reported that exposure to radioactive iodine emissions, from "16 nuclear power reactors" within a 90-mile radius, are likely causing a rising incident in rates of thyroid cancer. So, the only problem to be concerned about is not just a major incident at one of these sites, but the everyday fallout. There's a report on the internet of "The 25 Most Polluted Places on Earth" that provides horrendous pictures of what can happen in the U.S. if we don't get a grip, sooner rather than later. Is this why the nuns were imprisoned?

The "Garden State" has a great deal to be concerned about when it comes to pollution. The mindset of these polluters is akin to what Good Old Boy Lee Iacocca, former CEO and Chairman of Chrysler Corporation, said years ago when the "Clean Air Act" was on the agenda: *"We've got to pause and ask ourselves: How much clean air do we need?"* Wow!

I worked for the paint company National Lead (NL) Industries in Sayreville, New Jersey in their titanium dioxide plant with about 2,500 blue-collar employees and a small group of white-collar management employees. The company paid us fifty cents for our nylon stockings and a couple of dollars for nylon shirts that were ruined by the titanium dioxide that poured out of the stacks daily. When the wind blew, the sirens went off, and we all ran for cover, trying to protect our eyes and faces. Our cars were parked under sheds, but the paint was eventually eaten off. When the union had a strike, management would stay in the factory and order food we brought by boats across the waterway so we didn't cross picket lines. The paint on the boats was eaten off.

The accident rates in the plant were high and the pollution was even higher. Two new policies were set by the GOB all-white management to curb both. An employee believed that birth dates correlated with men's accident rates when overtime and shift-work were considered. It sounded crazy, but it actually worked when men were restricted from overtime when they were more likely to have an accident. A new policy was set and accident rates dropped.

Another problem was the high number of pollution complaints received from drivers as they drove over the Edison Bridge looking down on the manufacturing plant. Huge amounts of titanium dioxide spewed out of stakes during the day shift, when production was highest. A policy was set to increase production at night, so the pollution was less visible. Viola – Fixed!

Years later, NL Industries moved permanently from the site. The polluted land and waterway with its deserted buildings remained, like a deserted ghost town on the horizon. Then, magically, across the chemically-polluted water, a new housing development was built for the "unknowing." The ads boasted of beautiful homes with "Waterfront Views." A boat was offered initially, but was later rescinded. Caveat emptor ("Buyer Beware") should have been their marketing motto.

The 42,000 residents of Sayreville on their 19-square miles, and those in surrounding areas, have been exposed for decades to dangerous pollutants, including asbestos. The U.S. EPA designated the area as a "Superfund" site and NL Industries was directed to remove lead from the property and Raritan Bay. But the company paid a meager $79 million to remediate the lead contamination and cleanup of the toxins. The little blue Dutch Boy, modeled after a young Irish-American boy, should be ashamed of himself. The Dutch Boy Group was sold to Sherwin-Williams in 1980, three years after the manufacture of lead house paint was banned. Recent articles proudly announced a major park planned for the site.

This is only one example of what is going on in the U.S. And EPA rarely holds polluters accountable, so we remain unprotected. Many EPA employees believe the agency is simply a good front, while management gets in bed with the polluters. EPA has failed to process civil rights complaints from community groups and organizations being used as "chemical dumping grounds."

The Judge's decision in *Rosemere Neighborhood Association v EPA* said some complaints languished in EPA for up to 15 years -- and EPA didn't even follow their own regulations. EPA foxes remain in industrial chicken coops where they are knee deep in chicken crap. Someone needs to get serious about reversing EPA's cozy relationship with polluters and their retaliation against employees who blow the whistle on them. Dr. Marsha Coleman-Adebayo's book, *No Fear: A Whistleblower's Triumph Over Corruption and Retaliation at the EPA,* represents only one example of what happens to whistle blowers at EPA with over 1,000 attorneys and billions of taxpayer dollars being used to protect the culprits and destroy dedicated employees.

We cannot continue to suffer from cancers, breathing problems, poisoning and other health and mental problems. As the country mulls over the legality of marijuana, the drug dealers and legal polluters in the U.S. are wreaking havoc with our mental and physical health and bodies. Let's hold them accountable! We don't need any more sick adults or children – the private sector doesn't take care of them – we do.

C Round'em Up, Move 'em Out

"No, all we need to do is buy up the ground from under their feet –
and evict them."
David Marusek

Gentrification is coming to your ghetto… To gentrify is to change a place, such as an old neighborhood, by improving it and making it more appealing to people with money or making it more refined or dignified. But what's so dignified about kicking poor people out of their homes?

Powerful J&J "gentrified" New Brunswick, NJ calling it "New Brunswick Tomorrow." They wanted to move their corporate headquarters within walking distance of Rutgers University, but would only do so if the county agreed to extend Route 18 highway around their facility. So, two local Good Old Boys, John Heldrich and Ralph Voorhees, were involved in bringing the gentrification to fruition. At the same time, because of economic downturns and unemployment, the Department of Labor (DOL) funded a jobs program with an office located in downtown New Brunswick.

Eventually, the two GOBs destroyed the black male Executive Director and Federal program. When I asked why, I was told because they could. When I said it would destroy an outstanding program, they said they'd just build it up again. I have learned since that time that this is a major strategy used by the GOBs to seize something they want. Cut off the head, rip out the middle – gut it like a fish, then fry it up and eat it. Use happy, up-lifting words while you're doing it.

Almost 40 years later, an article shows a new $120 million mixed-use property hotel, meeting, and conference center named after John Heldrich. Surprise! Speeches at the ribbon-cutting ceremony said the entire project was "the culmination of years of planning and civic leadership," by him; a photo of the event showed only eight white males. Middlesex County assisted by issuing $70 million in bonds to finance a major portion of the construction costs.

And, as with American history books, all the hard work done by the DOL Executive Director and over 150 women and minority employees faded into oblivion. The positive work accomplished is still in New Brunswick because we, my boss and I, funded the start-up of the well-known 30-year-old African American "Crossroads Theater." Not even a small plaque has been hung because only the Good Old Boys are worth accolades, hotels, and worthy of keeping the flames glowing by the Voorhees at Rutgers University. New Brunswick Tomorrow was such a success that other cities are lining up to get gentrified -- cities like Newark, New Jersey.

Newark was once a thriving and bustling city just across from Manhattan. As demographics changed, whites moved out to the suburbs. After the huge migration to the "burbs," Newark stayed on a downhill spiral, trying to survive as the commuters passed through the city on their way to New York City. But, it's a major hub, close to transportation sites like Newark International Airport, and Port Authority Trans-Hudson (PATH) trains. Cultural activities include the New Jersey Performing Arts Center and the New Jersey State Opera.

Since 2005, the demographics of the quarter million people changed only slightly: 57% speak English and 28% speak Spanish; 50% are Black; 33% are Hispanic; 12% are White. The median age is 32, and only 41% of population is married. The median household income is $35,659 and over 25% of the residents live in poverty.

Just as J&J used the "New Brunswick Tomorrow" theme, Newark is calling their gentrification "The New Newark - A happening city is turning heads," touting hotels, offices, apartment buildings, and shops. There are stylish buildings, old classic makeovers, and opportunity. Panasonic is moving its North American corporate headquarters to a 250,000 square foot new office tower in Newark with residential apartments and lofts for downtown dwellers. The BUMs are tired of commuting; their children have left the nests; and they want to be close to Manhattan.

The women, Blacks, Hispanics and other minorities better hold onto their bootstraps. The GOBs are on their way to reclaim their land and bulldoze some tenements. We were told many Portuguese already moved out – maybe they went back to beautiful Portugal. The rest should do their best to dig in, find another place, scatter, leave the state or drop dead. They don't care because they have to go – for the sake of "progress." This is "Tomorrow" for New Brunswick and "Today" for a New Newark.

D Robbery – Inside Jobs

"Fraud, robbery, and murder have characterized the English usurpation of the government... Why, for the last fifty years we have been robbed in the matter of taxes of hundreds of millions."

John Edward Redmond

The John Dillinger Gang and Bonnie & Clyde had nothing on the U.S. banks and the banking industry or our U.S. tax system. These robberies are inside jobs. These thieves and gang members weren't even shot or jailed. And Americans still haven't gotten over the robberies committed legally against them by the Greedy Old Bastards.

Family members who came through the Great Depression often hid their money under the mattress of their bed. My grandmother hid her money in a coat pocket, then hung it on the line where thieves couldn't reach it. My grandmother's coat was still there when she died with her hard-earned money in her pockets.

Americans put their money in banks and let the banks steal it right out of their accounts. The banks in this country are legal institutions filled with big-time crooks. Wells Fargo's earnings rose by 16% to $22 billion dollars, making it the top annual profit maker among banks. Poor J.P. Morgan dropped to number two. Number 2 has always been used for children when they want to poop -- that's exactly what the banks and government did to Americans – crapped on us – particularly the middle-class.

President Ronald Reagan's conservative trickle-down economic theory (Reaganomics) was supposed to give tax breaks to the wealthy, creating such a flood of wealth that some would trickle down to the poor souls below – like those housekeepers. But Reagan's people were careful to call it "supply-side" economics, which sounds more palatable.

Famous economist John Kenneth Galbraith said trickle-down economics had been tried unsuccessfully in the 1890s under the name "horse and sparrow theory." The premise was that if you "feed the horse enough oats, some will pass through to the road for the sparrows," which led to the Panic of 1896. Basically then, trickle-down economics is: the wealthy eat everything, crap out what they don't want; then the middle-class and poor eat their feces.

As my brother-in-law Maurice used to say, "Who am I to tell a sparrow they can't fly?" I think he meant eat horse dung. Economists say that money invested in business is first paid to employees and suppliers so that the money then goes up, not down. So, how about using this strategy in reverse? Let them eat some of our crap for a change and see how they like it when it gets there. They'd probably pass a law with a poop loophole.

The Tea Party (TP) movement, a "loose as a goose" affiliation of groups with varying platforms and agendas, is based on principles of free enterprise, limited government, and reliance on a free market system or trickle-down capitalism. Unfortunately, the TP lacks the movie star appeal of Ronald Reagan to spout out their agenda. Since TP is also used for toilet paper, it's appropriate that the TPers are an anti-movement movement and since its "loose as a goose," it's pure diarrhea coming out of their mouths.

The TPers are anti-spending, anti-Obama, anti-tax, anti-immigration, anti-health care, and anti-women's rights. They pulled out some Good Old Girls, such as Sarah Palin and Michele Bachmann, so their positions are easier to understand and digest. But crap is crap no matter how you want to dress it up and put perfume on it.

Quotes attributed to TP Republicans from their bully pulpits include: There is no proof carbon dioxide is a harmful gas (Bachman); the moon might be as intimidating as Obama care (Ted Cruz); the unemployed are children who won't do their chores (Steve King); and business just can't find enough sober and drug free workers (Dave Joyce). The TP needs some researchers and speech writers before they spew their oats to the sparrows.

Conservatives and TPers don't want our first black President to be successful, so they've thrown all they could at him, putting every obstacle in his way. President Obama is extremely intelligent, so he found ways around them, such as Executive Orders and the "oops excuse," just incensing them more. TPers want the history books to show that he failed – not that he was instrumental in bringing about a major health insurance program, Obama care, with his name on it.

Economic forecasters are saying the U.S. economy is about to hit the skids again, so bar up those penthouse windows. As a country, we refuse to decrease our debts and keep borrowing money. We don't need more taxes or burdens on the middle-class, we need the Greedy Old Bastards to stop what they are doing and think about this nation. Instead of coming together to fix our problems, they are digging us into deeper holes.

The U.S.'s credit rating was downgraded by Standard & Poors, losing its AAA rating, with the caveat that it would be restored if Congress could get its act together. Good luck. Russia, China and North Korea are also teaming up to do in the U.S. economically, if they can. They see our weaknesses and will exploit them.

We have to remember that women always get the short end of the stick and they don't count at all in those countries who want ultimate power and control. Can you imagine having to face Vladimir Putin and his policies every day as a man or woman – how about being just one of the everyday workers? I better watch my back and check my mail for poison pen letters from Russia without love.

So far, I have to worry about lots of people because of this book – the mafia is starting to look benign and I'm used to them anyway coming from NJ.

3 Sports

"You wouldn't have won if we'd beaten you."

Yogi Berra

The Sports Industrial Complex (SIC) takes in over $422 billion a year, not including some separately-sponsored sports. And it's no different from every other sexist Greedy Old Bastards' club when it comes to their mindset on women. Billionaire Mark Cuban, owner of the National Basketball's Dallas Mavericks, asked a female entrepreneur on the *Sharks* TV show if she had a business meeting on her son's birthday, which one would she attend, the meeting or her son's birthday? This is the same old white male, anachronistic, chauvinistic tripe that puts women in their places. Mark didn't ask male entrepreneurs the same question of what's more important his son or his job.

With almost half a trillion dollars at stake, everyone wants to own a sports club. Saturday and Sunday television shows are filled with sports; males are watching Major League, Little League and college games; football, basketball, soccer, golf, tennis, boxing, wrestling… They also attend games, cheering from the sidelines. Women are their cheerleaders, fans and groupies. The choice is to join them, cheer them on, serve them, or go shopping.

Military planes have flyovers at sports events. Flyovers of five F-18s at Super Bowl games cost taxpayers about $450,000. The Air Force's Thunderbirds performed at the Daytona 500 at a cost of $80,000. Military services receive more than 850 requests annually for flyovers or parachute jumps for every conceivable sports event and ceremony. The excuse for this extravagance is that each flyover represents a training exercise. Oh – get real.

Because there are now 10 commercial ads on TV for every break and repeats all the time, I am thinking of canceling my cable TV. Recently I read that many others are doing the same. We must be the ones who remember when TV shows were for free, not this monopolistic or GOBolistic rip-off we have now. We should be called the "Private Sector Advertising Generation" because it's everywhere we turn – and there's no relief.

Among sports rift-raft – you just have to be big, tall, and accurate, not educated or too bright – there are murderers, rapists, sexual abusers, womanizers, child molesters, animal abusers, sexists and racists. Some of the players are criminals making appalling amounts of money. Many of them can't even curb their illegal and immoral acts and mouths.

The recent comments of Donald Sterling of the LA Clippers reminded me of when my Army supervisor, a Good Old Boy Chief of Staff, saw me in the Officer's Club with a few of my friends after work one night. He was across the room and called me over. I knew he was having marital problems, and he looked slightly inebriated. It was dark in the bar, so he asked me who I was with; I motioned to a group of my friends who were Black, Hispanic and Asian. After he glanced over, he turned back to me and slurred, *"What's the matter with you – don't you know you're white?"*

Didn't I know I was white? It's hard not to know you're white if your entire family is white. My fraternal grandparents came over on the boat from the Ukraine; my material grandparents from England. At first, I missed his point. Then I realized he was not only referring to my crowd, but must have heard that I was dating a black male, my current husband. This was not going over well since I was the senior woman on the base – fraternizing with Blacks and other minorities. But as President Obama said about Don Sterling's racist comments, *"When ignorant folks want to advertise their ignorance, you don't really have to do anything. You just let them talk."*

The depraved acts of sports athletes and their GOB support can be seen by what happened to Michael Vick, one of the National Football League's (NFL) highest paid players, under contract with the Falcons. He and his buddies ran a dog fighting ring, watching the poor animals tear each other apart, so there is no question these guys are psychologically damaged. We know that children who abuse animals have serious problems – so how about these pathetic guys? At first, they tried to shield Vick, and then he was charged, but would receive a 3-year suspended sentence and a $2,500 fine. Even his court costs would be suspended if he promised to be a good boy. This is called a "slap on the wrist" for being a bad boy. The public and animal rights advocates were outraged, which led to Vick's serving two years in Leavenworth. Many of the dogs were dead and buried or sent to recuperate at rescue facilities, some becoming therapy dogs and family pets.

But don't worry about Vick -- he's a star athlete! He declared bankruptcy in prison, the Judge reduced the amount he would pay back the Falcons of his $37 million signing bonus, his debts were paid off and he's back playing football again with the Eagles. The dog-killer even does endorsements. As one sport's idiot said, "…It's time to have fun again" as Vick touted his fleet of new vehicles.

Your college tuition money is hard at work for these low-life guys too. Penn State paid $59.7 million to settle the 26 cases of sexual abuse of sports Coach Gerald "Jerry" Sandusky. Another $50 million will be paid for attorneys' fees, public relations expenses, and they will be instituting new policies and procedures. What the hell were the old ones? Sandusky, a really smarmy-looking 69-year-old man, was allowed to destroy many lives because he could – just like the Ripper and pedophile priests. His buddies covered up for him, three former administrators and renowned football coach Joe Paterno. Sandusky was convicted of 45 criminal counts, but is appealing his case while serving his 30-60 year term, living off us. He probably has a large-screen TV so he can watch sports.

USA Today reported some of the worst sports scandals. They include: "Ponzi" schemes, prostitutes, "pay-for-play" systems, academic fraud, drugs, and sex. And the list goes on and on with no sport above corruption. Finally, women's sports have never commanded the attention or salaries of male sports because many women are not into them. Interest has increased, but until as much money comes in, they will not be worth as much as male sports -- and will never have as many scandals.

A Pistol Packers

"All you need for happiness is a good gun, a good horse, and a good wife."

Daniel Boone

Most women are smart enough to know not to mess with guys who are packing pistols! In men's minds, women are like material possessions, such as wine, songs, cars, horses, and guns. The mere mention of "gun control" creates a firestorm and brings out the big guys with guns. Only a few friends of mine are armed, and if anything goes down, I'm going to their house.

But is there anything scarier than anti-government, racist, sexist, homophobic, mentally ill and testosterone-filled macho men armed to the teeth? Most women are pacifists and unarmed -- but not for long, if the National Rifle Association (NRA) has anything to say about it.

The NRA is an extremely powerful organization with a huge lobby, backed by macho men and movie stars like John Wayne, Clint Eastwood, and Chuck Norris. Political opponents of gun control include: Senator Rand Paul of Kentucky, Senator Mike Lee of Utah, Governor Rich Perry and Senator Ted "Crazy" Cruz of Texas. Fewer women are gun-toters – two well-known pistol-packing mamas are Sarah Palin and Angelina Jolie. There are right-wing radicals, skin-heads, and sick maniacs mixed in with everyday hunters and gun owners.

A recent battle took place in Colorado – the marijuana-approval State. Someone please check the chemical pollution in Colorado and Florida and the impact on their residents. State Senator Angela Giron and Senate President John Morse, both Democrats, backed gun control legislation. The NRA poured their strength and money

($360,000) into having them recalled. The head of "Basic Freedom Defense Fund" bragged when they were ousted. The victory was based on complacency (probably due to "Mary Jane"). The recall votes were extremely slim, but the message was -- as Trump would say – Huge! 'Don't mess with the NRA or gun-lovers.'

The NRA was born as a way to improve rifle marksmanship and training of soldiers, just after the Civil War. Two Good Old Boy warriors founded the organization in 1871. Almost 150 years later, the NRA has over 5 million members (2013) and a budget around $231 million from membership dues, voluntary donations, and grants from gun manufacturers. By the way, the Founders were worried about slave revolts when they inserted the language in the Second Amendment of the Constitution that called for a 'well-regulated militia for the security of a free State.' So, it's hardly a healthy guide for us in the 21st century.

Controversy stems from the term "militia," which is an army or fighting force of citizens, to be called up to take arms in defense of the community, territory or property. One of the best-known militiamen was Teddy Roosevelt, a Texas "Rough Rider." We now have a U.S. National Guard and Reserves consisting of "citizen soldiers" with rules, regulations and controls like those of the other permanent military services. Without these controls, a militia that went haywire might degenerate into an armed mob. This reminds me of the old joke about how to prevent airplanes from being hijacked: "Arm all the passengers."

The NRA is probably the most powerful lobbying group in the U.S. And its lobbyists fight dirty when it comes to retaining the right to bear arms based on the Second Amendment of the Constitution. What we all have to realize is that we'll have more and more mass shootings until we take action to fix our mental health problems and stop giving mentally unstable shooters the ability to gun us down in our homes, work, schools, churches, and malls.

B Pistol-Packing Mamas

"America is at that awkward stage. It is too late to work within the system, but too early to shoot the bastards."

Claire Wolfe

Annie get your gun – and Suzie, Mary, Tina, Jackie, Alice, and Nancy, too. The goal of the NRA is to arm us, along with all of our citizens; crazy or not here we come. They are now on the look-out for an untapped resource - women. It will no longer be guns for boys and dolls for girls, but pretty little pink guns for us.

Their marketing to raise female membership and gun sales includes an online NRA women's channel, new and improved guns for women and, of course, dragging out the token gun-toting Good Old Girls. Their marketing strategy has names for us ("Armed and Fabulous," instead of "armed and dangerous"). There's also the "Pistol Packing Ladies," a women's shooting club, and "Guns, Gear, Grub and Girl's Night Out." Nothing like a little champagne, some food and loaded guns for the girls. One female advocate said that right now is the time for women to get out, buy a gun and you'll feel empowered. Just imagine some of the women you know packing a pistol. Hope you're not having an affair with any of their husbands.

The NRA won't say how many women are members, but their poster can be the same as the one used for military recruitment – "The NRA Wants You!" They probably have something to do with the movie "Bonnie & Clyde" being rerun recently.

Republican state legislator John Payne, an older white male with a large, down-turned mustache, wearing an American flag lapel pin, inserted $38 million into a budget bill going through the General Assembly to be used to lure to his state gun manufacturers from states with strict gun-control laws. A Pennsylvania newspaper reported that one of the gun manufacturers has already moved from Connecticut to the Good Old Boy state of South Carolina.

The firearms and ammunition industry is a $33 billion industry in the U.S., which generates over $2.1 billion in taxes from property, income and sales. Following the money, the gun industry and corporations have funneled $20 - $52.6 million into the NRA. (Again, we can't seem to count; that's a $32.6 million gap.) They received another $20.9 million selling advertising to companies marketing products. There are almost 100,000 people in the U.S. in manufacturing, distributing or selling firearms, ammunition and hunting equipment. Another 120,000 jobs are with gun suppliers and ancillary industries. No wonder the reality show *Duck Dynasty* is so popular.

Most Americans don't seem to be worried about all guns, just the type of guns which can mow down lots of people at once without reloading. Three types of guns were used in mass shootings in 2012 and 2013. They were a Glock Model 22, $500 semiautomatic handgun with 15 rounds; a Bushmaster AR-15, $1,200-400 semiautomatic rifle with 30 rounds by Bushmaster; and a Ruger Mini 14. This is an $800-1,100 lightweight semiautomatic or "poor man's assault rifle" that killed 69 people in 2011.

I don't know much about guns, but I learned that semi-automatic or self-loading firearms fire again with the cartridges feeding automatically from the device or magazine. The single-action, double-action, pump-action, bolt-action, or lever-action firearms, allows semi-automatics to fire continuously as long as the trigger is held under the magazine or when the feed device runs out of ammunition.

In other words, a semi-automatic is a firearm that uses the force of the recoil or gas to eject the empty case and load a fresh cartridge for the next shot and allows repeat shots by just pulling the trigger, making it easier to kill many people at once.

Gun control advocates want to make it harder for disgruntled or sick people to get these types of guns. But who knows who is mentally sick, unstable, insane or evil in our society? As the Pope said about not having sexual orientation stamped on the Vatican's ID cards, we don't have sanity stamped on any either. I'm not against citizens being armed in the U.S. Our democratic rights as citizens are being routinely infringed upon by increased surveillance, data collection, and police actions. There have been recent videos of male police officers beating the hell out of women. I believe women are so vulnerable in our society that more and more of us will be buying guns for protection, and pink is good.

A 95-year-old woman was raped in her home in downtown Washington, D.C. a month ago. She sympathized with her rapist; she said he "needed help." Better yet, she needed a gun! Just not one constructed to do mass murder.

4 Department of Defense

"A nation that continues year after year to spend more money on military defense than on programs of social uplift is approaching spiritual doom."

Martin Luther King, Jr.

The Military-Industrial Complex
Airplanes, Tanks, Guns & Drones

President Dwight Eisenhower said "The problem with defense is how far you can go without destroying from within what you are trying to defend from without."

I'm with the next person when it comes to defending our country. I'm a true-blue patriotic American. My mother and father were proud Americans. My father served in the U.S. Army during World War II. Whenever he was asked what nationality he was, he would always say American and he was proud to be a veteran. My brother served in the U.S. Navy during the Cuban Missile Crisis.

My husband retired from the U.S. Air Force Reserves as a Colonel after serving 31 years and worked 52 years as a civilian for the U.S. Army. I worked for the U.S. Army as a civilian for over a decade. My family is as blue as it gets! But that doesn't mean I want to continue down the road this country is going and I agree with former President Dwight D. Eisenhower when he said:

"Every gun that is made, Every warship launched, Every Rocket fired, signifies in the final sense a theft from those who hunger and are not fed, those who are cold and are not clothed.
This world in arms is not spending money alone. It is spending the sweat of its laborers, the genius of its scientists, the hopes of its children. This is not a way of life at all in any true sense. Under the clouds of war, it is humanity hanging on a cross of iron."

As he left office, Eisenhower was even more profound when he said: *"A people that values its privileges above its principles soon loses both."* In his 1961 Farewell Address, he told the nation he was worried about the future and knew Americans believed and expected compromise between its President and the Congress to find agreement beneficial to the nation. But with the immense military establishment, with its large arms industry, new to America, it would impact on our economy, politics and spirits, and be felt in every city and state and in our federal government.

As a soldier, Eisenhower recognized the imperative for our military, but said we should never *"fail to comprehend its implications."* He told Americans they had to guard against unwarranted influence by the military-industrial complex because of its potential to increase misplaced power. And he said we must not let democratic processes and liberties be endangered. In order to avoid that, Americans would have to be alert and knowledgeable citizens so that our liberty and security could prosper, while the huge industrial and military machinery operated in our defense.

The President then cautioned us not to live only for today and for our own convenience and ease, mortgaging the assets of our grandchildren, our precious resources, and losing our political and spiritual heritage:

"We pray that peoples of all faiths, all races, all nations, may have their great human needs satisfied; ....that those who have freedom

will understand, also, its heavy responsibilities; …that the scourges
of poverty, disease and ignorance will be made to disappear from
the earth….by the binding force of mutual respect and love."

President Eisenhower was a prophetic man, and his fears have
come to fruition. Our military-industrial complex is eating away at our
wealth and welfare. Our President and the Congress have shown they
cannot compromise on behalf of the citizens they claim to represent.
There has been a diminution of our personal freedoms, privacy and
liberties under the threat of terrorism and guise of security, as shown
by Edward Snowden, who exposed the National Security Agency. As
citizens, we are often ignorant and complacent, living for the moment
in a throw-away society that squanders our resources and our futures,
for the sake of the here-and-now.

The U.S. Department of Defense (DOD) is huge. It employs
about 718,000 civilians and close to 800,000 contractors, along with
1.6 million on active duty, 1.1 million in the National Guard and
Reserves. Another 2 million military retirees and their families receive
benefits. President Barack Obama submitted an increased budget to
Congress with Revenue of $2.902 trillion and Expenditures at $3.803
trillion requested; about a $901 billion Deficit. The DOD will eat
up about 60% of it. But add on 5.5% for Veteran's benefits, and the
hidden and Black Programs, along with costs for the spooks in the
CIA, NSA and Homeland Security, it's way beyond 60%. So what
does that leave for the rest of us schmucks?

To improve our weak public schools (6%), housing and community (5.5%), energy and the polluted, chemically-laden environment
(3%), our ancient infrastructure and transportation system (2%),
labor and lost jobs (2.5%), our tainted food and agriculture (1%), and
our serious health problems (5%). All told, we get a measly 25%. The
Government (6%), Science (2.5%), and International Affairs (4%)
take up the rest.

One smart writer asked how we can allow the Pentagon to have
$2.5 billion left over from a canceled program and let them keep it,

while politicians and others bemoan "military budget cuts." He doesn't think any other program could get away with that stuff. He's right, but he didn't factor in the Greedy Military Old Bastards (MOB). The $2.5 billion was supposed to be used during Donald Rumsfeld's term. Then the Army shifted priorities. The only thing new about this is someone was sleeping in the Pentagon and let the secret out that there was money left over.

The military knows if it doesn't spend every dollar it's given, it could disappear. The strategy is to keep this "close hold," -- away from the media and hardworking schmucks. Men with tanks and missiles engage in big business and so far no one has been big or bad enough to stop them. You'd think that with all this money, once we sent Americans to fight, they'd be cared for when they return. And most citizens assume the military takes care of its own. But it depends whom you consider to be your own.

Ask our Veteran's and they'll tell you a story that you probably won't believe or won't want to hear.

A Collateral Damage

"Asymmetrical warfare is a euphemism for terrorism, just like collateral damage is a euphemism for killing innocent civilians."

Alan Dershowitz

Many of our soldiers don't make it home and others come home seriously injured and damaged – physically, mentally and emotionally. Instead of taking care of them, we allow cover-ups and deny many of their illnesses to minimize or avoid liability and payments. Vietnam Veterans were exposed to Agent Orange and other herbicides, but were ignored because their treatment was going to be so expensive. Agent Orange was the blend of herbicides the U.S. sprayed in the jungles to remove trees and dense foliage where the enemy hid, resulting in "collateral damage" by poisoning our own soldiers.

Soldiers had to file claims under a "presumptive rule" to be eligible for benefits and show a direct connection to their service in Vietnam and illnesses such as leukemia, Parkinson's disease and ischemic heart disease. This seems to be modeled after U.S. insurance companies not insuring Americans for preexisting conditions, raising your premiums if you use it, and hoping you die before sucking out any money.

The Vietnam War lasted from 1959 to 1975, yet the Veteran's Administration did not begin adjudicating some of the claims until late 2010. By the time they got around to Vietnam veterans, many were already dead from "friendly chemical exposure."

This reminds me of a recent case of a U.S. soldier sent as a first responder on a ship to Japan after its nuclear disaster. He said he was suffering from respiratory problems because he was exposed to radiation when the wind shifted. He is now suffering from many ailments and he can't move his legs. His case is like first responders at Ground Zero after the WTC terrorist attack. During the Bush administration, EPA assured these workers that their work environment was safe. Thousands later suffered from serious respiratory illnesses from working or living near the site. All it would have required was adequate safety measures.

The "prove it" and "drag it out" strategies are used by the government in dealing with many types of cases. Employees die waiting for their discrimination and whistle blower cases to be adjudicated. Many just give up, knowing they're fighting against attorneys funded by unlimited taxpayer money. Most Americans were shocked to learn that soldiers buried at Arlington Cemetery were misplaced, put in mismarked graves, or buried on top of each other. The corpses of some veterans wait 3-4 months to be buried.

A former friend of ours, George, a retired senior Army civilian and Army Reserves Colonel, has been in a box somewhere for months awaiting his honor of being buried in Arlington Cemetery. What kind of honor allows you to disintegrate in a coffin for four months or more, then maybe get buried in the wrong place? With our soldiers being sent everywhere and used for everything throughout the world, we can't dig burial sites and bury our men and women soldiers promptly? They would probably be honored to do this for their fellow and female soldiers who put their lives on the line for the U.S. The disrespect we have shown and continue to show these brave men and women is despicable.

"Wreaths Across America" seeks to place 55,000 wreaths on grave sites, some at Arlington National Cemetery. After my husband and I donated, we drove by Arlington and noticed there were only wreaths in a few sections near the street. Is it possible that no wreaths are laid on some graves unless Americans donate -- when the military has over $2.9 trillion? Why are donations necessary for our "Wounded Warriors?" How about taking some money away from the double-dippers and big-bellied military contractors?

And, the military scandals for the top brass are handled differently than for "regular" DOD soldiers and women civilians. In 1997, John Ralston was the top candidate to succeed John Shalikashvili as the Chairman of the Joint Chiefs of Staff, the highest position in the military. Once Ralston's adulterous affair with a CIA employee was exposed, it was all over – sort of. He said he was separated from his wife at the time. She denied it and said the affair had caused their divorce. A woman who stood up for herself! Kudos. I'd go to war with her.

Ralston was backed by his military cronies, and Defense Secretary William Cohen. But an adulterous lower-level soldier was discharged a month before Ralston's scandal so there was a concern for a double standard, and Ralston did not get that job.

But, as they say in Jamaica, "No problem, mon." Ralston later became the Supreme Allied Commander in Europe, the highest-ranking officer in NATO, until he retired. Men understand that cheating on your wife doesn't matter, particularly if you're a big shot!

Retired 4-Star General David Petraeus had an adulterous affair which led to his downfall and resignation as head of the CIA, George Bush's place. He was crucified by the media for having the affair because it could have jeopardized and compromised national security.

One writer asked – does anyone care? Petraeus was back giving speeches at dinners honoring veterans and their families. He followed scandal protocol by apologizing, being contrite, asking for forgiveness and marching on. And by now, we all know the drill.

B Contracting Vultures

"Don't play dead with a vulture. That's exactly what they want."

Kevin Nealon

You can see and hear the contracting buzzards circling every military base in this country. The Pentagon awarded them contracts valued at almost $40 billion dollars in one month – March 2013. Not one year, but one month! That was 71% more than in the previous month, despite budget cuts that started to take effect. But it was below $46 billion awarded in a month the previous year. Even with sequestration, the DOD will spend at least $300 billion on contracts in 2013, with sweet deals to Lockheed Martin for $697 million, and overall "potential value" to them of $1.8 billion. Austral will get a $682 million "agreement" and BAE Solutions will get $781 million, to name just a few. There are major contractors and subcontractors. There are subcontractors to the subcontractors. Everyone wants a piece of the huge DOD pie.

A smart whistleblower, who chose to remain anonymous, reported that the new budget continued to be a "fat cow" because it still included $10 billion more for maintenance and operations. Six billion dollars in "penalty" cuts were spared. Furloughs, scheduled for almost all Federal agencies, were reduced for DOD from 22 to 14 days. Defense Secretary GOB Chuck Hagel said the funds for DOD "fell short of what they needed to maintain current spending levels," the operative words being "to maintain the current spending levels."

We have this trick down, too. Years ago, in a staff meeting, the Chief Counsel, who everyone thought was connected to the you know who, told all senior staff to hire as many new people as they could because a freeze was coming due to budget shortfalls and the military never falls far. I objected to hiring people just to turn around and lay them off, but was ignored, then chastised, as a naïve senior female, the only one at the time. I was slow to realize: That's how the game is played! The Chief Counsel filled us in: filled spaces would be used as a guideline for the cuts; if we were over ceiling, our cuts would start there. Then when you cut back, you'll be right back where you started.

This major Military Old Boy (literally or figuratively – he even owns a restaurant) worked for years on the inside, then retired and became a contractor on the outside, until the base closed. It's a gift that keeps on giving because he'll get 80% of his Federal high pay and a Social Security offset. This double-dipping goes on all the time in the military, especially for men. Soldiers retire and receive positions, which civilians have waited years to fill. And as they say in the service: "Once a General, always a General." The system is so entrenched that the regulations stating that civilians can't work for a contractor for five years in the same "field" or "area" is an utter joke. It happens all the time. There are contracts and jobs for lovers, friends and family.

The DOD has prime property and every amenity known to man and woman. The list of installations and bases owned and used by the U.S. armed forces in the Continental U.S. (CONUS) include: 160 Army; 60 Navy; 71 Air Force; and 18 Marines. They have banks, golf courses, theaters, bowling alleys, community centers, swimming pools, water views, boats, and cars with or without drivers, vans, houses, barracks, VIP quarters, commissaries and post exchanges. The Base Realignment and Closure Commission (BRAC) recommended base closures that were a pittance of the total number and didn't include some of the more fabulous ones, like Ft. Meyer, Ft. Belvoir and those in Florida, Hawaii and Puerto Rico.

When all sites are added together, the DOD uses over 30 million acres of land -- about the size of the state of New York. The Pentagon is one of the world's largest office buildings, twice the size of the Merchandise Mart in Chicago. It has almost 18 miles of corridors. The DOD also manages an inventory of installations and facilities at over 5,000 different locations.

Contractors sit in offices around these military bases like scavengers waiting to pluck out money from rotting carcasses. The skinheads are also supposed to be around U.S. bases, I guess hoping for discarded or unguarded armaments. It's a big revolving door worth billions. A list of government contracts is published regularly by *Capital Business* showing where your money is being squandered. "Operational, core functions and professional, administrative, and management support services" are listed. What the hell are the Federal employees being paid salaries for doing if not operational, core functions and admin?

Contracting has resulted in many scandals over the years, but the GOB mindset is to privatize as many functions as possible in a military trickle-down or flush-down method, washing their hands from a faucet of billions of dollars. Privatization is the wrong approach to take in these terrorist times – and we have several huge scandals to prove it. But the fat cat has to be skinned.

Finally, the government sets aside $500 million for Federal contracts to Fortune 100 companies and their subsidiaries as "small business" awards. The following companies don't look small to me: General Dynamics ($215.7 million), Lockheed Martin ($110.5 million), Apple ($29 million), Boeing ($25.6 million), Citigroup ($5.5 million), and General Electric ($1.9 million). What about the real small businesses in this country – the little "Moms & Pops?" They're can't compete with the big Military Old Bastards or the real MOB.

5   Government – The Big G

"It is to be regretted that the rich and powerful too often bend the acts of government to their own selfish purposes."

Andrew Jackson

FRAUD, WASTE & LOTS OF ABUSE

Cutting government is a political mantra, particularly for conservatives – but, it ain't happening! The Federal government employs 2.1 million civilian workers with a total in wages and benefits of about $24.8 billion in 2013 and average pay of $81,704 in 2012. Over a 5-year period, beginning in the Bush administration and moving into Obama's, the number of Federal government employees rose by 267,885 (14.4%) – so much for cutting the Federal government! The DOD employs over 40% of those employees, with growth concentrated in a few agencies, such as Veterans Affairs, and Homeland Security.   Slower growth is in the internally focused agencies, like Agriculture, Housing and Urban Department, and Treasury.

During our period of 9-11 shock, not surprisingly, President George W. created the huge Department of Homeland Security (DHS), which is now the third-largest Cabinet Department with a 2015 budget request of $38.2 billion. There are 240,000 employees in jobs ranging from aviation to border security. This Department is a Good Old Boys' haven. Its website has a photo of 10 white males receiving the Secretary's Award for Valor. I guess females are devoid of bravery. President Bush then increased surveillance of Americans, and privatized some security ventures.

The new security requirements included outsourcing, contracting, and funneling big money into specific private coffers. This is Old World, not New World stuff. A decade ago, there were 3,512 security contracts; after Bush's DHS there were over 115,000 security contracts. It's become a secret $200 billion dollar industry -- and it couldn't have come about without citizens being shocked, then exploited, then shocked again – with everything hidden under the cloak of darkness – as taught to and by the Yale Bonesmen. There was nothing "Bush league" about this.

Trust me – there's no job like a Federal government job! I've worked for industry and I've worked for government – and government wins, hands down! The most important difference is that in private industry, employees are trying to make money and in government, employees are trying to spend it. While budgets are being cut, many government employees are still pulling down top salaries, with tremendous benefits, travel, per diem, education, training, conferences and meetings. That non-performing lying supervisor I talked about is earning over $170,000 doing work that could be done by an admin officer.

Federal employees take their lead from our Congress, planning and attending lavish conferences. The Internal Revenue Service (IRS) had a conference that cost $4.1 million dollars for luxury rooms, speakers and leadership training including a *Star Trek* spoof. About 2,600 attendees received more perks, like baseball tickets and stays in presidential suites that normally cost up to $3,500 a night. The 15 outside speakers cost $135,000 in all. One was paid $17,000 to discuss "leadership through art." A government watchdog said the IRS spent $50 million to hold at least 220 conferences just in the years 2010-2012. Who's going to audit these people? Seize their desks!

The General Services Administration (GSA), which oversees Federal real estate, blew $822,000 at a Las Vegas conference with penthouse suites, a mind reader, a clown, a bicycle training exercise, and catering. The conference was mocked by GSA employees -- but 50 officials got bonuses from $500-$1000 for arranging this mess. Awards and bonuses should also be publicly posted – it's our money because some Feds are getting $10-25,000/year. And this is only the tip of government fraud, waste and abuse of taxpayer money.

When my grandfather cut off the heads of our pet chickens, we watched through the small cellar window as they ran around without their heads on. We were sick and it got worse when our grandmother cooked and served our friends for dinner that night. Where did she think she was – the Old Country? Her grandchildren didn't want to know this stuff. Now U.S. whistleblowers are running around screeching without their heads on, asking for some justice, and afraid someone will be eating them for dinner. Instead of protecting them, we offer them up on a platter to management to munch on and spit them out after severe retaliation, termination, exile and even imprisonment. Where are Obama's people at the OSC, EEOC and MSPB, agencies created to protect these employees?

Most Americans can't even name the Federal departments -- but they shape our daily lives. Times have changed since the first departments were formed around 1780, and the old way of doing business must also change. No more authoritarian white male leadership. Let's embrace democracy, and a highly diverse workforce including women and the young. Then, let the good, productive, committed public servants be rewarded and the "duds" or bad people moved out. We can call those horrible public servants who squander and misuse our money in government - Putrid People in Government or PIGs. Know any?

One final thought on PIGs. As a senior management official and advisor for years, I noted that male supervisors would often ask newly-appointed female subordinates to do something the men would not do. A female supervisor called me for advice when she was asked by her male boss to fire a nonperforming employee. I asked how long the employee worked for the agency and learned that he could have been fired by his previous male supervisors for decades, but wasn't. She was now the "fall girl" who would soon be entangled in a web of problems and complaints. I also saw female leaders given poor advice by the males around them, so they were just "sitting ducks" waiting to get shot off their perches. Often women will be sent "out front" to field questions when the going gets rough, while the males duck for cover. So, whether a woman is in industry or the public sector, at the top or bottom, they have got to watch their backs and fronts because the "boys will get you if they can."

A Of the People, For the People

"You can lead a man to Congress, but you can't make him think."

Milton Berle

Our Presidents and representatives develop amnesia or dementia after they get elected. They change, and begin to represent themselves, lobbyists and special interests. They get rich on our backs. Salaries paid to House and Senate members are $174,000, the Speaker of the House earns $223,500, and the Majority-Minority leaders earn $194,400. Yet many of them leave public service as multi-millionaires. How is that possible?

A recent CBS *60 Minutes* expose on Congress showed insider trading, stock tips, stock offerings, tax cheats, fraud, prostitution, bribery, accepting gifts, taking trips, and spending most of their time gathering money, and leaving rich. "It's a venture opportunity....in public service... to enrich yourself and your family," said Peter Switzer at Stanford University. He called it "honest graft" that allows them to become rich. It's not honest graft – it's dishonest and immoral. They make the rules, and they get rich, shilling for the rich and powerful -- legally. Say it ain't so, Nancy.

Nancy Pelosi is a Good Old Girl with family roots in politics. She and her husband exploited eight Initial Public Offerings (IPOs), one by Visa. They bought 5,000 shares at $44 a share; two days later it was up to $64 and, for some reason, the legislation on credit cards never made it to the house. On *60 Minutes*, Steve Kroft asked Pelosi: "Did you consider this to be a conflict of interest?" Clearly nervous and annoyed, she replied: "Is there some point you want to make?" Good political strategy, Nancy! When Kroft asked if it was right for the Speaker to make money from a company, as a major piece of legislation affecting that same company was going through Congress, Nancy said she would put her record up against anyone on the credit card issue.

Well, 'I'm less crooked than the next guy' isn't good enough. Nancy Pelosi could also have bragged that she's less crooked than Al Capone and Bernie "Made Off with the Money" Madoff. Steve Kroft reported that Congress finally passed the Stock Act barring them from trading during their time in Congress. But don't worry – there are probably loopholes in the Act. Congressional leaders will still find ways to get rich and spend our money. Our Presidents do.

The costliest each year has been George W. Bush at $1.3 million; Bubba Bill Clinton comes in second at less than a million; Papa Bush costs us $850,000; and, as expected, Jimmy Carter costs the least: a half million dollars. The widows get a pension and the Presidents get $200,000/year for life – and they are living longer along with us. More money is paid for office space, travel and postage; then there are Secret Service costs. George W. needed 8,000 square feet of office space, $85,000 for telephones and $60,000 to travel; Bill needed almost a half a million dollars for 8,300 square feet in Harlem and more money for travel and postage. We need more women on this wealthy wagon because everyone comes in or goes out rich, just like our representatives.

Women have served in Congress since 1917 when Republican Jeannette Rankin threw in her hat in Montana. In the 97 years since then, only about 300 women have joined her, a tiny number compared to all the men. The U.S. House of Representatives has two houses – theirs and ours. They're rich and we're poor. Really, it's bicameral, with two separate groups making laws – the House and the Senate. The upper house Senate, the more "deliberate" body, consists of 50 Senators (2 per State) serving 6-year terms. The lower House has 435 voting representatives serving 2-year terms. They are elected directly by the people to be "of the people" -- to represent our views and opinions. But write a letter to them and you'll be amazed at how much they don't do. There's a system in place in which you write to them, they write to the culprits, and the evil-doers write back. It's "Kiss off by Representative" or "Congressional Catch 22."

As of 2013, there were 38 widows who won their husband's seats. And there are only 79 women representatives in the House today or 18%. Some states have still never elected one woman to the House of Representatives (Alaska, Delaware, Iowa, Mississippi, North Dakota and Vermont), although Alaska and North Dakota have elected women Senators. Without female representatives, how the hell can women expect to have our interests represented? With over 40 presidents elected, and none of them female, how can women consider themselves equal? Any man trumps a woman in the U.S. I figure Hispanic men will be throwing in their hats soon. And that's great but... what about us?

B Immigration

"President Bush also said last night we do not yet have full control of the border. Full control? If we had any less control, there'd be an easy-pass lane."

Jay Leno

U.S. immigration laws are a joke. So – what's the problem? Could it be that Caucasian Americans, the Good Old Boys, and those considered the "old immigrants" need the underpaid workers, but don't want them to cause a shift in the demographic hegemony? There are currently 41.8 million Hispanics in the U.S., representing 14.2% of the population; there are 223 million Caucasians or 72.4% based on the 2010 census when Hispanic whites are included and 63.7% when excluded. Germans, Irish, and English head the population of Caucasians. Hispanics are supposed to become the largest minority group based on their birth rates and immigration.

The latest crisis is related to the recent flood of illegal immigrants, mainly women and children, crossing the U.S. borders; about three-fourths of the children are from Central America: Honduras, Guatemala, El Salvador, and the rest are from Mexico. These children are supposed to be fleeing from crime, gang violence and poverty or to reunite with their families who reside in the U.S. One of the arguments made against providing them with asylum is the possibility of their bringing diseases from South and Central America. I guess what goes around really does come around because this is nothing new.

When the U.S. opened its doors to white immigrants in the millions, the government took action to process them quickly and efficiently. In 1892, Ellis Island was opened as a Federal immigration station and processed newly-arrived immigrants primarily from Northern and Western Europe. Only 2% out of over 12 million immigrants were denied entry due to disease, criminal background, or insanity by the time it was closed in 1954. Over 40% of all current U.S. citizens can trace their ancestors to these early immigrants.

Meanwhile, the country was dealing with immigration problems by passing various laws. In 1790, a century before Ellis Island opened, the first Federal immigration law, the Naturalization Act, was passed. It allowed all white males living in the U.S. for two years to become citizens. Then starting in 1875, prostitutes and criminals were banned from immigrating; and in 1882, the *Chinese Exclusion Act* was passed that also included restricting "lunatics" and "idiots." I think some slipped through.

Controversies and other restrictive laws continued in order to preserve the "old immigrant" population (Caucasians) in the U.S. In 1965, sanity prevailed when President Lyndon B. Johnson signed a new immigration and nationalization bill that abolished the earlier quota system based on national origin, and allowed more immigrants from third-world countries, including previously-barred Asians. He also declared Ellis Island part of the Statue of Liberty National Monument.

I was working for the Department of the Interior, National Park Service, in Manhattan when President Ronald Reagan appointed Chrysler Corporation's Lee Iacocca to head the Statue of Liberty-Ellis Island Foundation for the restoration of the Island in 1982 that was a huge money-maker. A colleague of mine said that she was denied entrance to the U.S. with her parents because she had ringworm. She was held until it was effectively treated and then reunited with her parents. We allow everything and anything in now.

There are solutions to problems, when and if we are willing to intelligently deal with them. And why do we keep reinventing the wheel? Because we can't count on our representatives and the Good Old Boys who appear to be suffering from severe logorrhea, paralysis and greed. If we can prepare and process millions of immigrants when they are wanted and needed, what is so difficult with processing about 90,000 Hispanic children and mothers this year crossing the borders as they flee from abuse and poverty? Why can't they find refuge – is it because they can't see the Statue of Liberty in all her glory?

In the 1960's during the Cuban revolution led by Fidel Castro, over a 2-year period, 14,000 Cuban children arrived in the U.S. alone. The program was called "Operation Peter Pan" and the children were sent to live with relatives, into foster homes, boarding schools and other facilities until their parents could leave Cuba and unite with their children. In 1966, Congress passed the Cuban Adjustment Act and provided more than $1.3 billion for direct financial assistance. The Cuban immigrants were also eligible for public assistance, Medicare, free English courses, scholarships and low-interest loans. Unfortunately, during the exodus from Cuba twenty years later in 1980, Castro supposedly emptied his jails and sent criminals, drug addicts and the mentally ill to the U.S.

Of course, decisions by the U.S. are politically and economically motivated, therefore, many women and children without a return or benefit to us are often left to horribly suffer and die. Countless children are currently "dropping dead on the long trek to refugee camps" says the United Nations – "the number of people under threat has now reached 11 million" because of the food crisis in the Horn of Africa. Starving and desperate women bind their stomachs to reduce hunger pains in order to feed their children. A million and a half children are in danger of starvation in West Africa because of climate change, conflict and poverty. This is not a new crisis, but has been going on for years. Even the most heartrending photographs have not changed the U.S. and international priorities to stop this inhumane situation.

Man's inhumanity to man is well-known. We continue to observe and endure it, so it goes on and on. I believe it will take women with resources, such as those in advanced countries like ours, to stop the intentional and unintentional deaths. The distinction between doing harm and allowing it to occur has been philosophically dealt with in terms of morality. In other words, what's the difference between people being killed in war or bombings or allowing many millions to die from malnutrition, dehydration and starvation through a lack of intervention? The former is often considered justified, intentional and proactive, while the latter is thought acceptable because it is unintentional passive acceptance. Our failure to prevent and stop the deaths of millions of children throughout the U.S. and world are not only acts of commission, but omission, with the same results.

C The New World Order

"We must move as quickly as possible to a one-world government, one-world religion, under a one-world leader."

Robert Mueller, Former Assistant Attorney General of UN

Papa George Bush said, "We have before us the opportunity to forge for ourselves and for future generations a new world order... When we are successful, and we will be..." Sounds like a Yale Bonesman and good for the Greedy Old Bastards to me.

Women have to be particularly concerned about a New World Order because it is more sinister than it appears. Human population control is about artificially altering, up or down, the human population using various methods. China's one-child per family is just one example. This requires using contraceptives, practicing abstinence, increasing or decreasing infant mortality rates, allowing or disallowing abortions, passing laws, rules and penalties, and manipulating women into and out of the workforce. And, this is nothing new.

White women have to stay alert to strategies and tactics aimed specifically at them. Birth rates for Caucasians dropped significantly to replacement level or below (2 or less), while other races continued to reproduce at higher rates. But, there are even more important things to be concerned about on a national and global basis.

In 1798, economist and British clergyman, Thomas Malthus, theorized in his book *An Essay on the Principle of Population* that when population goes unchecked, it increases geometrically, but "subsistence" only increases arithmetically. He considered positive checks on this to be: war, disease, famine and disasters. Preventative checks were: abstinence, birth control and restraint. The latter he believed would save humanity from itself and the misery of overpopulation. Also, he believed the increase in population subjects the lower classes to distress and prevents any permanent amelioration of their condition. In other words, the proliferation of births among the poor prevents them from getting out of poverty because they cannot sustain themselves. Malthus' theories have been expanded to include decreasing the population of the "unfit," and increasing death rates through war and famine.

Not many of us pay attention to the United Nations (UN) and what they are doing unless something significant occurs. They look like a bunch of boring bureaucrats sucking up air. This is a mistake because it represents a powerful body of men, and a few women, coming together to make decisions on a global basis that significantly impacts on us. For example, the UN developed a "World Population Plan of Action" that deals with internationally adopted "strategies for national and international progress." Sounds good, doesn't it?

They also developed "Agenda 21," a 21st century voluntary comprehensive program and plan of action, "to be taken globally, nationally and locally by organizations of the UN system, governments, and major groups in every area in which human impacts on the environment," or "sustainable development." Sustainable development is similar to Malthus' subsistence or "survival," which means that the population may need to be reduced in order for the planet to sustain all of us. We are now at slightly over 7 billion and may reach 16 billion by 2100.

Conspiracy theorists say the plans are designed to reduce the current world population of just over 7 billion humans to only half a billion or less. I am not generally a conspiracy person, but I do believe that in order for the elite to maintain their consumption and wealth, nationally and globally, without major fallout caused by the masses, something has to be done to curb the populations to "sustainable" levels. Some of the passages and sections in the UN plans sound great, but the end result is that actions are being recommended, voluntarily of course, that focus and impact mainly on "women, youth, local and marginalized communities." And, you can't trust the Greedy Old Bastards, as we know.

Passages to worry about include: strengthening domestic resource mobilization (what is this?), sustainable human settlement planning (human settlements?), and increase significantly the availability of high-quality, timely and reliable data disaggregated (human data collection) by income, gender, age, race, ethnicity, migratory status, disability, geographic location and other characteristics relevant in national contexts (NSA and Snowden?). George Orwell's novel *1984,* written in 1948 about his vision of the world within 40 years, seems to be off by 30 years.

6 Family Clubs

"Family is the most important thing in the world."

Princess Diana

The family should be the most important club, the nucleus of our lives. And let me say here that we can't and don't want to live without men in our lives. There are many, many good men out there, intermingled with the bad ones. As Rodney Dangerfield said, *"I tell you, I don't get no respect. The way my luck is running, if I was a politician, I'd be honest."* We just want some respect, happiness, love, and a good life. Not "The good life" depicted in the *Twilight Zone*, but a reasonably peaceful existence, handling only life's ordinary bumps, not those sexist ones created purely for us.

It's the exception when people find a soul mate. Most of us select a mate we think is compatible with us and we carry on from there. But as we go along, too often we forget why we married this person in the first place. Two of my girlfriends wanted to marry just to find out what it was like. One husband drank up all their money, and bankrupted them. She sent him back to his mother. Another married a couch-potato dud and he's still on the couch.

Many of my friends were abandoned with children, but they've all survived - barely. Many had no education beyond high school, which made it hard to make more than minimum wage after their "better half" spouses' skipped town. One returned after the kids were 18. Two went on welfare until they could get themselves together. Some went from rich, fulfilling lives to lives with just the bare essentials.

A few of my friends made bad decisions while married, letting the macho-control freaks handle all the decisions and finances. Two signed away everything at their husbands' insistence, and both ended up with nothing. They're both living with their daughters, taking care of their grandchildren. After her husband lost their entire fortune, another friend refused to sign away her upscale house across from Manhattan.

She was a school teacher so she worked into her 70's to maintain the house and pay the taxes. Two of the husbands died, one is in an assisted-living facility, and none of them left any retirement income for their wives, so they expect to live on minimum Social Security, a little over $400/month.

My friends are part of the "Sandwich Generation" taking care of their parents, mainly their mothers, without their brothers or other family members helping. I have many friends who are single and living alone. Only a few are still married, which makes us all wonder when the next breakup will occur. The number of older women in assisted-living facilities compared to men is astonishing, so men are still dying earlier. My life is surrounded by women doing the best they can in a man's world. What I love about them is the profound love they have for their children and their ability to keep giving even as they struggle for their own survival. Before ending this book, let's get back to Natalie and Charlie.

NATALIE & CHARLIE

Abused women usually suffer from PTSD, like soldiers in combat. It develops after horrific ordeals involving actual, or threatened, physical harm. Many batterers are also cheaters and Natalie suffered all of that, along with kicks, marital rape, and severe beatings. Charlie was a beast – malevolent, devious, and manipulative. If you met him, you would think he's one of the nicest men. But, not too far under his surface skin, he smells foul, putrid, and evil. On one occasion, he slit his arm with a knife from elbow to wrist, called the police and said Natalie did it. Another time he told the police she was trying to run him down with her car and got a restraining order against her. While driving, he smashed Natalie in the face until she was unconscious while their son sat in the back seat. He isolated Natalie away from her family and friends.

For 40 years, Charlie sucked the blood and money out of Natalie and her family. Thankfully, he finally turned her in for a younger model that had asset-sucking potential. Unfortunately, Charlie's divorce attorney, Natalie's attorney, the judges, and the experts were all white males. So Charlie hid money and assets with his paramour long before the divorce took place. He was in the driver's seat right to the end. Happily, he looks very old, while Natalie is still a sexy-looking woman and free at last. She lives in a high-cost area in her own condominium with her dog and cat. She has a car, a job, and alimony he begrudges her. In one of his recent tyrannical texts he wrote that she was an ugly bitch that deserved to die and hopefully his daughter and husband would die a day later. Poor thing, he just can't give up or believe – "He's dead to us!"

CHAPTER X

1 The Train of Life

"I'm an idealist. I don't know where I'm going, but I'm on my way."

Charlie Sandburg

The journey of life is really short – shorter for some than for others.
I often think of us all getting on "The Life Train." Some are on the
high-cost, high-class Acela Express, some in business class on the
Metroliner, and most of us on the local commuter trains. Some of
us jump off the train at various stops along the journey. One of my
girlfriends still has a 1960s bouffant hairdo; she jumped off in 1965.
Others stay on to the end of the line. We mix with, and join up with,
various people; after many miles we wonder why we hooked up with
them in the first place (husbands), or lose track of them as they move
to other cars (friends). Some of the other passengers even start to look
better than others (infidelity).

Many of us are yelling, "Stop the train, I want to get off," but the
alternative is worse. We don't need to get off the train; we need to fix
the one we're on. Henry David Thoreau said "The mass of men lead
lives of quiet desperation." Too often women are taking what's handed
out silently, quietly and desperately; some of us are screaming our
bloody heads off and suffering from all kinds of stress and maladies.
Resignation can kill you. Better to let it out than to hold it in and ruin
your insides and your mind.

Laughing is a great cure for what ails us and my girlfriends and I
get together and laugh every chance we can. But, after all is said and
done, we'd better laugh or we'd be crying all the time for the plight of
women and children in the U.S. and all over the world.

2 What Now?

"You simply have to put one foot in front of the other and keep going. Put blinders on and plow right ahead."

George Lucas

I watched the Belmont Stakes rooting for "California Chrome" just as if he were my own horse. Horses have their eyes on the sides of their heads for hunting, so they have blinders on to keep them focused ahead and ready to take chances they would not normally take – like running their asses off. That's what we women have to do and the middle-class in this country have to do: stay focused and run our asses off! Focus on what's going on in this country that is ours – not that amorphous "theirs," "them," and "they."

We need expertise and input from all of our people, not just that little sneaky elitist group at the top using their strategies against us; we have to outsmart, outpace, and out race them. Let's start where it all begins and ends - the Systemic War on Women (and the middle-class) in the U.S. It needs to be fought vigorously, openly and vehemently. So, what did we learn from all of this -- and what can we do?

First and foremost, we have to fight the Greedy Old Bastards, staying alert to their strategies that include The Shock Doctrine, Constructive Confusion and Chaos, Pete & Repeat, and High Visibility Syndrome, to name a few. We need to pay attention to their plans and programs, such as those geared towards the "New World Order," and "Population Control." Let's unearth their dens and shed light on their secret societies by pulling them out of their dark enclaves and exposing them. And, let's stop allowing a few American dynasties and the elite from running us and everything around us.

The question is what Americans, particularly the middle- and lower-classes, are going to do to stop the drain on their lives and well-being. We cannot allow a "New World Order" to take over as we watch moronic sit-coms, reality TV shows, and listen to a bunch of people tell us what to feel and think. We need better role models for our children and they need good educations if we are going to succeed. Our polluted environments and decadent lives need to be cleaned up. We have to stop being uninformed, oblivious, and scared. As President Franklin D. Roosevelt said at the depth of the Great Depression, "*The only thing we have to fear is fear itself.*"

The American middle-class pays, pay, and pays some more. You can't do anything without being charged or barraged by money-suckers – they're everywhere with their hands out. Yet, you never get your money's worth. Our willingness and ability to work and pay taxes has been abused and is being squandered. We have to stop the madness of allowing over 60% of our budget to be spent on the Military-Industrial Complex and black programs, while our infrastructure and social services continue to deteriorate. We have to stop the Prison Industrial Complex from incarcerating our people for profit, particularly Black and Hispanic males. We have to change our judicial system and go after bad judges and lawyers, who are never held accountable for their putrid actions, advice and decisions.

We deserve safe day care, flexible work schedules, job sharing, lactation centers, and other family-friendly policies and practices. Women and men have to stop the rape and abuse of our women and children. We also have to insist on safe havens for them, and our homeless, mentally ill and displaced veterans. Our systems need to be fixed for the benefit of all of us, not for just a select few. We really need change – not just be promised it by our ineffective and self-serving politicians.

I hope I've said something in this book that will be helpful to you and yours. I am extremely grateful for everything I have, which is much more than most and more than I ever expected. I am proud of everything I've been able to achieve and give to others on my Train of Life. Not that I'm done yet – I'm out protesting and trying to make some major changes happen in my country. I have been blessed with wonderful friends and family members, and I am truly blessed for having a wonderful, kind, intelligent, and loving man in my life, my husband.

In the Appendix I have included a few steps that may be helpful to you in overcoming glossophobia or fear of public speaking. I have no solution to Pteromerhanophobia, or the fear of flying except… Close your eyes, and as my mother Helen would say – Just do it!

Appendix A

Overcoming Glossophobia

"Make sure you have finished speaking before your audience has finished listening."

Dorothy Sarnoff

Many of us have Glossophobia, but mine was the shaking-in-your-boots type. At an executive session with J&J executives, I had to be rescued by the trainer because no words would come out of my mouth. The trainer waited patiently, staring at me. I've never gotten over that humiliating experience. So, maybe I can help others.

Arrrg. Fear resides in the self. Over many years speaking in public, before small and large audiences, I've learned that most of us are afraid of embarrassing and making a fool of ourselves in front of people. I'm not sure you can make a fool of yourself to yourself – you need an audience for that. It's like the sound of the tree falling in the forest when no one is there.

Fearless. A young female intern at that regional conference did what we're all afraid of – tried to speak at the microphone, but came out with an enormous fearful sound, like a beastly animal growl. She scared the hell out of us. We all felt her anguish and embarrassment. It seemed to be imbedded in us and kids probably added to it when we were younger. Whenever I see Arrrrg (an aqueous reactor release result), I think of her fear and her body's reaction. But, as they say, it's not how you start, but how you finish that counts. One of my gentle male employees on the dais went to the intern, called the next student speaker, and gently sat her back down. We heard from the rest of the interns and we all gasped when only that young tongue-tied terrorized female intern was left.

Brave Heart and Soul. But, youthfully and bravely, she was going to try again. Watching her approach the microphone was painful.

She started very slowly and timidly – but then she got her groove on. When she finished, we all gave her a standing ovation. What she said was unimportant – the fact that she pushed past her fear made us all extremely proud.

Don't Rush: Being surrounded by people with no fear of public speaking doesn't seem to help. My mother, my husband, my girlfriends, my staff, my bosses, all seemed to have this gift to walk up to a microphone and spill their guts. My husband takes extra pains to add a little poetry or spice to his presentation. He's warm, thoughtful and sincere, which helps. No one can rush him, either, and he forces you to pay attention to him. He's really kind of weird because he also doesn't interrupt people when they are speaking.

Draft It. To anyone with the same fear and inclinations, I suggest starting with something easy, like introducing someone else. Prepare a draft of what you want to say about that person. Put your remarks on one page or on numbered cards (in case you drop them). You are now ready. Stay close to where you will be speaking because your legs and hands may be shaking and you don't want to trip. A friend of mine tripped and fell flat on her face coming into the General's meeting. She did what she had to do; she picked herself up and those who understood her anguish clapped for her as she walked to the front of the room.

Breathe. Take deep breaths. This will calm your nerves as you walk up to the podium or microphone. Walk slowly – there's no rush. Think of my patient husband. Everyone will wait for you. Stop and get your bearings, and take heart if you have a podium to hide behind. Keep your head down and your ass up! Look at your paper or cards for a minute, or two, or three. Too long is not good because they may think you slipped into a catatonic state. Then raise your head slightly and say "Good morning," or "Good afternoon" or "Good evening." Even if you get the time of day wrong, it's okay. Another thing we all know – It happens! You have begun speaking in public, and, the hardest part is over.

Head Up – Head Down. The next part, which I often forget, is to say your name. If you can manage to say: Good morning, my name is so and so….take another rest. Then, if you can't pick your head up – just read the cards or paper you prepared, loud enough to be heard, with something like: It's my pleasure to introduce to you so and so. Be sure to include something personal about why you are introducing this person or something you've learned about them. After reading and picking your head up now and then while people are trying to learn about the person who is the real speaker, you're done. So, you simply say: And now let me introduce to you…..

Get Up Here! That's the audience's clue to welcome the main speaker by clapping. You start it by clapping yourself. It's the announced guest's cue to come forward, and your clue to shake their hand, or hug them – and walk away relieved. Believe me; each time you do it, it becomes easier. One day, you'll realize it's become second nature, just as pushing your foot on the brake pedal has become.

Take Small Steps. A few more pointers may help: After learning to make introductions, imparting needed information is the next easiest thing to do. Remember to keep the attention off yourself and onto what you have to share with the audience. Leave the big speeches to people egotistical enough to make them. If you do have to give a speech, be sure to follow the way I was taught by a professional orator. Step one: Tell them what you're going to tell them; Step two: Tell them; and, Step 3: Tell them what you told them.

Keep it Short. Don't go on too long. I tried to keep this book short, but it didn't work! Try to be warm, and tell a personal story that people can identify with and remember. Many of us tune out, daydream with added sexual fantasies, and we don't remember much except bits and pieces or the main thrust of the story. Leave jokes to the comedians. I hope this helps because it's one of the things people dread most.

Enjoy your success!

Appendix B

Glossary

1. GOBs - Greedy Old Bastards or Good Old Boys

2. GOBlins – Young GOBs

3. GOBligook – GOB BS

4. GOBliarchy – Systems built by GOBS

5. GOBonomics – Economics for GOBS

6. GOBism - Good Old Boyism

7. GOBish – Good Old Boyish

8. GOGs -- Good Old Girls

9. AUXILIARIES – Women

10. BANs – Business Anns

11. BUMs – Businessmen GOBs

12. MOBs – Military Old Boys

13. PIGs – Putrid People In Government

14. SLOBs – Sex & Leisure-time GOBs

15. COGs – Congressional GOBs

16. CRAP - Congressional Rip-offs and Pork

Appendix C

Bibliography

Airplane! Dirs. Jim Abrahams, David Zucker, Paramount,1980.

American Association of University Women. *Gender: Major Issues, Major Impact Questionnaire.* Wash, DC: 2014.

Anti-Violence Resource Guide: Facts About Violence--U.S. Statistics. Feminist.com, 2013. http://www.Feminist.com/ antiviolence/facts/html.

Baker, Russ. *Family of Secrets: The Bush Dynasty, the Powerful Forces That Put it in the White House, and What Their Influence Means for America.* New York: Bloomsbury, 2008.

Bernards, Michelle. "With women in combat will military finally address epidemic of sexual assaults." *Washington Post,* 24 Jan 2013.

Browne, Sylvia. *Secret Societies:…and How They Affect Our Lives Today.* CA: Hay House, 2007.

Cocker, Joe. *You Can Leave Your Hat On.* Songwriter: Randy Newman. Warner/ Chappell Music.

Coleman-Adebayo, Marsha. *No Fear: A Whistleblower's Triumph over Corruption and Retaliation at the EPA.* New York: Hill, 2011.

Coontz, Stephanie. *A Strange Stirring: The Feminine Mystique and American Women at the Dawn of the 1960s.* New York: Basic Books, Jan 2011.

Cramer, Clayton E. *My Brother Ron: A Personal and Social History of the Deinstitutionalization of the Mentally Ill.* Create Space, 2012.

De Beauvoir, Simone. *The Second Sex: Complete and Unabridged Edition.* New York: Knopf Doubleday, Apr 2010.

Dedman, Bill and Paul Clark Newell, Jr. *Empty Mansions: The Mysterious Life of Huguette Clark and the Spending of a Great American Fortune.* New York: Ballantine, 2013.

Dershowitz, Alan M. "Wives Also Kill Husbands – Quite Often." Iowa: University of Iowa, 19 Sept 2012.

Fastenberg, Dan. "Fearful Women Shun Maternity Leave, Study Reveals." *Career Builder,* 10 May 2013.

Federal Register. "Executive Orders Disposition Tables 1929 – 2014." Wash, DC: National Archives http://www.archives.gov/federal-register/executive-orders/disposition.htp.

Francis, Theo and Joann S. Lublin. "The Annual CEO Pay Survey." *Wall Street Journal,* 28 May 2014.

French, Marilyn. *The History of Women in the World: From Eve to Dawn.* New York: Feminist Press, 2002.

Freud, Sigmund. *The Psychopathology of Everyday Life.* New York: Norton, 1990.

Friedan, Betty. *The Feminine Mystique.* New York: Norton, 1963.

Gardner, Amanda. "Who Says the Sexes are Planets Apart?" *Health Day News,* 7 Feb 2013.

Garofoli, Joe. "Why do Political wives stand by their man?" *San Francisco Chronicle,* 12 Mar 2008.

Gents Without Cents. "Niagara Falls." Three Stooges, Columbia, Short Subject, 1944.

Gilbert, Daniel and Joann S. Lublin. "Oxy, Irani Settle Pay Dispute." *Wall Street Journal,* 24 Dec 2013.

Gladwell, Malcolm. *Outliers: The Story of Success.* New York: Little, Brown, 2008.

Good Hair. Dir. Chris Rock Productions, HBO Films, 2009.

Grough, Mark and Toby Goldbach. "Relationship between Pimps and Prostitutes." New York: Cornell University Law School, 2010.

Harvey, Steve. "How God and Wife Marjorie Renewed His Faith." *Essence Magazine,* 5 Nov 2009.

Harvey, Steve and Denene Millner. *Act Like a Lady, Think Like a Man.* New York: Harper Collins, 2009.

Hemphill, Paul. *The Good Old Boys.* New York: Simon and Schuster, 1974.

Hockman, David. "The Best is Yet to Come." *AARP Magazine,* Oct-Nov 2013.

Holiday, Billie. *Lady Sings the Blues.* Eleonora Fagan and William F. Duffy. New York: Doubleday, 1992.

Holmes, Anna. "Divorce Makes Women Poorer, Man Lonelier." *Gawker Media,* 2013. http://jezebel.com.

Ibarra, Herminia and Nancy M. Carter, Christine Silva. "Why Men Still Get More Promotions Than Women." *Harvard Business Review,* Sept 2010.

Johnston, Peter. *Choice Words.* 2013. http://choicewordsbookclub. weebly.com/the-book.h.

Joyce, Amy. "Still Outside the Good Ol' Boys Club: Women Continue to be Diminished in the Workplace, Study Finds." *Washington Post,* 18 Jul 2004.

Klein, Naomi. *The Shock Doctrine: The Rise of Disaster Capitalism.* New York: Metropolitan, 2007.

Knute Rockne, All American. Dir. Lloyd Bacon, Warner Home Video, DVD, 2006

LaTorre, R.A. *Sexual Identity: Implications for Mental Health.* Berkeley: 1981.

Lawrence, Jill. "Congress full of Fortunate sons – and other relatives." *USA Today,* 8 Aug 2006.

Leamer, Lawrence. "The Last Days of Mary Kennedy." *Newsweek,* 18 Jun 2012.

Linn, Allison. "Who Uses Food Stamps? Millions of Children." *NBC News Business/Economy,* 17 Mar 2014.

Little Shop of Horrors. Dir. Frank Oz, Warner Bros, 1986.

Malthus, Thomas Robert. "An Essay on the Principle of Population." Library of Economics & Liberty. London: J. Johnson, 1798.

Mangano, Joseph J. "Geographic Variation in the U.S. Thyroid Cancer Incidence, and a Cluster Near Nuclear Reactors in New Jersey, New York and Pennsylvania." National Institutes of Health, 2009.

Maslow, Abraham. "A Theory of Human Motivation." *Psychological Review,* 1943. *Mother Jones: Investigation.* "U.S. Mass Shootings, 1982-2012. https://docs. google.com/spreadsheet/ccc?key.

National Coalition Against Domestic Violence. *Domestic Violence Facts.* Wash, DC: 2013.

National Poverty Center. *Poverty in the U.S.* University of Michigan. http://www. npc.umich. educ/poverty.

National Rifle Association. NRA Digital Network. "A Brief History of the NRA." http://home.nra.org /home/document/about. *Network.* Dir. Sidney Lumet, United Artists, 1976.

Oppenheimer, Jerry. *Crazy Rich: Power, Scandal and Tragedy Inside the Johnson & Johnson Dynasty.* New York: St. Martin, 2013.

Pegg, David. "The 25 Most Polluted Places on Earth." *Geography & Travel.* http:// list25.com/the-25-most-polluted-places-on-earth/

Pfaff, Leslie Garisto. "It Takes a Woman: Women are the poorest of the poor." NJ: *Rutgers Magazine,* Winter 2010.

PolitickerNJ. "America's Top 53 Political Scandals." 13 Mar 2008. http://www. politickernj.com.

Rampell, Catherine. "U.S. Women on the Rise as Family Breadwinner." *New York Times,* 29 May 2013.

Rape, Abuse & Incest National Network (RAINN). "Violence Against Women online Resources and Statistics." https://www.rainn.org/.

Romano, Lois. "The Huma Abedin survival guide." *Politico,* 25 July 2013. http:// politi.co/1aKHPmd. *Rosemere Neighborhood Association v EPA,* U.S. Court of Appeals for the Ninth Circuit. No. 08-35045. DC No. CV-07-5080. 14 Apr 2009.

Rummel, R.J. "Democide: Nazi Genocide and Mass Murder: 20,946,000 Victims: Nazi Germany 1933 to 1945. https://www.hawaii.edu/ powerkills/nazi.chap1. htm.

Sandberg, Sheryl and Nell Scovell. *Lean In: Women, Work, and the Will to Lead.* New York: Knopf, 2013.

Sasoon, Jean. *Princess: A True Story of Life Behind the Veil in Saudi Arabia.* GA: Windsor-Brooke, 2001.

Simon, Stephanie. "Protesters back US nuns on standoff with Vatican." *Reuters,* 24 May 2012.

Smith, Joan. *Misogynies.* New York: Ballantine, 1990.

Sutton, Anthony C. *America's Secret Establishment: The Order of Skull & Bones.* eBook, 2013. *The Catholic Encyclopedia.* List of Popes, Vol. 12. New York: Appleton, 30 Jul 2013. *The Fact File.* "The Size of the Federal Workforce: Rapid

Growth for Some, Stagnation for Others." 23 Jan 2012. http://www.thefactfile.com/2012/01/23.

The Library of Congress. "Women of Protest: Tactics & Techniques of the National Woman's Party Suffrage Campaign."

The Master. Dir. Paul Thomas Anderson. 2012.

The Sewall-Belmont House & Museum. Home of the National Woman's Party. Wash, DC. http://sewallbelmont.org/suffrage/nwp/.

The War of the Roses. Dir. Danny DeVito, Gracie, 20th Century Fox, 1989.

Tiron, Roxana. "US House Passes $625.1 Billion Defense Policy Measure." *Bloomberg,* 13 Dec 2012. http://atrtiron@bloomberg.net.

Tobin, Frances. "Sara Palin: Embracing Feminism, or Co-opting it for Conservatives." *Politics,* 10 Jun 2010.

Troianovski, Anton. "Vatican Suspends German 'Bishop of Bling'." *Wall Street Journal,* 24 Oct 2013.

U.S. Bureau of Census. *Population Statistics.* http://www.census.gov/population

U.S. Centers for Disease Control and Prevention. *Marriage and Divorce.* http://www.cdc.gov/nchs/fastats/ marriage-divorce.htm.

U.S. Central Intelligence Agency. *CIA World Factbook.* Wash, DC: CIA, 2009.

U.S. Department of Defense. *DOD FY 2014 Budget Proposal.* Wash, DC. http://www.defense.gov/home /features/2013/ 04134_budget

U.S. Department of Homeland Security. *FY 2014 Budget.* http://www.dhs.gov/dhs-budget.

U.S. Department of the Interior. *DC List of Sites.* Wash, DC: http://www.nps.gov/.../sitelist.htm

U.S. Department of Justice. *Commercial Sexual Exploitation of Children: Special Report.* http://www.ojp.usdoj.gov/nij.

U.S. Department of Justice. *Statistics Factbook: 2000 National Crime Victimization Survey.* http://www.usdoj.gov.

U.S. Department of Labor, Bureau of Labor Statistics. *Highlights of Women's Earnings.* Wash, DC: July 2013.

U.S. Department of Labor, Women's Bureau. *Quick Stats of Women Workers, 2010.* http://www.Dol.gov/wb/factsheets/QS-women work2010.htm.

U.S. Environmental Protection Agency. *Superfund Sites Where You Live.* http://www.epa.gov/superfund/sites/.

U.S. Federal Bureau of Investigation. *Uniform Crime Reports: Crime in the U.S, 1995-2013.* http://www.fbi.gov/about-us/cjis/ucr/ucr-.

U.S. Federal Bureau of Investigation. *Serial Murder: Multi-Disciplinary Perspectives for Investigators.* http://www.fbi.gov/stats-services/publications/serial-murder.

U.S. General Services Administration. *Federal Travel Regulations.* Wash, DC. http://www.gsa.gov/portal/content/104790?utm.

U.S. Office of Personnel Management. *Federal Employment Reports.* Wash, DC. http://www.opm.gov/policy-data.../data.../federal-employment-reports/.

Vicini, James. "U.S. Has the Most Prisoners in the World." *Common Dreams,* 24 Mar 2013.

Warren, Elizabeth. *A Fighting Chance.* New York: Metro, Holt, 2014.

Welles, Orson. *I Know What It is to be Young.* CD Grip Crescendo Label, 2002

White, Lee C. *Government for the People: Reflections of a White House Counsel to Presidents Kennedy and Johnson.* New York: Hamilton, 2008.

Whitlock, Craig. "Two Admirals face probe in Navy bribery scheme." *Washington Post,* 2013.

Wolf, Naomi. *The Beauty Myth: How Images of Beauty are Used Against Women.* New York: Morrow, 1990.

Worldwide Guide to Women in Leadership. "Female Heads of State & Government; Female Presidential Candidates." http://www.guide2womenleaders.com/.

Zirin, Dave. "Condi Rice's membership at Augusta National is nothing to celebrate about." *CBS News,* 8 Sept 2012.

CPSIA information can be obtained at www.ICGtesting.com
Printed in the USA
BVOW06*1315111114

374621BV00003B/4/P

.